PENGUIN BOOKS

THE LONG MARCH
OF EVERYMAN
1750–1960

Theo Barker is Professor of Economic History at London University. He was educated at Cowley School, St Helens, Jesus College, Oxford, and Manchester University. His books include *A Merseyside Town in the Industrial Revolution* (1954, with J. R. Harris), *A History of London Transport* (Vol. 1, 1963, and Vol. 2, 1974, with Michael Robbins), a new edition of Christopher Savage's *Economic History of Transport* (1974) and the histories of three London livery companies (the Girdlers, 1957; the Carpenters, with B.W.E. Alford, 1968; and the Pewterers, with John Hatcher, 1974). He helps to run a seminar on the history of diet at Queen Elizabeth College, London, and has edited (with J. C. McKenzie and John Yudkin) *Our Changing Fare: 100 Years of British Food Habits* (1966). His latest book, *The Glass-makers. Pilkington: The Rise of an International Company, 1826–1976*, appeared in 1977. He is Secretary of the Economic History Society and Treasurer of the British National Committee of the International Congress of Historical Sciences.

THE LONG MARCH
OF EVERYMAN
1750–1960

EDITED BY
THEO BARKER

PENGUIN BOOKS

in association with André Deutsch and the
British Broadcasting Corporation

Penguin Books Ltd, Harmondsworth, Middlesex, England
Penguin Books, 625 Madison Avenue, New York, New York 10022, U.S.A.
Penguin Books Australia Ltd, Ringwood, Victoria, Australia
Penguin Books Canada Ltd, 2801 John Street, Markham, Ontario, Canada L3R 1B4
Penguin Books (N.Z.) Ltd, 182–190 Wairau Road, Auckland 10, New Zealand

—

First published by André Deutsch Limited and the
British Broadcasting Corporation 1975
Published in Penguin Books 1978

—

'The Iron Machine' copyright © John F. C. Harrison, 1974; 'The Dignity
of Danger 1: The Army' copyright © Brian Bond, 1974; 'The Dignity of
Danger 11: The Navy' copyright © Christopher Lloyd, 1974; 'True Born
Britons' copyright © Gwyn A. Williams, 1974; 'The Two Nations:
Industrialization and its Discontents' copyright © George Rudé, 1974;
'The Early Railway Age', 'Poverty and Progress, 1870–1914' and Preface
copyright © Theo Barker, 1974; 'High Imperial Noon' copyright © V. G.
Kiernan, 1974; 'The Inferno, 1914–18' copyright © John A. Terraine,
1974; 'The Hungry Years, 1918–40' copyright © Donald Nicholl, 1974;
'Semi-Detached' and 'The People's War and Peace' copyright © Asa Briggs,
1974; 'Between Two Worlds' copyright © Stuart Hall, 1974.

—

Made and printed in Great Britain by
Richard Clay (The Chaucer Press) Ltd, Bungay, Suffolk
Set in Monotype Baskerville

Contents

Preface

The BBC Radio 4 series, *The Long March of Everyman*, succeeded in bringing British history to life for many people who previously had not been particularly interested in the past. This volume attempts to translate into book form the second half of the series, covering the period from about 1750 down to the present day. The original programme directors are the authors of these chapters and much of the material included here is the material from which the broadcast extracts were selected. But here the similarity ends, for the radio series was (to quote a familiar phrase frequently on the lips of its resourceful originator, Michael Mason) 'total audio'; that is to say, not just the spoken word but music and sounds to support and add atmosphere to the spoken word. As a result, the remarks of Everyman were usually brief, and sometimes repeated for effect. Here we take the opportunity to quote him more fully and to provide a longer commentary. We hope that this fuller treatment may go some way towards compensating for the contribution of the Radiophonic Workshop – those splendid sounds of tramping, note-counting, coin-dropping, and hunting horns; lists of stately homes or steam locomotives individually declaimed; music and folk singing – all of which gave the radio series its real character. Within the same general framework of presentation, we have each chosen the blend of commentary and quotation which seemed most suitable for our own particular contributions; and we are each responsible for our own particular parts of the book.

These radio programmes were a unique venture. History had never been presented to such a large audience from quite this angle and certainly never on such a generous scale. Each of the twenty-six 45-minute programmes was a 'sound symphony' composed from almost every category of sound which it is possible to record, and some idea of the scope and complexity of the operation can be got from the fact that one ingredient alone – the 'vox pop' dialect voices – involved the recording of about 800 speakers all over Great Britain, and the feeding of the 500 tapes of these voices into the twenty-six separate 'symphonies'.

Radio still has a special part to play in mass communication. It is particularly well placed to communicate sustained arguments and ideas to a wide audience; and it is difficult to think of any radio organization but the BBC, which over the years has given such prestige to its serious programmes, that would have been prepared to make such a bold venture or was in a position to enlist the help of so many scholars. On their side, the participating historians were made to think afresh about their sources, their research methods and the whole art of presenting history to non-specialists. In this way BBC Radio may be said to have made a contribution to learning which was of some historiographical and educational importance. The BBC also opened to us for these programmes the rich resources of its Sound Archives. Over fifty extracts from these recordings are printed here for the first time. The reader's attention is also drawn to the appendix at the end of the book, which gives details of the radio programmes, together with a short explanatory note by Michael Mason.

To capture the authentic voice of Everyman, even today with more students of the subject on his trail with their tape recorders, is a formidable task, for Everyman is often reluctant to talk to strangers or at least to say what is really in his mind. Those who do talk often belong to the more politically motivated or socially active minority who may or may not express what the majority thinks. This majority is not necessarily so keenly concerned with the great issues of the day. Problems peculiar to particular families or particular places may loom larger in their scale of values. And so may the influence of particular friends or groups to which they belong, or the hobbies or pastimes or good causes which take up their spare time. These features of people's lives, which may differ at various stages in their life cycle, are very difficult to capture and even more difficult to generalize about.

The more we venture into the past and the less Everyman's views were sought by others – and the less he himself wrote – the greater become the historian's difficulties. The opinions of leaders and political activists inevitably command more attention. Yet many of the extracts in this volume do nevertheless capture the less strident and more authentic voices of ordinary people telling their own story in their own way. Even so, a volume such as this can do no more than catch glimpses and convey insights. Its basis remains the same as that of the broadcasts: themes and variations from the history of the people in Britain, not an attempt at a comprehensive portrait.

THEO BARKER

I

The Iron Machine

JOHN F. C. HARRISON

Great as were all the changes in the life of Everyman in previous times, they are completely eclipsed by the magnitude of the changes between 1760 and 1830. Possibly the only parallel to this period is to be found in the Neolithic age, when man discovered how to become a settled agriculturist and herdsman instead of a hunter and nomad. Within the short span of one man's lifetime Britain was changed more fundamentally by the Industrial Revolution than it had been for hundreds of years before. Until about 1760 Britain was basically an agricultural country, with a small population, a low standard of living for the majority of the people, an hierarchical social system and an aristocratic oligarchy in political control. As a result of the Industrial Revolution she became a nation dependent on her manufacturing and extractive industries, with a large population, great urban centres, vastly increased wealth (some of which slowly percolated down to the lower classes), an increasing degree of social mobility, and political democracy. It can be said without exaggeration that virtually no institution or aspect of life was unaffected by these changes.

The Industrial Revolution was more than a series of technological innovations and economic changes. It offered to men, for the first time in human history, the way towards controlling their environment instead of being at its mercy. The possibility of material abundance for all was no longer an idle dream, though it took time before the full implications of this were grasped by any large number of people. With the appearance of these new practical possibilities men's ideas and assumptions also changed. The Industrial Revolution was a new way in which men looked at themselves, at society and at the world at large. Ultimately it offered a new dimension of freedom.

But to Everyman at the time it did not look this way at all. On the contrary, the vast social upheaval to which he was suddenly subjected represented a loss of freedom. For thousands of labouring men and women the process of social and economic change was painful, bewildering, frustrating and degrading. The transformation of British society in the late eighteenth and early nineteenth centuries was complex, uneven and unplanned. Contemporaries seized upon those aspects of change with which they were familiar, and used such parts to interpret the whole. The growth of machine industry was one such aspect, and is illustrated by the extracts in this chapter.

Before the Industrial Revolution industry was mainly on a small scale and was carried on in the homes of the people, who used only simple tools and machinery. The whole family worked together as an economic unit. Cloth-weaving, stocking-knitting, nail-making, for instance, were carried on in this way, using material supplied by a middle man (or 'putter-out') who also marketed the product. The hours of labour were long and earnings modest, but the handworker could set his own rhythm of work and enjoy a sense of independence. He could, if he chose, take a holiday at the beginning of the week ('St Monday') and work long hours later to compensate for it. Some of the delights and distresses of domestic industry are indicated in Section I of this chapter.

This system was disrupted, and ultimately destroyed, by a series of inventions in the textile, iron and engineering industries. The techniques and economic organization of first one and then another sector of an industry were revolutionized; and in all cases the result was away from the domestic system and towards the use of more elaborate machines, driven by water or steam power, in large 'manufactories'. The impact of the new machines was felt first in the cotton and then in the woollen industry; and so the extracts in Section II are from textiles, which was the leading sector of the economy in the first stages of the Industrial Revolution.

Section III shows how high was the price in terms of social and individual misery that Everyman paid for this industrial development. The 'manufacturing system' found few defenders among labouring men. Its inhumanity was vividly sketched by James Kay-Shuttleworth in his pamphlet, 'The Moral and Physical Condition of the Working Classes employed in the Cotton Manufacture in Manchester' *(1832):*

'Whilst the engine runs the people must work –
men, women and children are yoked together with
iron and steam. The animal machine – breakable
in the best case, subject to a thousand sources
of suffering – is chained fast to the iron machine,
which knows no suffering and no weariness.'

1: DOMESTIC INDUSTRY

A Hand-loom Weaver's Life

'My uncle's domicile, like all the others, consisted of one
principal room called "the house"; on the same floor with
this was a loom-shop capable of containing four looms, and
in the rear of the house on the same floor, were a small
kitchen and a buttery. Over the house and loom-shop were
chambers; and over the kitchen and buttery was another
small apartment, and a flight of stairs. The whole of the
rooms were lighted by windows of small square panes,
framed in lead, in good condition; those in the front being
protected by shutters. The interior of this dwelling showed
that cleanly and comfortable appearance which is always to
be seen where a managing Englishwoman is present. There
were a dozen good rush-bottomed chairs, the backs and
rails bright with wax and rubbing; a handsome clock in
mahogany case; a good chest of oaken drawers; a mahogany
snap-table; a mahogany corner cupboard, all well polished;
besides tables, weather-glass, cornice, and ornaments ...

'The family were, at that time, chiefly employed by
Messrs Samuel and James Broadbent, of Cannon Street
[Manchester], and as the work was for the most part
"pollicat" and "romoll" handkerchiefs, with a finer reed,
occasionally, of silk and cotton "garments", or handkerchiefs, the "bearing-home wallet" was often both bulky and
heavy; and when it happened to be too much so for one
person to carry, a neighbour's wallet would be borrowed,
the burden divided into two, and I would go with one part

over my shoulder, behind or before my uncle. He being, as already stated, rather heavy in person would walk deliberately, with a stick in his hand, his green woollen apron twisted round his waist, his clean shirt showing at the open breast of his waistcoat, his brown silk handkerchief wrapped round his neck, a quid of tobacco in his mouth, and a broad and rather slouched hat on his head ...

'The warehouse of Messrs Broadbent was nearly at the top of Cannon Street, on the right-hand side. We mounted some steps, went along a covered passage, and up a height or two of stairs, to a landing place, one side of which was railed off by the bannister, and the other furnished with a seat for weavers to rest upon when they arrived. Here we should probably find some half-dozen weavers and winders, waiting for their turn to deliver in their work and to receive fresh material; and the business betwixt workman and putter-out was generally done in an amicable, reasonable way. No captious fault-finding, no bullying, no arbitrary abatement, which have been too common since, were then practised. If the work were really faulty, the weaver was shown the fault, and if it were not a serious one he was only cautioned against repeating it; if the length or the weight was not what it should be, he was told of it, and would be expected to set it right, or account for it, at his next bearing-home, and if he were a frequent defaulter he was no longer employed ...

'It would sometimes happen that warp or weft would not be ready until after dinner, and on such occasions, my uncle having left his wallet in care of the putter-out, would go downstairs and get paid at the counting-house, and from thence go to the public-house where we lunched on bread and cheese, or cold meat and bread, with ale, to which my uncle added his ever-favourite pipe of tobacco. This house, which was the "Hope and Anchor", in the old churchyard, was also frequented by other weavers; the putter-out at Broadbents generally dined there in the parlour, and when he had dined he would come and take a glass of ale, smoke his pipe, and chat with the weavers, after which, my uncle would again go to the warehouse, and getting what material he wanted, would buy a few groceries and tobacco in the town, or probably, as we returned through the apple market, to go down Long Mill Gate, he would purchase a peck of apples, and giving them to me to carry, we wended towards home.'

(Samuel Bamford, *Early Days*, 1849. Bamford (1788–1872) was a silk weaver from Middleton, Lancashire, and in this passage from his autobiography he describes the domestic system of industry in its last prosperous days around the turn of the century.)

Distress among Weavers

'About the close of the French wars there was a very great fall in the price of wool, and consequently in the price of cloth. This, with other unfavourable events, caused a great and general panic amongst the cloth manufacturers, and perhaps amongst tradesmen generally. My father could not sell his cloth at times for much more than the wool had cost him. He was unable to go on any further without involving himself and his family in ruin, so he gave up. He was in some debt at the time, but he paid every person his own in full. After that we were very poorly off at times indeed. We had to begin to earn our bread by labouring for other people at a time when work was exceedingly scarce, and for several years we were in very great difficulties, and had to suffer grievous hardships. Sometimes we had no work, and when we had work, wages were very low, while provisions were very high. I believe that for a year together the whole family, consisting of nine or ten persons, did not earn more than twenty shillings per week. Out of that sum, from four to five would go in rent, and something would have to go for coals and taxes. And at that time flour was seven shillings and sixpence per stone, and oatmeal was dear in proportion. We were, of course, unable to obtain sufficient to supply our daily wants. I recollect being for years together, during that period of my life, without ever having sufficient to satisfy the cravings of hunger, except on rare occasions . . .

'The silent streets and houses told their own melancholy tale, and the downcast and haggard looks of the men, as they stood in groups at every street-corner, confirmed it. In ordinary times, hundreds of looms would be busy at work in Bramley alone. The click of the shuttle and the regular and steady stroke of the weaver's beam, could be heard from one end of Bramley to the other. But now you could walk through the whole length of the village, and not hear more than two or three looms going. There were scores and hundreds of families entirely without work and completely destitute . . .

'After this the cloth trade itself began to improve, and work became more regular. Wages also rose a little, and flour and the like got cheaper. But here was another evil: we were so anxious to be straight with all the world, we were so wishful to be completely out of debt, that we worked beyond our strength. I many a time rose in summer by three or four o'clock in the morning, and kept at my work with scarcely any intermission till eight or nine in the evening.'

(Joseph Barker, *Life, by Himself*, ed. J. T. Barker, 1880. Barker, at this time a handloom weaver in Bramley, Leeds, describes the unemployment and distress following the ending of the Napoleonic Wars.)

A Shoemaker's Apprentice

'One day in June [1820] I met Tom Aram in the street. He had become a shoemaker's apprentice, he said; and he liked his place much, and they wanted another lad – Would I come? Tom was an old crony, and we had known each other from the time that we were four years old. I told him I would ask my mother.

'She seemed hurt by the proposal. She had witnessed all my tendencies from my infancy, and had fostered and cherished all the buddings of intelligence, and formed a very different ideal for her child's future than that of his becoming a lowly labourer with the awl. But I entreated her to yield to me, and told her I could not endure the daily torment of being pointed at as an idle good-for-nothing. At last she yielded – saying, "The Lord's will be done! I don't think He intends thee to spend thy life at shoemaking. I have kept thee at school, and worked hard to get thee bread, and to let thee have thy own wish in learning, and never imagined that thou wast to be a shoemaker. But, the Lord's will be done! He'll bring it all right in time."

'So on the 10th of June, 1820, I sat down, in Clark's garret, to begin to learn the art, craft, and mystery of shoemaking . . .

'I found that I must not expect any regular apprenticeship as a shoemaker; for Clark often quarrelled with his mother, and threatened to leave her, and go back to London. In one of his haughty fits, I took offence and left him. From about the age of sixteen and a half to seventeen, I sat and worked with another small master; and then, for another year, sat in a shop with others, and worked for the Widow Hoyle. My work, of course, was very imperfect; and so, when it was rumoured that "Don Cundell" had come to the town, and took young men under his instruction, I told my mother that I must become one of his pupils. "Don", in my time, was the title always given to a first-rate hand; and usually to one who was known to all the members of the trade who had "tramped", or travelled for improvement.

'Under Don Cundell I learned to make a really good woman's shoe; but could not get any work from the best shops, because I had not served an apprenticeship to the trade. When Cundell left the town, I retired to a corner of my mother's humble house; and, as long as I continued at shoemaking, I worked for the Widow Hoyle, who sold her goods in the market, cheap, and therefore could only pay low wages. To the end of my short shoemaker's life, I could never earn more than about ten shillings weekly. But what glorious years were those years of self-denial and earnest mental toil, from the age of nearly nineteen to nearly three-

and-twenty, that I sat and worked in that corner of my poor mother's lowly home!'

(Thomas Cooper, *Life, by Himself*, 1872. The setting is Gainsborough, Lincolnshire.)

II: THE COMING OF THE NEW MACHINES

The Change to Cotton

'In the year 1770, the land in our township was occupied by between fifty to sixty farmers; rents, to the best of my recollection, did not exceed 10s. per statute acre, and out of these fifty or sixty farmers, there were only six or seven who raised their rents directly from the produce of their farms; all the rest got their rent partly in some branch of trade, such as spinning and weaving woollen, linen, or cotton. The cottagers were employed entirely in this manner, except for a few weeks in the harvest. Being one of those cottagers, and intimately acquainted with all the rest, as well as every farmer, I am the better able to relate particularly how the change from the old system of hand-labour to the new one of machinery operated in raising the price of land in the subdivision I am speaking of. Cottage rents at that time, with convenient loom-shop and a small garden attached, were from one and a half to two guineas per annum. The father of a family would earn from eight shillings to half a guinea at his loom, and his sons, if he had one, two, or three along side of him, six to eight shillings each per week; but the great sheet anchor of all cottages and small farms, was the labour attached to the hand-wheel, and when it is considered that it required six to eight hands to prepare and spin yarn, of any of the three materials I have mentioned, sufficient for the consumption of one weaver, – this shews clearly the inexhaustible source there was for labour for every person from the age of seven to eighty years (who retained their sight and could move their hands) to earn their bread, say one to three shillings per week without going to the parish. The better class of cottagers and even small farmers also helped to earn what might aid in making up their rents, and supporting their families respectably . . .

'From the year 1770 to 1788 a complete change had gradually been effected in the spinning of yarns, – that of wool had disappeared altogether, and that of linen was also nearly gone, – cotton, cotton, cotton, was become the almost universal material for employment, the hand-wheels, with the exception of one establishment were all thrown into lumber-rooms, the yarn was all spun on common jennies, the carding for all numbers, up to 40 hanks in the pound, was done on carding engines . . . In weaving no great alteration had taken place during these 18 years, save the introduction of the fly-shuttle, a change in the woollen looms to fustians and calico, and the linen nearly gone, except the few fabrics in which there was a mixture of cotton. To the best of my recollection there was no increase of looms during this period, – but rather a decrease . . .

'The fabrics made from wool or linen vanished, while the old loom-shops being insufficient, every lumber-room, even old barns, cart-houses, and outbuildings of any description were repaired, windows broke through the old blank walls, and all fitted up for loom-shops. This source of making room being at length exhausted, new weavers' cottages with loom-shops rose up in every direction; all immediately filled, and when in full work the weekly circulation of money as the price of labour only rose to five times the amount ever before experienced in this sub-division, every family bringing home weekly 40, 60, 80, 100, or even 120 shillings per week!!! . . .'

(William Radcliffe, in this passage from his *Origin of the New System of Manufacture, commonly called Power Loom Weaving*, 1828, describes the early effects of machine spinning in the cotton industry, as he observed them in Mellor, Lancashire.)

The Decline of the Hand-loom Weavers

'It was some time before power-looms for weaving woollen cloths were introduced, and then very slowly, though it was plain enough to all thoughtful-minded people that the doom of hand-looms was fixed. Many of the old weavers might be heard saying that "power-looms might do for narrow goods such as cotton and stuffs, but never for broad cloths". Meanwhile, unheeded, power-looms for weaving broad cloths steadily marched on, being introduced first by one large manufacturer and then another; and it was well for the hand-loom weavers that the introduction was not more rapid, or the shock and suffering for the time would have been much more severe. Slubbers had been displaced, but they were not such a numerous class as the weavers. Spinners on jennies had been superseded by mule spinners, but many of them could weave, and jennies were taken down and looms put up in their places, while some of the most skilful and enterprising learnt to spin on the mule. But when both billy, jenny, and hand-loom were rendered useless, the old weavers saw nothing in the world worth living for, and began to feel there was nothing for them to do. The hand-loom weavers formed a large class of men, and women, as well as boys and girls in their teens. Many years before, when cloth began to be made broader, the old ten and eleven quarter looms had been taken down and put on the "balks" next to the roof, with a strong faith that before long they would be wanted again when the temporary whim was over. But that time never came, and the old looms lay piled there to rot (as cotton and worsted looms had done), and were ultimately used to light the fire, or for other base uses never thought of by their once owners. But in the case of power-looms it was not a question of width or strength of the hand-looms, – good, bad, and indifferent were all the same. Power-looms spoke as with a voice of thunder to all who had ears to hear: "Get out of our way; ye have had your day; see the march of your superiors."

'The change had a terrible effect on the minds of some

old hand-loom weavers. Many an old weaver had become as much attached to his favourite loom as a warrior to his old steed.'

(Joseph Lawson, *Progress in Pudsey during the last Sixty Years*, 1887. The introduction of power-loom weaving in the Yorkshire woollen industry was later than in cotton; but its effects on the hand-loom weavers were no less disastrous.)

A Protest against Machinery

'TO the Merchants, Clothiers and all such as wish well to the Staple Manufactory of this Nation.

'The Humble Address and Petition of Thousands, who labour in the Cloth Manufactory.

'Sheweth, That the Scribbling-Machines have thrown thousands of your petitioners out of employ, whereby they are brought into great distress, and are not able to procure a maintenance for their families, and deprived them of the opportunity of bringing up their children to labour ...

'The number of Scribbling-Machines extending about seventeen miles south-west of Leeds, exceed all belief, being no less than one hundred and seventy! and as each machine will do as much work in twelve hours, as ten men can in that time do by hand, (speaking within bounds) and they working night and day, one machine will do as much work in one day as would otherwise employ twenty men.

'As we do not mean to assert any thing but what we can prove to be true, we allow four men to be employed at each machine twelve hours, working night and day, will take eight men in twenty-four hours; so that, upon a moderate computation twelve men are thrown out of employ for every single machine used in scribbling; and as it may be supposed the number of machines in all the other quarters together, nearly equal those in the South-West, full four thousand men are left to shift for a living how they can, and must of course fall to the Parish, if not timely relieved. Allowing one boy to be bound apprentice from each family out of work, eight thousand hands are deprived of getting a livelihood . . .

'How are those men, thus thrown out of employ to provide for their families; – and what are they to put their children apprentice to, that the rising generation may have something to keep them at work, in order that they may not be like vagabonds strolling about in idleness? Some say, Begin and learn some other business. – Suppose we do; who will maintain our families, whilst we undertake the arduous task; and when we have learned it, how do we know we shall be any better for all our pains; for by the time we have served our second apprenticeship, another machine may arise, which may take away that business also; so that our families, being half pined whilst we are learning how to provide them with bread, will be wholly so during the period of our third apprenticeship.'

(*Leeds Intelligencer*, 13 June 1786. The scribbling-machines referred to were used for teazing out the wool and straightening the fibres before spinning.)

The Case for New Machines

'The Cloth Merchants of Leeds, being informed that various kinds of Machinery, for the better and more expeditious dressing of woollen-cloth, have been lately invented, that many such Machines are already made and set to work in different Parts of this County . . . thought it necessary to meet together on the Eighteenth of October, to take into their most serious Consideration what Steps were needful to be taken, to prevent the Merchants and Cloth-Dressers in other Parts, from diminishing the Staple Trade of this Town, by the Enjoyment of superior Implements in their Business.

'At the said Meeting, attended by almost every Merchant in the Town, the above Facts did clearly appear, and after a Discussion of the Merits of various Inventions, and the Improvement in Dressing likely to be derived from them, it appeared to them all, absolutely necessary that this Town should partake of the Benefit of all Sorts of Improvements that are, or can be made in the Dressing of their Cloths, to prevent the Decline of that Business, of which the Town of Leeds has for Ages had the greatest Share . . .

'At a time when the People, engaged in every other Manufacture in the Kingdom, are exerting themselves to bring their Work to Market at reduced Prices, which can alone be effected by the Aid of Machinery, it certainly is not necessary that the Cloth Merchants of Leeds, who depend chiefly on a Foreign Demand, where they have for Competitors the Manufacturers of other Nations, whose Taxes are few, and whose manual Labour is only Half the Price it bears here, should have Occasion to defend a Conduct, which has for its Aim the Advantage of the Kingdom in general, and of the Cloth Trade in particular; yet anxious to prevent Misrepresentations, which have usually attended the Introduction of the most useful Machines, they wish to remind the Inhabitants of this Town, of the Advantages derived to every flourishing Manufacture from the Application of Machinery; they instance that of Cotton in particular, which in its internal and foreign Demand is nearly alike to our own, and has in a few Years by the Means of Machinery advanced to its present Importance, and is still increasing . . .

'In the Manufacture of Woollens, the Scribbling Mill, the Spinning Frame, and the Fly Shuttle, have reduced manual Labour nearly One-third, and each of them at its first Introduction carried an Alarm to the Work People, yet each has contributed to advance the Wages and to increase the Trade, so that if an Attempt was now made to deprive us of the Use of them, there is no doubt, but every Person engaged in the Business, would exert himself to defend them.

'From these Premises, we the undersigned Merchants . . . declare that we will protect and support the free Use of the proposed Improvements in Cloth-Dressing by every legal Means in our Power . . .'

(This proclamation by the Leeds cloth merchants was issued as a broadsheet in 1791.)

III: THE MANUFACTURING SYSTEM

The Effects of Competitive Industry

'Those who were engaged in the trade, manufactures, and commerce of this country thirty or forty years ago formed but a very insignificant portion of the knowledge, wealth, influence, or population of the Empire.

'Prior to that period, Britain was essentially agricultural. But, from that time to the present, the home and foreign trade have increased in a manner so rapid and extraordinary as to have raised commerce to an importance, which it never previously attained in any country possessing so much political power and influence . . .

'This change has been owing chiefly to the mechanical inventions which introduced the cotton trade into this country, and to the cultivation of the cotton tree in America. The wants which this trade created for the various materials requisite to forward its multiplied operations, caused an extraordinary demand for almost all the manufactures previously established, and, of course, for human labour. The numerous fanciful and useful fabrics manufactured from cotton soon became objects of desire in Europe and America: and the consequent extension of the British foreign trade was such as to astonish and confound the most enlightened statesmen both at home and abroad . . .

'The manufacturing system has already so far extended its influence over the British Empire, as to effect an essential change in the general character of the mass of the people. This alteration is still in rapid progress; and ere long, the comparatively happy simplicity of the agricultural peasant will be wholly lost amongst us. It is even now scarcely anywhere to be found without a mixture of those habits which are the offspring of trade, manufactures, and commerce . . .

'The inhabitants of every country are trained and formed by its great leading existing circumstances, and the character of the lower orders in Britain is now formed chiefly by circumstances arising from trade, manufactures, and commerce; and the governing principle of trade, manufactures, and commerce is immediate pecuniary gain, to which on the great scale every other is made to give way. All are sedulously trained to buy cheap and to sell dear; and to succeed in this art, the parties must be taught to acquire strong powers of deception; and thus a spirit is generated through every class of traders, destructive of that open, honest sincerity, without which man cannot make others happy, nor enjoy happiness himself . . .

'But the effects of this principle of gain, unrestrained, are still more lamentable on the working classes, those who are employed in the operative parts of the manufactures; for most of these branches are more or less unfavourable to the health and morals of adults. Yet parents do not hesitate to sacrifice the well-being of their children by putting them to occupations by which the constitution of their minds and bodies is rendered greatly inferior to what it might and ought to be under a system of common foresight and humanity . . .

'In the manufacturing districts it is common for parents to send their children of both sexes at seven or eight years of age, in winter as well as summer, at six o'clock in the morning, sometimes of course in the dark, and occasionally amidst frost and snow, to enter the manufactories, which are often heated to a high temperature, and contain an atmosphere far from being the most favourable to human life, and in which all those employed in them very frequently continue until twelve o'clock at noon, when an hour is allowed for dinner, after which they return to remain, in a majority of cases, till eight o'clock at night . . .'

(In these extracts from his *Observations on the Effect of the Manufacturing System*, 1815, Robert Owen wrote with all the authority of one of the most successful pioneer cotton spinners in the kingdom.)

Factory Slavery

'Before this infernal system was known in England; before this system, which has corrupted every thing, was known in this country, there were none of those places called Manufactories. To speak of these places with any degree of patience is impossible. It is to be a despicable hypocrite, to pretend to believe that the slaves in the West Indies are not better off than the slaves in these manufactories.

'Some of these lords of the loom have in their employ thousands of miserable creatures. In the cotton-spinning work, these creatures are kept, fourteen hours in each day, locked up, summer and winter, in a heat of from Eighty to Eightyfour degrees. The rules which they are subjected to are such as no negroes were ever subjected to.'

(William Cobbett, in his *Political Register*, 20 November 1824.)

Child Labour in the Mills

'[The 'Prentice House] was a large stone house surrounded by a wall from two to three yards high with but one door, which was kept locked. It was capable of lodging about one hundred and fifty prentices. When we went, there were about an hundred altogether, girls and boys. We all ate in the same room, and all went up a common stair case to our bed-chamber; all the boys slept in one chamber and all the girls in another. The beds were in rows along the wall, a second tier being fixed over the first. The beds were thus made double by a square frame work – one bed above, the other below. This was done to save room. There were about twenty of these beds, and we slept three in one bed. The girls' bed-room was of the same sort as ours. There were no fastenings to the two rooms and no one to watch over us in the night or to see what we did.

'We went to the mill at five o'clock without breakfast, and worked till about eight or nine, when they brought us our breakfast, which consisted of water porridge with oat-cake in it and onions to savour it with, in a tin can. This we ate as we best could, the wheel never stopping. We worked on till dinner time, which was not regular, sometimes half-past twelve, sometimes one. Our dinner was thus served to us. Across the door way of the room was a cross-bar like a police bar, and on the inside of the bar stood an old man with a stick to guard the provisions. These consisted of Derbyshire oat-cakes cut into four pieces, and ranged in two stacks. The one was buttered and the other treacled. By the side of the oat-cake were cans of milk piled up – butter-milk and sweet-milk. As we come up to the bar one by one the old man called out "Which'll 'ta have, butter or treacle, sweet or sour?" We then made our choice, drank down the milk and ran back to the mill with the oat-cake in our hand, without ever sitting down. We then worked on till nine or ten at night without bite or sup. When the mill stopped for good, we went to the house to our supper, which was the same as the breakfast – onion porridge and dry oat-cake. But even this was not always ready for us.'

(J. Brown, *A Memoir of Robert Blincoe*, 1832. This passage relates to Blincoe's experiences as a 'parish apprentice' at Litton Mill in Derbyshire, in 1815–16. He was then ten years old.)

Overwork

'In the details of employments, I have frequently had to animadvert on the *excess of labour*. From this cause a great proportion of town-operatives prematurely sink. "Worn out" is as often applied to a workman as a coach-horse, and frequently with equal propriety . . .

'It is especially incumbent on masters to regard the health of the persons they employ; to examine the effects of injurious agents, to invent and provide remedies and to enforce their application. This to me appears not only a call of humanity, but a direct duty. The attention of masters is too exclusively engaged with the manufacture itself – the means of effecting it at the least expense – and the market for its productions. The work-people are less thought of than the machinery: the latter is frequently examined to ascertain its capabilities – the former is scarcely ever. Care is seldom taken that the animal machine sustain as little injury as possible, and that it will bear the work imposed. Enough if the man, the woman, or the child be at work the requisite time, and perform what is required. If persons be disqualified for labour, fresh hands are promptly found. The master rarely knows what becomes of the persons dismissed, or the cause of their dismissal.'

(C. Turner Thackrah, *The Effects of Arts, Trades and Professions . . . on Health and Longevity,* 2nd edition, 1832.)

2

The Dignity of Danger

I: THE ARMY

BRIAN BOND

The extracts quoted in this chapter were selected with the aim of illustrating some of the salient characteristics of life in the Army in the late eighteenth and early nineteenth centuries. At this time there was still an enormous social gulf between the officer corps (the majority of whom purchased their commissions until 1871), and the rank and file, who were still mostly drawn from the dregs of society.

To say that life in the ranks was harsh and hazardous would be an understatement. Naïve youngsters were often inveigled into the service by false promises of bounty money, rapid promotion and glory. Barrack-room conditions could be abominable, pay was inadequate and punishment draconian. Worse still, treatment of the sick and wounded was all too often primitive and callous, while as yet there was little concern with pensions and aftercare in retirement. It has to be remembered, however, that the life of the common people was also exceedingly harsh; many old soldiers survived appalling experiences to recall the comradeship of the ranks as their happiest experience.

A point which must strike any student of the subject is the variety of the rank and file – they were certainly not an anonymous mass of robots without individuality. It is significant that so many rankers were sufficiently educated to write their memoirs, even allowing that those of a few, like Rifleman Harris, were written up from conversations. "71st", for example, came from a bourgeois Edinburgh home: he distressed his parents by becoming an actor and then sought refuge in the ranks after completely muffing his first appearance on the stage. William Cobbett was another unusual ranker and NCO, who later achieved fame as an author and politician. Moreover, since until 1871 most commissions had to be purchased, there was always a sprinkling of 'gentlemen rankers' who hoped eventually to be officers. There were also men like John Shipp, who loved the service so much that when he was obliged to sell his commission because of a debt, he re-enlisted in the ranks.

Another aspect which will impress the contemporary reader is the soldier's habitual fatalism or stoicism in conditions that would now be regarded as intolerable. Not only was there no Welfare State, but even the Englishman's basic rights, on which the orators lavished so much rhetoric, were scarcely in evidence when it came to soldiering. Press-ganged or deceived by recruiting sergeants, consigned to foul, disease-ridden quarters, undernourished, weighed down by huge packs, and callously treated when sick or wounded – how could men endure these conditions without rebelling (as indeed part of the Navy did in 1797)? How could they stand passively by while a comrade suffered several hundred lashes (sometimes dying) for some often petty offence? Worst of all, perhaps, how could the people tolerate a system which used its rank and file as cannon fodder and then turned the survivors, sick, wounded and elderly, on the streets with only a meagre pension, or perhaps none at all? Towards the end of this chapter the soldier from the 71st Regt decides in despair to emigrate to South America because he is destitute and cannot find employment in Britain. We can only conclude that civil life was so 'nasty, brutish and short' for many men that they were glad to find a temporary haven in the regiment – an enlarged family in which they found comradeship, a sense of purpose and self-respect. These extracts should cause us to reflect, as Kipling did so often in his Barrack Room Ballads, *on the contrast between the soldier's social standing in war and in peace.*

'For it's Tommy this and Tommy that, and Chuck him out, the brute!
But it's "Saviour of his country" when the guns begin to shoot.'

The social aspect of soldiering is one that deserves more attention from historians to counterbalance the great flood of publications on generalship and battles.

Social Structure and Social Authority

Sgt-Major William Cobbett instructs his officers on the new regimental drill books (late eighteenth century):

'To make this change was left to me, while not a single officer in the regiment paid the least attention to the matter; so that, when the time came for the annual review, I had to give lectures of instruction to the officers themselves, the Colonel not excepted; and, for several of them, I had to make out, upon large cards, which they bought for the purpose, little plans of the position of the regiment, together with lists of the words of command, which they had to give in the field. There was I, at the review, upon the flank of the grenadier company, with my worsted shoulder-knot, and my great high coarse, hairy cap; confounded in the ranks amongst other men, while those who were commanding me to move my hands or my feet, thus or thus, were, in fact, uttering words, which I had taught them; and were, in every thing except mere authority, my inferiors; and ought to have been commanded by me. It was impossible for reflections of this sort not to intrude themselves; and, as I advanced in experience, I felt less and less respect for those, whom I was compelled to obey.

'But I had a very delicate part to act with those gentry; for, while I despised them for their gross ignorance and their vanity, and hated them for their drunkenness and rapacity, I was fully sensible to their power. My path was full of rocks and pitfalls; and, as I never disguised my dislikes, or restrained my tongue, I should have been broken and flogged for fifty different offences, had they not been kept in awe by my consciousness of their inferiority to me, and by the real and almost indispensable necessity of the use of my talents. They, in fact, resigned all the disciplines of the regiment to me, and I very freely left them to swagger about and to get roaring drunk.'

(William Cobbett, *The Progress of a Ploughboy to a seat in Parliament*, 1835. Paperback edition of *The Autobiography of William Cobbett*, ed. W. Reitzel, 1967.)

By contrast Rifleman Harris, who served through the Napoleonic Wars, says the other ranks respect gentlemen as officers:

'It is indeed, singular, how a man loses or gains caste with his comrades from his behaviour, and how closely he is observed in the field. The officers too, are commented upon and closely observed. The men are very proud of those who are brave in the field, and kind and considerate to the soldiers under them. An act of kindness done by an officer has often during the battle been the cause of his life being saved. Nay, whatever folks may say upon the matter, I know from experience, that in our army the men like best to be officered by gentlemen, men whose education has rendered them more kind in manners than your coarser officer, sprung from obscure origin, and whose style is brutal and over-bearing.'

(*Recollections of Rifleman Harris*, ed. Capt. Henry Curling, 1848. New edition ed. Christopher Hibbert, 1970.)

A bugler of the 71st Foot describes an incident on the retreat to Corunna, 1808–9:

'We had to march early in the morning. I put a pair of dry stockings and shoes on to keep my feet comfortable. But we had not gone far when we came to a river. There was no bridge. We had to go into it, and pass over. One of our officers got his servant to carry him on his back. Our Colonel came riding to him, crying out "Put him down, put him down," for he was very angry. We were well pleased at it.'

('Peninsular Private: Bugler John MacFarlane of the 1st Bn, 71st Highland Regt', *Journal of the Society for Army Historical Research*, Vol. XXXII, 1954.)

Public Attitudes to the Other Ranks

*Private Wickins describes the callous ingratitude of the English
ladies rescued at Lucknow (1857) towards the ordinary soldier:*

'The Ladies, women and children were all brought out in
safety without a single casualty. And now let us see what
thanks we got from the ladies for all that we had done for
their safety and personal comfort. We, the relieving force,
were called all sorts of foul names – dirty, ill-looking
fellows, not in any way to be compared to the clean respectable and ever-obliging sepoy. The reader will scarcely
believe that in 1857 there were at Lucknow Englishwomen
who actually refused to help a poor fellow-countryman to a
drop of water. Yes, I assure you it is a fact, these Englishwomen, who had been rescued from a fate too horrible to
think of and had been protected during their imprisonment
with the beleaguered garrison of Lucknow by the ever-
brave and generous English soldier! And so protecting them
he had met with his death wound and now he is unable to
rise from his cot. He calls on his countrywomen for a drop
of water, either to quench his parched lips or otherwise to
wash his wounds. But what must have been the consterna-
tion of the poor dying soldier to have these women reply to
him in words to this effect? Pointing to the well they said,
"There is the well, my man, and you can get the water
yourself." And this to a dying man! And all likewards this
man had his death wound through rendering some assistance
to his ungrateful countrywoman.'

('The Indian Mutiny Journal of Private Charles Wickins, 9th
Regt', *Journal of the Society for Army Historical Research*, Vols.
XXXV and XXXVI, 1957 and 1958.)

*By contrast, the survivors from Corunna (1809) were well treated
by the people of Kent:*

'The people were looking at the regiment passing, but when
they saw me, I was looked on as an object of pity. Well
might they say, "Here is a representative of what we have

heard about the Corunna retreat." I was stopped; shoes and stockings were brought to me, and as I was putting them on, they were asking questions about me at the Corporal, for he was a countryman of their own. The English showed no small kindness to the soldiers that came from Corunna. When they came into the towns after marching, some of the people took them to their houses without billets. We came away, and I was very thankful for the kindness shewed to me. My comrade and I was billeted in a public house. After getting our supper, the people that came in to drink were asking us questions about what we had come through, and what we had seen.'

('Bugler of the 71st', op. cit.)

On Active Service

'*71st*' *outside Montevideo, 1806:*

'This was the first blood I had ever seen shed in battle; the first time the cannon had roared in my hearing charged with death. I was not yet seventeen years of age, and had not been six months from home. My limbs bending under me with fatigue, in a sultry clime, the musket and accoutrements that I was forced to carry were insupportably oppressive. Still I bore all with invincible patience. During the action, the thought of death never once crossed my mind. After the firing commenced, a still sensation stole over my whole frame, a firm determined torpor, bordering on insensibility. I heard an old soldier answer, to a youth like myself who inquired what he should do during the battle, "Do your duty."'

(*Journal of a Soldier of the 71st Regt, Highland Light Infantry, from 1800 to 1815, 1822.*)

Plundering the dead and wounded was a commonplace practice. Here Rifleman Harris describes an incident at Vilalero (1808) in the Peninsular War:

'After the battle I strolled about the field in order to see if there was anything to be found worth picking up amongst the dead. The first thing I saw was a three-pronged silver fork, which, as it lay by itself, had most likely been dropped by some person who had been on the look-out before me. A little further on I saw a French soldier sitting against a small rise in the ground or bank. He was wounded in the throat, and appeared very faint, the bosom of his coat being saturated with the blood which had flowed down. By his side lay his cap, and close to that was a bundle containing a quantity of gold and silver crosses, which I concluded he had plundered from some convent or church. He looked the picture of a sacrilegious thief, dying hopelessly, and overtaken by Divine wrath. I kicked his cap, which was also full of plunder, but I declined taking anything from him. I felt fearful of incurring the wrath of Heaven for the like offence, so I left him, and passed on. A little further off lay an officer of the 50th regiment. I knew him by sight, and recognized him as he lay. He was quite dead, and lying on his back. He had been plundered, and his clothes were torn open. Three bullet-holes were close together in the pit of his stomach: beside him lay an empty pocket-book, and his epaulette had been pulled from his shoulder. [Harris was twice fired on and then knocked over his assailant at about twenty paces.]

'It was a relief to me to find I had not been mistaken. He was a French light-infantryman, and I therefore took it quite in the way of business – he had attempted my life, and lost his own. It was the fortune of war; so, stooping down, with my sword I cut the green string that sustained his calabash, and took a hearty pull to quench my thirst.

'After I had shot the French light-infantryman, and quenched my thirst from his calabash, finding he was quite dead, I proceeded to search him. Whilst I turned him about in the endeavour at finding the booty I felt pretty certain he had gathered from the slain, an officer of the 60th approached, and accosted me.

'"What! looking for money my lad," said he, "Eh?" "I

35

am, sir," I answered; "But I cannot discover where this fellow has hid his hoard."

' "You knocked him over, my man," he said, "in good style, and deserve something for the shot. Here," he continued, stooping down and feeling in the lining of the Frenchman's coat, "this is the place where these rascals generally carry their coin. Rip up the lining of his coat, and then search his stock. I know them better than you seem to do."

'Thanking the officer for his courtesy, I proceeded to cut open the lining of his jacket with my sword bayonet and was rewarded for my labour by finding a yellow silk purse, wrapped up in an old black silk handkerchief. The purse contained several doubloons, three or four napoleons and a few dollars.'

'71st' describes a similar experience at Sobral, 1810:

'Here I first got any plunder. A French soldier lay upon the ground dead; he had fallen backwards; his hat had fallen off his head, which was kept up by his knapsack. I struck the hat with my foot, and felt it rattle; seized it in a moment, and, in the lining, found a gold watch and a silver crucifix. I kept them; as I had as good a right to them as any other. Yet they were not valuable in my estimation. At this time, life was held by so uncertain a tenure, and my comforts were so scanty, that I would have given the watch for a good meal and a dry shirt. There was not a dry stitch on my back, at the time, or for the next two days.'

'71st' at Waterloo:

'The artillery had been tearing away, since day-break, in different parts of the line. About twelve o'clock we received orders to fall in for attack. We then marched up to our positions, where we lay on the face of a brae, covering a brigade of guns. We were so overcome by the fatigue of the two days march, that scarce had we lain down until many of us fell asleep. I slept sound for some time, while the cannonballs plunging in amongst us killed a great many. I was suddenly awakened. A ball struck the ground a little below me, turned me heels-over-head, broke my musket in pieces, and killed a lad at my side. I was stunned and confused, and knew not whether I was wounded or not. I felt a numbness in my arm for some time.

'We lay thus, about an hour and a half, under a dreadful fire, which cost us about 60 men, while we had never fired a shot. The balls were falling thick amongst us. The young man I lately spoke of lost his legs by a shot at this time. They were cut very close: he soon bled to death. "Tom," said he, "remember your charge: my mother wept sore when my brother died in her arms. Do not tell her how I died; if she saw me thus, it would break her heart: farewell, God bless my parents!" He said no more, his lips quivered, and he ceased to breathe.'

And his reflections on the morrow:

'Many an action had I been in, wherein the individual exertions of our regiment had been much greater, and our fighting was so dreadful, and the noise so great. When I looked over the field of battle, it was covered and heaped in many places; figures moving up and down upon it. The wounded crawling along the rows of dead was a horrible spectacle; yet I looked on with less concern, I must say, at the moment, than I have felt at an accident, when in quarters. I have been sad at the burial of a comrade who died of sickness in the hospital, and followed him almost in tears: yet I have seen, after a battle, fifty put into the same trench, and comrades amongst them, almost with indifference. I looked over the field of Waterloo as a matter of course – a matter of small concern.'

A 17th Lancer (Trooper Wightman) describes an example of heroic self-sacrifice after the Charge of the Light Brigade at Balaclava (1854):

'Not many of Corporal Morley's party got back. My horse was shot dead, riddled with bullets. One bullet struck me on the forehead, another passed through the top of my shoulder, while struggling out from under my horse a Cossack standing over me stabbed me with his lance once in the neck near the jugular, again above the collar-bone, several times in the back and once under the short rib; and when having regained my feet, I was trying to draw my sword, he sent his lance through the palm of my hand. I believe he would have succeeded in killing me, clumsy as he was, if I had not blinded him for the moment with a handful of sand. Fletcher at the same time lost his horse, and it seems was wounded. We were very roughly used. The Cossacks at first hauled us along by the tails of our coatees and our haversacks. When we got on foot they drove their lance-butts into our backs to stir us on. With my shattered knee and the other bullet wound on the shin of the same leg, I could barely limp, and good old Fletcher said "Get on my back, chum." I did so, and then found that he had been shot through the back of the head. When I told him of this, his only answer was, "Oh, never mind that, it's not much, I don't think." But it was that much that he died of the wound a few days later; and here was a doomed man himself, making light of a mortal wound, and carrying a chance comrade of another regiment on his back. I can write this, but I could not tell of it in speech, because I know I should play the woman.'

(J. W. Wightman, 'One of the "Six Hundred" in the Balaclava Charge', in *The Nineteenth Century*, May 1892.)

Conditions of Service Life

William Cobbett instances a typical piece of recruiting blarney, and the distressing effects of inadequate pay in the late eighteenth century:

'When I told the Captain that I had thought myself engaged in the marines, "By Jasus, my lad," said he, "and you have had a narrow escape." He told me, that the regiment into which I had been so happy as to enlist was one of the oldest and boldest in the whole army, and that it was at that time serving in that fine, flourishing and plentiful country, Nova Scotia. He dwelt long on the beauties and riches of this terrestrial paradise, and dismissed me, perfectly enchanted with the prospect of a voyage thither.

'I enlisted in 1784, and, as peace had then taken place, no great haste was made to send recruits off to their regiments. I remember well what sixpence a day was, recollecting the pangs of hunger felt by me, during the thirteen months that I was a private soldier at Chatham, previous to my embarkation for Nova Scotia. Of my sixpence, nothing like fivepence was left to purchase food for the day. Indeed not fourpence. For there was washing, mending, soap, flour for hair-powder, shoes, stockings, shirts, stocks and gaiters, pipe-clay and several other things to come out of the miserable sixpence! Judge then of the quantity of food to sustain life in a lad of sixteen, and to enable him to exercise with a musket (weighing fourteen pounds) six to eight hours every day . . . The best battalion I ever saw in my life was composed of men, the far greater part of whom were enlisted before they were sixteen, and who, when they were first brought up to the regiment, were cloathed in coats much too long and too large, in order to leave room for growing.

'We had several recruits from Norfolk (our regiment was the West Norfolk); and many of them deserted from sheer hunger. They were lads from the plough-tail. I remember two that went into a decline and died during the year, though when they joined us, they were fine hearty young men.

'I have seen them lay in their berths, many and many a time, actually crying on account of hunger. The whole week's food was not a bit too much for one day.'

Troubles of a raw recruit, 1806:

'On the 6th April 1806, I enlisted in the 43rd regiment of the line, and in company with several other recruits proceeded to Bristol, at which place, after a rough passage, we safely landed; and in a few days reached the town of Ashford in Kent, where the regiment was quartered.

'The sleeping room of which I was an inmate was an oblong building of unusually large dimensions, and was occupied by three companies, of an hundred men each ... many were Irish, and a few more were English, several Welshmen were intermingled, and a few Scotchmen came in to complete the whole. Most of these, and that was the only point of general resemblance, had indulged in excessive drinking. Some were uproariously merry; on others the effect was directly the reverse; and nothing less than a fight, it matter not with whom, would satisfy. Meantime, as they were unable to abuse each other in language mutually intelligible, exclamations profoundly jocular or absurdly rancorous ran through the building. Never will the occurrence of that night be effaced from my mind. Surely, I thought, hell from beneath is moved to engulf us all ...'

(*Memoirs of a Sergeant late in the 43rd Light Infantry Regiment*, 1835.)

Reasons for Enlistment in the 1840s

'1. Indigent – Embracing labourers and mechanics out of employ, who merely seek for support   80 in 120
'2. Indigent – Respectable persons induced by misfortune or imprudence   2 in 120
'3. Idle – Who consider a soldier's life an easy one   16 in 120
'4. Bad characters – Who fall back upon the army as a last resource   8 in 120
'5. Criminals – Who seek to escape from the consequence of their offences   1 in 120
'6. Perverse sons – Who seek to grieve their parents   2 in 120
'7. Discontented and restless   8 in 120
'8. Ambitious   1 in 120
'9. Others   2 in 120'

(J. MacMullen (late Staff Sergeant of the 13th Infantry), *Camp and Barrack Room; or, the British Army as it is*, 1846.)

Staff Sergeant J. MacMullen describes barrack life before the Crimean War:

'All recruits on their first arrival at Chatham, are sent to their several depots. The sleeping accommodations in this place were anything but of the best; no one being allowed sheets, because they are said to be retentive of a certain contagious disease, of a most disagreeable though not very dangerous character; and as to the beds, they were, as one of my companions facetiously expressed it, like the continent of Asia, thickly peopled with black, brown and white inhabitants. The origin and perpetuation of this nuisance, may be in part ascribed to the uncleanly habits of some prior to enlistment.

'Probably some reader may wish to know the daily routine of my duties and amusements at this period. I rose at five o' clock in the morning, and made up my bed; which occupied at the least a quarter of an hour, and was rather a troublesome job. I then made my toilet, and at six turned out for drill; had dinner at one, in the shape of potatoes and meat, both usually of the most wretched quality; and at two fell in for another drill, which terminated at four; after which hour my time was at my own disposal until tattoo, provided I was not ordered on picquet . . .'

Alexander Alexander enlisted in Glasgow in 1801 determined to assert his independence after family friction:

'The first man I saw punished my heart was like to burst. It was with difficulty I could restrain my tears, as the thought broke upon me of what I had brought myself to. Indeed, my spirits sunk from that day, and all hopes of bettering my condition of life fled forever. I had hitherto only seen the pomp of war – the gloss and glitter of the army; now I was introduced into the arcana of its origination, and under the direct influence of its stern economy. I felt how much I had been deceived.

'Another circumstance I must not omit before I leave Chatham; it made a great impression on me and all the troops. A poor fellow of the 9th regiment, said to be a farmer's son in Suffolk, had the misfortune to be found asleep on his post. General Sir John Moore had the command of the Chatham division at the time; he was a severe disciplinarian. The soldier was tried by a court-martial, and sentenced to be flogged; all the troops were paraded to witness the punishment. It was a very stormy morning; the frost, which had continued for some days, gave way during the night, and the wind and sleet drove most piteously: it was a severe punishment to stand clothed looking on, how much more so to be stripped to the waist, and tied up to the halberts. The soldier was a fine-looking lad, and bore an excellent character in his regiment; his officers were much interested in his behalf, and made great intercession for him to the General. But all their pleading was in vain, the General remained inflexible and made a very long speech after the punishment, in which he reflected in very severe terms on the conduct of the officers and non-commissioned officers present, observing, that if they did their duty as strictly as they had any regard for their men, they ought never to report them to him, for he would pardon no man when found guilty. The poor fellow got two hundred and twenty-nine lashes, but they were uncommonly severe. I saw the drum-major strike a drummer to the ground for not using his strength sufficiently. General Sir John Moore was present all the time. At length, the surgeon interfered, the poor fellow's back was black as the darkest mahogany, and dreadfully swelled. The cats being too thick, they did not cut, which made the punishment more severe. He was instantly taken down and carried to the hospital, where he died in eight days afterwards his back having mortified. It was the cold I think that killed him; for I have often seen seven hundred lashes inflicted, but I never saw a man's back so horrible to look upon.'

(*The Life of Alexander Alexander*, written by himself, ed. John Howell, 2 vols., 1830.)

Although social conditions in the Army gradually improved after the Crimean War, recruits were still drawn mostly from the lowest classes, so that illiteracy remained a problem:

'The 14th Hussars contained as fine a body of fighting men and as smart a set of soldiers as any in the British army, their only fault being a liking for pongelo, for, truth to tell, they were hard drinkers. It must also be admitted that they were not as clever with the pen as with the sword, and in the matter of "the three R's" could not be compared with the young soldiers of the present day, who are scholars by Act of Parliament. But it is an ill wind that blows nobody any good, and my education now stood me in good stead; for of the fifteen men in my room, not one could write, and only one could read, and my ability to do both soon proved to my advantage.'

(E. Mole, *A King's Hussar: Being the Military Memoirs for Twenty-five years of a Troop-Sergeant-Major of the 14th (King's) Hussars,* 1893.)

Retrospection and Reflections on the Military Life

Alexander Alexander was discharged in 1814, sick and with a pension of only ninepence per day. He had served four years longer than some of his fellows, who nevertheless received one shilling:

'No sooner had I got my discharge in my pocket than I felt I was a new man; I was once more free; I actually thought I stood a few inches higher, as I stretched myself like one who has just laid down a heavy load.'

A discharged soldier's sad farewell to his family, 1818:

'Edinburgh, May, 1818.
'Dear John,
'These three months I can find nothing to do. I am a burden on Jeanie and her husband. I wish I was a soldier again. I cannot even get labouring work. God will bless those, I hope, who have been good to me. I have seen my folly. I would be

useful, but can get nothing to do. My mother is at her rest –
God receive her soul! – I will go to South America . . . If I
succeed in the South, I will return and lay my bones besides
my parents: if not, I will never come back.'

(*Journal of a Soldier of the '71st' Regiment*, op. cit.)

Cobbett's reflections on the military life:

' "Once a soldier, always a soldier", is a maxim, the truth
of which I need not insist on to anyone who has ever served
in the army for any length of time, and especially, if the
service he has seen has embraced those scenes and occasions
where every man first or last, from one cause or another,
owes the preservation of his all, health and life not excepted,
to the kindness, the generosity, the fellow-feeling of his
comrades . . .

'Of this military feeling, I do not believe that any man
ever possessed greater portion than myself. I like soldiers, as
a class in life, better than any other description of men.
Their conversation is more pleasing to me; they have
generally seen more than other men; they have less of
vulgar prejudice about them. Amongst soldiers, less than
amongst any other description of men, have I observed the
vices of lying and hypocrisy.'

Rifleman Harris:

'The field of death and slaughter, the march, the bivouac,
and the retreat, are no bad places in which to judge of men.
I have had some opportunities of judging them in all these
situations, and I should say that the British are amongst the
most splendid soldiers in the world. Give them fair play,
and they are unconquerable. For my own part I can only
say that I enjoyed life more whilst on active service, than I
have ever done since; and as I sit at work in my [cobbler's]
shop in Richmond Street, Soho, I look back upon that
portion of my time spent in the fields of the Peninsula as the
only part worthy of remembrance. It is at such times that
scenes long passed come back upon my mind as if they had

taken place but yesterday. I remember even the very appearance of some of the regiments engaged; and comrades, long mouldered to dust, I see again performing the acts of heroes.'

II: THE NAVY

CHRISTOPHER LLOYD

When wars escalated from the 'temperate and undecisive conflicts' of Gibbon's day to the total war against the French Revolution and Napoleon, the strain on the nation's seagoing population became intense. It had been difficult enough to man a fleet of 30–40,000 men earlier in the century, but by the end of the Napoleonic war this had risen to 142,000, in addition to which there were Sea Fencibles (a maritime militia) and an expanding merchant marine.

There had never been any difficulty about the recruitment of officers, because they belonged to an honourable and comparatively lucrative profession, even though a naval officer joined as a boy in the humble capacity of Captain's Servant or Volunteer First Class. Roughly half a ship's company was also composed of volunteers, attracted by the bounties offered at the beginning of a war; but to fill the complement of over 100 ships of the line and 150 frigates necessitated stringent methods of impressment, i.e. conscription by force. By the Quota Acts passed early in the war every county and borough was required to send a proportion of its inhabitants to the fleet, so that many petty criminals and unskilled landsmen were drafted to the ships. They deserted or died of disease in large numbers, and in 1797 they mutinied. 'What were you to expect,' asked Admiral Collingwood, 'from the refuse of the gallows and the purgings of the gaols, when such make a majority of most ships' companies in such a war as this?'

To control such heterogeneous crews, discipline had to be harsh, nor were conditions at sea ever attractive. The mutineers did not complain of the frequent floggings because they realized their necessity, as well as the fact that such brutal punishments were common on shore. What they complained of was the monthly pay of nineteen shillings for an Ordinary Seaman (a wage which had not been increased since Cromwell's day) and the poor quality of their victuals. Food was indeed bad, largely because the art of preserving it was not discovered until the last year of the war, when canned meat and vegetables were first issued on a limited scale; but the quantity was generous – 6 lb. of salt beef or pork a week for men who seldom ate meat at home, and an issue of grog twice daily which made many who were not accustomed to it feel 'groggy'. Though pay was increased after the mutinies, other aspects of life at sea could not be improved until after the war was over.

The most fatal consequence of overcrowding such ships was the outbreak of epidemics of typhus or dysentery, though no longer of scurvy because of the adoption of the antidote of lemon juice. Over 80 per cent of the casualties were due to disease, only 6 per cent being due to enemy action. Furthermore, shore leave could seldom be permitted because men deserted in large numbers, hence the presence of women on board when ships were in port.

One result of drafting so many landsmen into the Navy was the presence of some literate persons on board, the professional seaman not being normally an articulate man. The type of evidence provided by men from the Lower Deck is very rare previous to this date, though there are plenty of reminiscences by naval officers. Most of our extracts come from memoirs written in later life by men who served and suffered in the war, hence their radical and critical tone.

It was only after the twenty years' war was over and the Navy was reduced to a manageable size that it became possible to render the seaman's life a little more tolerable with the spread of a more humanitarian spirit, largely due to the influence of the Evangelicals. The class structure and the hierarchy of the naval profession remained rigid, so that the gulf between the Quarter Deck and the Lower Deck was as insurmountable as ever; but the life of the true man-o'-war's seaman, mostly recruited from south coast towns, was immensely improved after the discharge of those impressed for hostilities only.

Joining the Navy – Volunteers

'Towards the autumn of 1782 I went to visit a relation at Portsmouth. From the top of Portsdown hill I, for the first time, beheld the sea, and no sooner did I behold it than I wished to be a sailor. I could never account for this sudden impulse, nor can I now; it would seem that, like young ducks, instinct leads them to rush to the bosom of the water.

'But it was not the sea alone that I saw; the grand fleet was riding at anchor at Spithead; I had formed my own ideas of a ship, but what I now beheld so far surpassed what I had ever been able to form a conception of that I stood lost between astonishment and admiration. My heart was inflated with national pride. The sailors were my country-men, the fleet belonged to my country and surely I had a part in it and all its honours.'

(William Cobbett, *The Life and Adventures of Peter Porcupine*, 1796. When Cobbett found his way on board, the captain advised him to return home. He later joined the Army.)

'In going across the harbour we passed close under the stern of the *Royal George*. It was the first time I ever floated on salt water, the first hundred-gun ship I ever saw. Ye gods! What a sight – what a sensation! I feel it now as I write. It is impossible to forget the breathless astonishment and delight with which my eyes were fixed upon this ship. Nothing so exquisitely touching has ever occurred to me since to pro-duce such frantic joy. After the first exclamation of ecstasy I for a time spoke not a word; until presently, as we approached nearer to the *Royal George* and went closely under her richly carved stern, I broke into a succession of questions, and jumping about and almost springing out of the hands of the strokesman of the boat, who held me as I stood upon the seat. I was told that I would tumble into the water if I was not quiet. What nonsense! Who could be quiet in such circumstances?'

(Journals of Admiral Sir T. Byam Martin, 1781; printed by the Navy Records Society. Martin later became an Admiral of the Fleet. The *Royal George* sank at Spithead the year after this incident.)

'On descending the hatchway, I turned to view the main deck. Ye gods, what a difference! I had anticipated a kind of elegant house with guns in the windows. Here were the tars of England, rolling about casks, without jackets, shoes or stockings. On one side provisions were received on board; at one port-hole coals, at another wood; dirty women, the objects of the sailors' affections, with beer cans in their hands, were everywhere conspicuous; the shrill whistle squeaked, and the voice of the boatswain and his mates rattled like thunder in my ears; the deck was dirty, slippery and wet; the smells abominable; the whole sight disgusting; and when I noticed the slovenly attire of the midshipmen, some without shoes, I forgot all the glory of Nelson, all the pride of the Navy or the bulwarks of Albion; and for nearly the first time in my life I took the handkerchief from my pocket, covered my face, and cried like the child I was.'

(Captain Frederick Chamier, *The Life of a Sailor*, 1834. Like his friend, Captain Marryat, Chamier joined as a Captain's Servant at the age of twelve.)

'On my introduction to my new shipmates I was shown down to the starboard wing berth. I had not long been seated before a rugged-muzzled midshipman came in, and having eyed me for a short time, he sang out with a voice of thunder: "Blister my tripes, where the hell did you come from? I suppose you want to stick your grinders (for it was near dinner time) into some of our à la mode beef"; and without waiting for a reply he sat down and sang a song that I shall remember as long as I live. The first verse, being the most moral, I shall give.

A Duchess from Germany
   Has lately made her will;
Her body she's left to be buried,
   Her soul to the devil in hell . . .'

(From the Recollections of James Anthony Gardner, edited under the original title of *Above and Under Hatches* by C. Lloyd, 1953. Gardner joined as a Captain's Servant in 1775.)

'All true-blue hearts of oak who are able, and no doubt willing, to serve their good King and Country on board his

Majesty's ships are hereby invited to repair to the Roundabout Tavern near New Crane, Wapping, where they will find Lieutenant James Ayscough, who still keeps open his right royal, senior and general Portsmouth Rendezvous for the entertainment and reception of such gallant seamen, who are proud to serve the ships now lying at Portsmouth, Chatham and Sheerness.

'Lieutenant Ayscough will be damned happy to shake hands with any of his old shipmates in particular, or their jolly friends. Keep it up boys!

'Able seamen will receive three pounds bounty, and Ordinary seamen two pounds, with conduct money and their chests and bedding rent free.

'For the encouragement of discovering Seamen that may be impressed, a REWARD of two pounds will be given.

'Success to his Majesty's Navy! With health and limbs to the jolly tars of old England.'

GOD SAVE THE KING

(Recruiting poster of 1780, printed in C. Lloyd, *The British Seaman*, 1968. Posters offering such bounties were displayed at recruiting centres called 'rendezvous'.)

Joining the Navy – Impressment

'As I crossed Tower wharf, a squat, tawny fellow with a hanger by his side and a cudgel in his hand, came up to me calling "Yo, ho, brother, you must come along with me". As I did not like his appearance, instead of answering his salutation I quickened my pace, in hope of ridding myself of his company; upon which he whistled aloud and immediately another sailor appeared before me, who laid hold of me by the collar and began to drag me along. Not being of a humour to relish such treatment, I disengaged myself from my assailant and with one blow of my cudgel laid him motionless on the ground and perceiving myself surrounded in a trice by ten or a dozen more, exerted myself with such dexterity that some of my opponents were fain to attack me with drawn cutlasses; and after an obstinate engagement, in which I received a large wound on my head, I was disarmed, taken prisoner and carried on board a pressing tender, where I was thrust into the hold among a parcel of wretches, the sight of whom well nigh distracted me.

'I complained bitterly to the midshipman on the deck, telling him that unless my hurts were dressed I should bleed to death. But compassion was a weakness of which no man can accuse this person, who, squirting a mouthful of tobacco upon me through the gratings, told me I was a mutinous dog and that I might die and be damned.'

(Tobias Smollett, *Roderick Random*, 1748. Smollett served as a surgeon's mate in the War of Jenkins' Ear.)

'I lament the unhappy necessity of providing for the safety of the state by a temporary invasion of the personal liberty of the subject. Would to God it was practicable to reconcile these important objects in every situation of public affairs. But I can never doubt that the community has a right to command as well as purchase the services of its members. I see that right founded originally upon a necessity which supersedes all arguments. I see it established by usage immemorial and admitted by more than a tacit assent of the legislature. I conclude there is no remedy, in the nature of things, for the grievance complained of; for if there were, it must have long since been redressed.'

(From the *Letters of Junius*, 1771.)

'In the distribution of the duties of society, those that are offensive and disagreeable public duties – among which we reckon personal service in the armies and navies of the state – must fall to the lot of that part of mankind which fills the lower ranks of life. In the advanced state of government which the British nation has reached, personal service is not, nor ought to be, the duty of *every* citizen.'

(Charles Butler, *On the Legality of Impressing Seamen*, 1778. A typical eighteenth-century defence of impressment.)

'Dear Wife. I should be glad to know how you live; where I am it is a prison. I would give all that I had, if it were a hundred guineas, if I could get on shore. I only lays on the deck every night. I hope my wife is easy in her mind as well as she can. There is no hopes of my getting to you. We are looked upon as a dog and not so good. It is worse than a prison. They flog them every day only if they get drunk. Dear wife, do the best you can for the children and God prosper you and them till I come back.'

(Letter from Richard Hall, pressed in 1800; printed in *Five Naval Journals*, ed. J. R. Thursfield, Navy Records Society.)

'Captain B-, Sir, there is a Desartar of yours at the upper water gate. Lives at the sign of the mansion house. He is an Irishman, goes by the name of Mack Mullins, and is trying to ruin a Widow and three Children, for he has insinuated into the old woman's favour so far that she must sartingly come to Poverty; and you by Sarching the books will find what I have related to be true and much oblige the whole Parish of St Pickles, Deptford. Nancy of Deptford.'

(Letter of 1771 in Public Record Office. Adm.1/1495. St Pickles is St Nicholas.)

Life on Board

'A ship is worse than a jail. There is, in a jail ... better company, better conveniency of every kind; and a ship has the additional disadvantage of being in danger. When men come to like a sea-life, they are not fit to live on land ... every man thinks meanly of himself for not having been a soldier, or not having been at sea. *Boswell* – Lord Mansfield does not. *Johnson* – Sir, if Lord Mansfield were in a company of general officers and admirals ... he would shrink; he'd wish to creep under the table ... Sir, the impression is universal; yet it is strange. As to the sailor, when you look down from the quarter deck to the space below, you see the utmost extremity of human misery: such crowding, such filth, such stench! *Boswell* – Yet sailors are happy. *Johnson* – They are

happy as brutes are happy, with a piece of fresh meat – with the grossest sensuality. But, Sir, the profession of soldiers and sailors has the dignity of danger . . .
'*Scott* – We find people fond of being sailors. *Johnson* – I cannot account for that, any more than I can account for other strange perversions of the imagination.'

(Boswell, *Life of Johnson*, 1791.)

'Seamen in the King's ships have made buttons for their jackets and trousers with the cheese they were served with, having preferred it, by reason of its tough and durable quality, to buttons made of common metal . . . The flour in the King's ships has been devoured by weevils, and so become intolerably musty and cemented into such hard rocks that the men have been obliged to use instruments to pulverise it . . . Their bread has been so full of large black-headed maggots and they have been so nauseated by thoughts of it as to be obliged to shut their eyes before they could bring their minds into a resolution of consuming it.'

(W. Thompson, *An Appeal to the Public*, 1761.)

'The sourkrout, the men at first would not eat, until I put into practice a method I never knew to fail with seamen, and this was to have some of it dressed every day for the Cabin table and left it to the option of the men either to take as much as they pleased or none at all. This practice was not continued above a week before I found it necessary to put everyone on board on an allowance. For such are the tempers and disposition of seamen that whatever you give them out of the common way, although it be ever so much for their good, it will not go down and you will hear nothing but murmurings against the man that first invented it; but the moment they see their superiors set value upon it, it becomes the finest stuff in the world, and the inventor an honest fellow.'

(Captain James Cook, *Journal of First Voyage*, 1768–71.)

'My Lords, We the seamen of his Majesty's navy, take the

liberty of addressing your Lordships in an humble petition, shewing the many hardships and oppressions we have laboured under for many years and which we hope your Lordships will redress as soon as possible. We do not boast of our good services for any other purpose than of putting you and the nation in mind of the respect due to us, nor do we ever intend to deviate from our former character.

'The first grievance we have to complain of is that our wages are too low and ought to be raised, that we might be the better able to support our wives and families in a manner comfortable.

'We, your petitioners, beg that your Lordships will take into consideration the grievances of which we complain and now lay before you.

'First, that our Provisions be raised to the weight of sixteen ounces to the pound and of a better quality.

'Secondly, that your petitioners request your honours will be pleased to grant a sufficient quantity of vegetables of such kind as may be most plentiful in the ports to which we go; which we grievously complain and lie under want of.

'Thirdly, that your Lordships will be so kind as to look into this affair, which is nowise unreasonable; and that we may be looked upon as a number of men standing in defence of our country; and that we may in somewise have opportunity to taste the sweets of liberty on shore, when in any harbour and when we have completed the duty of our ship after our return from sea.

'It is also unanimously agreed by the fleet that, from this day, no grievances shall be received, in order to convince the nation at large that we know when to cease, as well as to begin, and that we ask nothing but what is moderate and may be granted without detriment to the nation or any injury to the service.

'Given on board the *Queen Charlotte*, by the Delegates of the Fleet, the 18th day of April, 1797.'

(Petition of the Mutineers at Spithead, 1797, printed in C. Lloyd, *The British Seaman*, 1968.)

'For the Lords Commissioners of the Admiralty – Damn my eyes if I understand your lingo or long Proclamations, but in short give us our Due at once and no more at it, till we go in search of the Enemies of our Country. Henry Long. On Board His Majesty's Ship *Champion*.'

(Quoted in Peter Kemp, *The British Sailor*, 1970.)

'Sent Samuel Morgan, a prisoner for desertion, on board the *Barfleur*, and the next day he and two other men were tried by court martial and sentenced to 300 lashes. Poor Morgan was much to be pitied, being a good and mild creature and almost fainted when the sentence was pronounced. By the kind interference of the humane Lady Hardy he got reprieved, but the other two poor fellows were punished round the fleet; but did not receive the number of lashes because they could not bear it, so they were sent on board the flagship until they recovered to receive the remainder.

'Horrid work! Could anyone bear to see a beast used so, let alone a fellow creature? People may talk of negro slavery and the whip, but let them look nearer home and see a poor sailor arrived from a long voyage, exulting in the pleasure of soon being among his dearest friends and relations. Behold him just entering the door when a press gang seizes him like a felon, drags him away and puts him into a tender's hold, and from thence he is sent on board a man-of-war, perhaps ready to sail for some foreign station, without ever seeing his wife or friends. If he complains, he is likely to be seized up and flogged with a cat, much more severe than the negro driver's whip, and if he deserts he is flogged round the fleet nearly to death. Surely they had better shoot a man at once.'

(William Richardson, c. 1800, *A Mariner of England*, 1908.)

'On the arrival of a ship of war in port crowds of boats flock off with cargoes of prostitutes. Having no money to pay for their conveyance, the waterman takes as many as his boat will hold and hovers around the ship until she is secured at her anchors and the necessary work done, when he is permitted to come alongside. The men then go into the boats and pick out each a woman, paying a shilling or two to the boatman for her passage. The women are examined at the gangway for liquor which they are in the habit of smuggling aboard. They then descend to the lower deck with their husbands, as they call them. Hundreds come off to a large ship. The whole of the transactions of the lower deck it is impossible to describe – the dirt, filth and stench; the disgusting conversation; the indecent, beastly conduct and horrible scenes; the blasphemy and swearing; the riots, quarrels and fighting which often take place, where hundreds of men and women are huddled together in one room, as it were, and where in bed they are squeezed between the next hammocks and must be witnesses of each other's actions . . . Let those who have never seen a ship of war picture to themselves a very large low room with 500 men and probably 300 or 400 women of the vilest description shut up in it, and giving way to every excess of debauchery that the grossest passions of human nature can lead them to, and they see the deck of a ship the night of her arrival.'

(From an anonymous pamphlet, *A Statement of Certain Immoral Practices in H.M. Ships*, 1822; probably by Admiral Hawkins.)

Action

'Most of the crew were on deck, eagerly straining their eyes to obtain a glimpse of the approaching ship, and murmuring their opinion to each other on her probable character. Then came the voice of the Captain, shouting "Keep silence, fore and aft." He hailed the look-out, who replied "A large frigate, bearing down on us, sir." A whisper ran along the crew that the strange ship was the Yankee frigate *United States*. The thought was confirmed by the command "All hands clear the ship for action, ahoy!" The drum and fife beat to quarters; bulkheads were knocked away; the guns run out; the whole dread paraphernalia of battle was produced; and after a few minutes of hurry and confusion, every

man and boy was at his post, ready to do his best service for
his country . . .

'The cries of the wounded now rang through all parts of
the ship. These were carried to the cockpit as fast as they
fell, while those who were killed outright were immediately
thrown overboard. As I was stationed near the main hatchway I could catch a glance at all who were carried below. A
glance was all that I could indulge in, for the boys belonging
to the guns next to mine were wounded in the early part of
the action and I had to keep three or four guns supplied with
cartridges. Our men kept cheering with all their might. I
cheered with them, though I confess I scarcely knew for
what. Certainly there was nothing very inspiring in the
aspect of things where I was stationed, so terrible had been
the work of destruction around us.

'We kept on our shouting and firing. Our men fought like
tigers. Some of them pulled off their jackets and vests; some,
still more determined, had taken off their shirts and with
nothing but a handkerchief tied round the waistbands of
their trousers fought like heroes. Suddenly the rattling of
the iron hail ceased. We were ordered to cease firing. A profound silence ensued, broken only by the groans of the brave
sufferers below. The enemy had shot ahead to repair
damages, but we lay utterly helpless in a state of complete
wreck.'

(Samuel Leech, *A Voice from the Middle Deck*, 1844. Leech, the
son of a gardener at Blenheim, describes the action between
HMS Macedonian and *USN United States* in 1812. He became an
American citizen to escape a charge of desertion.)

The Happy Ship

'Then was the time for the frigate to revel in her falcon
speed. She darted down and along to the uttermost parts of
the scattered fleet, now whizzing to the east, throwing up
broad and spreading fountains of spray as she split the on-
coming billows in her eastward dash; then rocking from side
to side, till her yard arms pointed to the yeasty waves, as she

swung in balance before the wind in her northward run;
now bounding to this point, now darting to that, and
wheeling round with all the rushing sweep of an eagle round
a flock of swans that flap their wings in laboured motion,
until resuming her first position, she half enfolded her wings
and floated as she rested on her sea. Faith, I began to be
proud of my ship!'

(C. R. Pemberton, *Autobiography of Pel Verjuice*, ed. R. Partridge,
1929.)

'So I left the happy *Prompte*, a ship where there was none of
your browbeating allowed, nor that austere authority where
two men durst hardly be seen speaking together, as I have
since seen in the service. The *Prompte*'s crew were like a
family united and would, both officers and men, risk their
lives to assist each other. This I knew well, having belonged
to her more than five years in continual active service and on
many trying occasions, too.'

(W. Richardson, *A Mariner of England*, 1908.)

'It gave me great pleasure to find by your last letters that
you were so youthful and strong as to take walks, which I
believe are past my ability. We are going on here in our
usual way, watching an enemy who, I begin to suspect, has
no intention of coming out, and I am almost worn down by
impatience and the constant being at sea. I have devoted
myself faithfully to my country's service; but it cannot last
much longer, for I grow weak and feeble, and shall soon only
be fit to be nursed and live in quiet retirement; for, having
been so long out of the world, I believe I shall be found
totally unfit to live in retirement.

'Tell me, how do the trees which I planted thrive? Is
there shade under the three oaks for a comfortable summer
seat? Do the poplars grow at the walk, and does the wall of
the terrace stand firm?'

(*Memoirs and Correspondence of Lord Collingwood*, ed. Newnham
Collingwood, 1837. Collingwood, in command of the blockading
fleet in the Mediterranean in 1807, is writing to his wife.)

'A better friend of seamen never trod the quarter-deck. He [Collingwood] took especial care of the boys. Blow high, blow low, he had us arranged in line on the poop every morning and he himself inspected us to see that we were all clean and in good trim. No swearing, threatening or bullying was to be heard or seen. Boatswain's mates dared not to be seen with a rope's end in hand; nor do I recollect of a single instance of a man being flogged on board. Was discipline neglected then? By no means. There was not a better disciplined crew in the fleet.'

(From the journal of Landsman Hay, ed. M. A. Hay, 1953. Robert Hay ran away to sea in 1803 at the age of fourteen; he later deserted.)

'My life, for a period of twenty-five years, was a continued succession of change. Twice I circumnavigated the globe; three times I was in China; twice in Egypt; and more than once sailed along the whole landboard of America from Nootka Sound to Cape Horn; twice I doubled it. Old as I am, my heart is still unchanged and were I young and stout again I would sail upon discovery; but, weak and stiff, I can only send my prayers with the tight ship and her merry hearts.

'I can look to my deathbed with resignation, but to the poorhouse I cannot look with composure. I have been a wanderer and the child of chance all my days; and now look only for the time when I shall enter my last ship, and be anchored with a green turf upon my breast; and I care not how soon the command is given.'

(From *The Life of John Nicol, Mariner*, 1822.)

3

True-Born Britons

GWYN A. WILLIAMS

In the winter of 1791–2, as the powers of Europe moved towards war against the France of the Revolution, groups of like-minded men, artisans and working people, in Sheffield, Norwich, London and other centres came together in political societies to organize around the London Corresponding Society the first serious popular political movement in our history. Their programme was full political democracy, manhood suffrage, annual parliaments, vote by ballot.

Apprentices to Liberty

This was no failed French Revolution; the movement grew out of the long tradition of English libertarianism and specifically out of a reform movement precipitated by the crisis of American independence. Its bible was The Rights of Man *of 1792, written by the Englishman who had become America's spokesman, Thomas Paine, the Norfolk man without magic who yet created it, who did for the English political sentence in the eighteenth century what Ernest Hemingway was to do for the English literary sentence in the twentieth. With his American irreverence, his cocksure belief in reason and common sense, his blasphemy against the revered Constitution and his assertion of popular capacity, Paine became the very prototype of British populist radicalism and remained so, right through to the days of Lloyd George.*

But it was the impact of the French Revolution, in particular the second revolution of August 1792 which overthrew the French monarchy and created a vigorous and violent popular democracy, which charged the new English movement with enthusiasm, ideological bite and a drive for social equality. As middle-class sympathizers with the French Revolution fell away in droves, thousands of the new people, the artisans, journeymen, shopkeepers hitherto excluded

59

*from political life, swarmed into these unprecedented clubs, called
each other Citizen and copied French styles, brought out the first
popular political journals like* Hog's Wash *of 1793 (a reply to
Edmund Burke's dismissal of the 'swinish multitude') and fought
for democracy. In these societies they deliberately tried to establish
their own Common Wealth of Reason; in them they served what
Hazlitt called their apprenticeship to liberty.*

*They were defeated; tiny minorities within society, except in times
of crisis and food shortage, they were beaten by government repression,
patriotic hostility in the long wars against France, periodic outbreaks
of loyalist witch-hunting. But they established a precedent and a
presence.*

'To all real lovers of Liberty. Be assured that Liberty and
Freedom will at last prevail. Tremble O thou the Oppressor
of the People that reigneth upon the throne and ye Ministers
of State, weep for ye shall fall. Weep ye who grind the face of
the poor, oppress the People and starve the Industrious
Mechanic. My friends, you are oppressed, you know it. Lord
Buckingham who died the other day had thirty thousand
pounds yearly for setting his arse in the House of Lords and
doing nothing. Liberty calls aloud, ye who will hear her
Voice, may you be free and happy. He who does not, let him
starve and be DAMNED.

'N.B. Be resolute and you shall be happy. He who wishes
well to the cause of Liberty let him repair to Chapel Field at
Five O'Clock this afternoon, to begin a Glorious Revolution.'

(Confiscated broadsheet, Home Office papers, 1793.)

'The standard being raised, the nation was at once divided
into two bodies unequal and of an aspect in all respects
different from each other. I perceived that the great body was
composed of labourers, artisans, shopkeepers, of all the professions useful to society, and that in the small group there
were only priests, financiers, nobles, generals, in other words
nothing but the agents of government. And I saw indignation and rage spring up on the one hand, fear and dismay
on the other . . .

'PEOPLE: Why have you separated from us? Are you not then of our number?

'PRIVILEGED: No. You are but people. We are a different order of beings. We are the Privileged. We are men of a different race.

'PEOPLE: What work do you do in our society?

'PRIVILEGED: None. We are not made for work.

'PEOPLE: How then have you acquired your wealth?

'PRIVILEGED: By taking the pains to govern you.

'PEOPLE: What? You call this governing? We sweat and you enjoy. We produce and you squander. Privileged, who are not of the people form a nation apart and govern yourselves.

'PRIVILEGED: People! The King wills it! The Sovereign commands!

'PEOPLE: The King can will only the People's welfare.

'PRIVILEGED: The Law orders you to submit.

'PEOPLE: The Law is the General Will and we will a new order! . . . And the Military Governors stepping forward said "The people are timid. Menace them. They obey only force. Soldiers chastise this insolent rabble . . ."

'PEOPLE: Soldiers! You are of our own blood. Will you strike your own brothers?
And the soldiers, grounding their arms, said "We, too are the people." Whereupon the Ecclesiastical Governors said, "There is but one resource left. The people are superstitious. Frighten them with the name of God."

'PRIVILEGED: Dearly beloved brethren! Children! God has appointed us to govern you.

'PEOPLE: Show us your Divine warrant.

'PRIVILEGED: You must have faith. Reason will lead you astray.

'PEOPLE: Do you then govern without reason?

'PRIVILEGED: Man is born but to suffer.

'PEOPLE: Set us the example.

'PRIVILEGED: Will you live without Gods and without Kings?

'PEOPLE: We will live without Tyrants, without Impostors.

And the small group cried, "We are lost! The people are enlightened!" And the People answered, "You are saved. Since we are enlightened, we will not abuse our power. We have resentments but we forget them. We were slaves, now we might dictate. But we wish only to be free. And free we are!"

'Vox Populi Vox Dei. THE VOICE OF THE PEOPLE IS THE VOICE OF GOD.'

(From *Volney's Ruins*, a translation in 1793 of C. F. de Volney, *Les ruines*, 1791, a fantasy or piece of science-fiction, product of the first Utopian phase of the French Revolution. Chapter 15, 'The New Century', with this classic 'enlightened' dialogue, caught the imagination of thousands across the Channel. Between 1792 and 1822 there were at least eleven different English editions of Volney, who, for two generations and more, enjoyed a supremacy in the world of populist thought and sensibility not unlike that of William Morris or Jack London in a later generation. It was even translated into Welsh, and by a Baptist minister to boot.)

'For God's sake, send us the word of enlightenment and philanthropy. Huddersfield abounds in true patriots but we are beset by masses of ignorant aristocracy . . .'

(Letter from Huddersfield to the London Corresponding Society, 1793, among papers confiscated during the Treason Trials of 1794; Treasury Solicitor's Papers.)

'Aristocratic tirany and Democratic ignorance seem to pervade and over Awe the town of Leeds to that Amazing degree that in General we are beheld more like monsters than the Friends of the People. But our numbers amount to two hundred and we constantly keep increasing . . .'

(*Correspondence of the London Corresponding Society*, 1795.)

'Bradford may be ranked with the first in the West Riding for a domineering aristocracy but they have been much less liberal with their insults than formerly . . .'

(ibid.)

'From the situation of this place it is probable you have considered it one of the hives of aristocracy, but the reverse is exactly the case. The complexion of the great bulk of the inhabitants is purely democratical, though many who are good Citizens are prevented from avowing their principles publicly by the certainty of being discharged from their relative situations in the Dock Yard for so doing. Our newly formed society is chiefly composed of working men. Our hearts are with *all the family* and we fondly wish to be UNITED WITH THEM not only in *distant views* but in real *personal* union.'

(Portsmouth to the London Corresponding Society, ibid.)

'The usual mode of proceeding at these weekly meetings was this. The Chairman (each man was chairman in rotation) read from some book . . . and the persons present were invited to make remarks thereon, as many as chose did so, but without rising. Then another portion was read and a second invitation given. Then the remainder was read and a third invitation was given . . . Then there was a general discussion.'

(Papers of Francis Place, 'the radical tailor of Charing Cross', London, whose career in the working-class movement began in 'Jacobinism' and who took pains to expunge evidence of a youth he considered less than 'respectable' from memoirs he wrote a generation later as a 'Benthamite' luminary.)

'Almost everybody speaks and there is always a very great noise, till the delegate gets up. People grow very outrageous and won't wait, then the delegate gets up and tries to soften them.'

(Spy's report, 1794, Treasury Solicitor's papers.)

'You have treated our Delegate with contempt and reproach, you have despised and neglected our motions, consequently have broken the laws of the society; we, determined to be just and resolved not to establish a precedent of such base submission, do declare the social compact between us and you dissolved . . .

'Fellow Citizens of the Friends of Liberty, we cannot forebear remarking the concluding part of your letter in which you have asserted "It is true we are ranged under different *leaders*". On this point we deem it necessary to say that however the Friends of Liberty may be situated in this particular, the London Corresponding Society disclaims any such relation and assures you they recognise no *leaders* . . .

'Citizen Burks apologised for the term *leaders* which he said had accidently crept into the letter for that of names in the hurry of writing . . . Citizen Baxter in a speech of some length, reprobated the idea of *leaders* and declared there was not an individual in the Friends of Liberty but abhorred "leaders" as much as it was possible for the London Corresponding Society to do . . .

With respect to your offer to pay a higher subscription if your Division may restrict its membership to householders. It is the reproach of this as well as every other commercial country that property is too much respected . . . It can by no means be considered as a general test of moral rectitude . . . Reform will never be effected while men of different descriptions are studious of keeping distinct companies . . .'

(*Correspondence of the London Corresponding Society*, 1795.)

The tone was not always so urbane.

'For the Benefit of John Bull. At the Federation Theatre in Equality Square on the First of April 1794. Will be performed a new and entertaining farce called – La Guillotine, or George's Head in the Basket! Dramatis Personae – Numpy the Third by Mr Gwelp (being the last time of appearance in that character). Prince of Leeks by Mr Gwelp Junior. Duke of Dice by Mr Freddy from Osnabruck . . . Chancellor of the Exchequer by Mr Billy Taxlight . . . Banditti, Assassins, Cut-Throats and wholesale dealers in blood by the Tsar of All the Ruffians, Emperor of Harm-any, Thing of Prussia etc. . . . Tight-rope dancing from the Lamp-post by Messrs Canterbury, York, Durham etc. . . . In the course of

the evening will be sung in full chorus, Ça Ira and Bob Shave
Great George our * * * *.'

(London squib, 1794, Home Office papers. The Guelphs are
George III and his family; other targets are William Pitt
(window-tax), European rulers and the episcopacy. The blank
was apparently a raspberry.)

'Facts are seditious things
When they touch courts and kings
Armies are raised.
Barracks and bastilles built,
Innocence charged with guilt,
Blood most unjustly spilt,
God stands amazed.
God save great Thomas Paine . . . etc.'

(One of several parodies of the song that grew into a national
anthem directed at the 'knavish tricks' of Jacobins. During
1795–6, London theatres became cock-pits, with rival groups
bawling songs at each other.)

The message, however, was always the same.

'The Age of Reason has at length revolved. Long have we
been endeavouring to find ourselves men. We now find ourselves so. We will be treated as such.'

(Address of the sailors at the Nore during the naval mutinies of
1797; Admiralty papers.)

This, of course, was not to be tolerated.

'When you separate the common sort of men from their
proper chieftains, so as to form them into an adverse army,
I no longer know that venerable object called the People in
such a disbanded race of deserters and vagabonds. They are
terrible in such a manner as wild beasts are terrible. The
mind owes them no sort of submission. They are rebels.
They may be lawfully fought with and brought under.'

(Edmund Burke, *Reflections on the Revolution in France*, 1790.)

'A mob of several hundred people led by one Harrop, of

Barrowshaw, an atrocious ruffian, came in front of the house and with shouts of "Church and King for ever!" "Deawn with t'Jacobins!" began to smash the windows and break open the doors . . . every article of furniture was broken; the glasses, jugs, and other vessels were dashed on the floor and trampled under foot; the bar was gutted . . . others again were beating and kicking and maltreating in various ways the persons found in the house. Several of these were lamed; others were seriously crushed and injured in their persons . . . the parson of the place, whose name was Berry, standing on an elevated situation, pointed them out to the mob, saying – "There goes one; and there goes one! That's a Jacobin; that's another!"'

(From Samuel Bamford, *Passages in the Life of a Radical* (1893 edition), based on personal experience.)

'An officer of the Guards has been talking most demo-cratically in Chelmsford . . .
'Grocers in Middlesex have concocted an infernal Jacobin plot.'

(From letters in the papers of the Association for the Preservation of Liberty and Property from Republicans and Levellers, 1792-3.)

'The Hampshire Sedition Hunters think it proper to acquaint their brethren at the Crown and Anchor, that last Monday their Committee met – but having nothing to do – they ordered an effigy for Tom Paine to be made, dressed in black, the Church giving the coat, the College the waist-coat and breeches and the corporation the hat and wig . . . They also caused a mob to assemble to carry this effigy about the city, but the mob was not numerous, as the Militia men, now here, refused to join . . . We think it proper to inform you that when the mob got drunk some few did cry out "Tom Paine for ever", but they were very drunk and very few that did – for you may depend upon all in our list being of the right sort – having amongst us forty parsons . . .'

(ibid. This piece, though probably cocking a snook, does capture the spirit of the mushrooming Loyalist associations which mobilized the right-thinking. Even young William Hone, later a satirist-hero to radicals, offered his loyal services and in his best Sunday handwriting.)

'He recollects the day when he durst scarcely walk the streets. He can tell how he was hooted, pelted and spurned ... He makes younkers stare when he tells them about a time when there was no Habeas Corpus and the Attorney General went up and down the country like a raging lion ... He tells of a man who said ... that the king was born without a shirt, and was in consequence transported for sedition ...'

(From E. Sloane, *Essays, Tales and Sketches*, 1849, quoted in E. P. Thompson, *The Making of the English Working Class*, 1963; a perceptive and accurate portrait of the 'village Jacobin', appropriately a shoemaker.)

This first movement was defeated, succumbing to waves of repression and to the tide of traditional patriotism of the long French wars. But it established a tradition of its own, it established a presence.

'I am contending for the rights of the living and against their being willed away and controlled and contracted for by the manuscript assumed authority of the dead. Man has no property in man; neither has any generation a property in the generations which are to follow.'

(Thomas Paine, *The Rights of Man*, 1792.)

In Spite of Nadin Joe

Paine, like all these embattled democrats of the 1790s, was pre-industrial; democracy is a pre-industrial ideology. But as the new industry took hold in Britain, as the new, and to working people harsh and hypocritical, creeds of Political Economy and Evangelicalism won their hegemony, as old popular traditions, rhythms of life, sense of community crumbled, groups of working people, slowly and imperfectly growing aware of themselves as a distinct commonalty, built movements of resistance, and it was around Paine's democracy that they focused.

The democracy of the old pre-industrial régime bit deep into the mind and spirit of the politically conscious among industrial working people as they struggled to assert their value, their worth, their very presence in what was essentially a struggle for dignity. They fought in elemental tumult, bread riots, strike, arson; in the half-insurrection of Luddism during the Napoleonic Wars, in illegal and secret trade unions, in a sporadic but swelling surge of political action after the Wars, with its new explosion of working-class journalism, Cobbett's Register, Black Dwarf, The Republican, *its new heroes like Henry 'Orator' Hunt and villains like Joseph Nadin, the deputy constable of Manchester. In August 1819 a mass demonstration for democracy was cut down by yeomanry and cavalry at Manchester and the 'Peterloo Massacre' created a new myth and martyrology for people who were coming to think of themselves as a working class.*

'. . . all those new streets behind Mr Twist's and Mr Grab's and Mr Screw's . . . were all open fields and children used to be there at eight, nine, ten, eleven, aye, and twelve years of age idling their time at play . . . till the time when rich folk frightened poor folk out of their sense with "He's a cooming" and "They're a cooming".

'Who are "they", Robin?

'Why, Boney and the French, to be sure. Well, that time when rich folk frightened poor folk and stole all the land. This was all common, then, Mr Smith . . . All reet and left, up away to bastile and barracks was all common . . . They built barracks at one end and church at t'other . . . and, at last, almost all folk had to sell cow, to pay Lawyer Grind and Lawyer Squeeze and now the son of one of 'em is mayor and t'other is manager of bank . . .'

(Feargus O'Connor, the Chartist leader, in his *The Employer and the Employed*, 1844.)

'First then, as to the employers: with very few exceptions, these are a set of men who have sprung from the cotton shop without education or address, but to counterbalance that deficiency, they give you enough of appearances by an ostentatious display of elegant mansions, equipages, liveries, parks, hunters, hounds etc. . . . but the chaste observer of the beauties of nature and art combined will observe a woeful deficiency of taste . . . They bring up their families at the most costly schools, determined to give their offspring a double portion of what they were so deficient in themselves . . . their whole time is occupied in contriving how to get the greatest quantity of work turned off with the least expence . . . What then must be the men or rather beings who are the instruments of such masters? . . . observe the squalid appearance of the little infants and their parents taken from their beds at so early an hour in all kinds of weather . . . examine the miserable pittance of food chiefly composed of water gruel and oatcake broken into it, a little salt and sometimes coloured with a little milk, together with a few potatoes and a bit of bacon or fat for dinner; would a London mechanic eat this?'

(Address to the public of Manchester by a journeyman cotton spinner, *Black Dwarf*, 30 September 1818.)

'For the last 20 years wee have been in a Starving Condition to maintin your Dam Pride . . . So now as for this fire you must not take it as a front, for if you hadent been Deserving it wee should not have dont. As for you my Ould frend you dident hapen to be hear, if that you had been rosted I hear and if it had a been so how the farmers would lagh to see the ould Parson rosted at last . . . As for this litel fire dont be alarmed it will be a damd deal wors when we burn down your barn . . .'

(Anonymous letter from an arsonist, Isle of Wight, 1830; Home Office papers, quoted in E. P. Thompson, op. cit.)

'I was at yor hoose last neet and meyd mysel very comfortable. Ye hey nee family and yor just won man on the colliery, I see ye hev a greet lot of rooms and big cellars and plenty wine and beer in them which I got ma share on. Noo I naw some at wor colliery that has three of fower lads and lasses and they live in won room not half as gude as yor cellar. I dont pretend to naw very much but I naw there shudnt be that much difference. The only place we can gan to o the week ends is the yel hoose and hev a pint. I dinna pretend to be a profit, but I naw this, and lots of ma marrows na's te, that were not tret as we owt to be, and a great filosopher says, to get noledge is to naw yer ignerent. But weve just begun to find that oot, and ye maisters and owners may luk oot, for yor not gan to get se much o yor own way, wer gan to hev some o wors now . . .'

(Pitman's letter left in the house of a colliery manager in the North-east, broken into during a riot in 1831. Quoted in R. Fynes, *The Miners of Northumberland and Durham*, 1923.)

'I ham going to inform you that there is Six Thousand men coming to you in Apral and then We will go and Blow Parlement house up and Blow up all afour hus labring Peple Cant Stand it No longer dam all Such Roges as England governes but Never mind Ned lud when general nody and is harmey Comes We Will soon bring about the greate Revelution then all these greate mens heads gose of.'

(Paper left in Chesterfield market, 1812; Home Office papers.)

'When a member is admitted there are two rooms, in one of which the Lodge is assembled. The first operation was to blindfold him; he was then conducted into the Lodge by two members; he was then required to give the pass word which on that occasion was Alpha and Omega; he was then walked around the room, during which time a great rumbling noise was made by a sheet of iron – a hymn was then sung . . . they then took the bandage from his eyes and the first thing he saw was a picture of death as large as a man, over which was the inscription "Remember Thy End". Over this picture there was a drawn sword . . . he was then ordered to kneel down beside a table, and the bandage was again taken from his eyes, when he saw a large bible before him, his hand having been placed upon it . . . the 94th Psalm was then read, when the oath was administered . . . (Lord, how long shall the wicked, how long shall the wicked

triumph? . . . They break in pieces thy people O Lord . . .
Who will rise up for me against the evildoers? . . .)'

(*Leeds Mercury*, 12 December 1832; description of initiation into
a trade union, quoted in E. P. Thompson, op. cit.)

'Hunt sat on the box-seat . . . continually doffed his hat,
waved it lowly, bowed gracefully and now and then spoke
a few kind words to the people; but if some five or ten
minutes elapsed without a huzza or two or the still more
pleasing sound – Hunt for Ever! – he would rise from his
seat, turn around cursing poor Moorhouse in limbs, soul or
eyes, he would say "Why don't you shout, man? Why dont
you shout? Give them the hip, damn you, dont you see
they're fagging? . . ."'

(Description of Henry (Orator) Hunt in Samuel Bamford's
memoirs, op. cit.)

' . . . a Motion was made, "That no person but Leaders of
Sections should vote" – one Gentn, got up and spoke as
follows – Mr Chair! Mr Chair!! Mr Chair!!! I *desire* you
will do Your Duty in keeping Order – after he had repeated
this so often I was afraid of his Lungs, the Chairman called
out Order! Order!! and with such a voice that made me
tremble . . . He then proceeded, Mr Chair I look upon *us*
here, as being Members sent to *this here* place, to transact the
business of Reform, in same manner as our business should
be done in Parliament . . . up started two or three others . . .
one of them saying he had only a few words to say in
Opposition to that Gentn. who had compared this place to
the House of Commons – that House of Corruption, that
Den of Thieves as Cobbett properly called it, if he thought
they resembled that Company in any way he would never
come into this place again . . . at this moment presented
themselves two Country-Men, one of which got up and
wished to know if this was the Union – it was some time
before any one spoke. – at last some person said it should be
– the Stranger then said he came from Flixton, to see how
Reform was going on – some one cried out, "did Justice

Wright send you?" the Old Man took no Notice but continued that in their Country hundreds were daily joining their Sections, and if he was to tell them what he had seen this Night they would never put any confidence in the Manchester Union. Several of the Leaders got round the Strangers and persuaded them not to mention what they had seen that Night.'

(From a description of a meeting of Manchester political union, 1819, Home Office papers.)

'By eight o'clock on the morning of Monday, the 16th of August 1819, the whole town of Middleton might be said to be on the alert . . . First were selected twelve of the most comely and decent-looking youths, who were placed in two rows of six each, with each a branch of laurel held presented in his hand as a token of amity and peace; then followed the men of several districts in fives, then the band of music, an excellent one . . . Our whole column, with the Rochdale people, would probably consist of six thousand men. At our head were a hundred or two of women, mostly young wives and mine own was amongst them. A hundred or so of our handsomest girls, sweethearts to the lads who were with us, danced to the music or sung snatches of popular songs . . .

'At Newtown we were welcomed with open arms by the poor Irish weavers who came out in their best drapery . . . We thanked them by the band striking up St Patrick's Day in the morning . . . we wheeled quickly and steadily into Peter Street and soon approached a wide unbuilt space occupied by an immense multitude which opened and received us with loud cheers. We walked into that chasm of human beings . . .'

(From Samuel Bamford's description of the mass march on Manchester in support of parliamentary reform, dispersed by yeomanry and cavalry at Peterloo; in his memoirs, op. cit.)

'With Henry Hunt we'll go, we'll go,
With Henry Hunt we'll go,

We'll raise the cap of liberty
In spite of Nadin Joe.'

(J. Morland, *Ballads and Songs of Lancashire*, reprinted in
Socialist Songbook, 1898.)

'On the cavalry drawing up they were received with a shout
of good-will as I understood it. They shouted again, waving
their sabres over their heads; and then, slackening rein, and
striking spur into their steeds, they dashed forward and
began cutting the people . . . their sabres were plied to hew
a way through naked held-up hands and defenceless heads;
and then chopped limbs and wound-gaping skulls were seen
and groans and cries were mingled with the din of that
horrid confusion. "Ah! Ah! for shame!" was shouted. Then
"break! break! they are killing them in front" . . .

'For a moment the crowd held back as in a pause; then
was a rush, heavy and resistless as a headlong sea; and a
sound like low thunder with screams, prayers and impreca-
tions from the crowd-moiled and sabre-doomed who could
not escape . . .'

(Bamford, op. cit.)

'I picked up a cap of liberty; one of the cavalry rode after me
and demanded it; I refused to give it up. Two others then
came up and asked what was the matter, when the first
said, this fellow wont give up this Cap of Liberty. One of the
others then said, damn him, cut him down. Upon this, I
ran . . .'

(From the *Inquest on John Lees*, 1820.)

'In ten minutes from the commencement of the havoc the
field was an open and almost deserted space. The sun looked
down through a sultry and motionless air . . . The hustings
remained with a few broken and hewed flagstaves erect and
a torn and gashed banner or two dropping; whilst over the
whole field were strewed caps, bonnets, hats, shawls, and
shoes. The yeomanry had dismounted – some were easing

their horses girths, others adjusting their accoutrements, and some were wiping their sabres . . .'

(Bamford, op. cit.)

'To our brethren in Lankaster Shire. Dearly Beloved. We hope you are comeng on pretty well though your Captifeity is painful. Our Musick in Yorkshire as played twise where yours in Lankashire has never struck at all, is your Musicians sick?

'Melancholy, melancholy, melancholy Yorkshire, your Reformers stand true . . . About 300 at Grange Moor, they marched all night, each man had is Blanket, Spare or Gon and well filed with ammunition poor Men to be so deceived by short sighted men it would have tuck an afect on your feelings to have seen the brave men stand under their arms all that wet neet after a march of twelve miles and Not one man to meet them according to Appointment . . . All at a loss to know what to do. Return to Barnsley they could not think of but when there was no other prospect they all began to shed tears Most bitterly with crys of the most distracted . . . I hope that we may all meet in one Body and one Voice yet . . .'

(Letter of Joseph Tyas, weaver, found on him after his arrest near Huddersfield during the troubles after Peterloo, April 1820; Home Office papers, quoted in E. P. Thompson, op. cit.)

One Body and One Voice

During the 1820s this thrust for unity and search for community grew more powerful and sophisticated. In clubs, discussion groups, free-thinking Zetetic societies grouped around journals like the atheist Republican *with its book club (the first Left Book Club), active minorities wrestled with the new science, brought out Voltaire in penny weekly parts and groped after a new vision. The labour theory of value of dissident economic thinkers registered among them; Robert Owen's co-operative socialism penetrated trade unions struggling into a fitful legality after 1825. It swept them into a mass syndicalist movement in the early 1830s which left another clutch of martyrs, those of Tolpuddle. Driven by such impulses, working people created for themselves an extraordinarily rich and dense culture, alive with an anti-capitalist morality and sensibility, teeming with unlawful and unstamped newspapers, clubs, mechanics' institutes, co-operatives, trade unions, friendly societies, factory reform movements and political organizations of all kinds, from Republican to Orange. Particularly after the onset of simultaneous economic and political crisis in 1829, they moved into a multiplicity of movements increasingly organized on a national scale, through the Reform Bill crisis of 1831, the great union movement, the fight for a free press and against the new Poor Law, into the climax of the Chartist movement, fashioned around the People's Charter of 1838. This, the first serious working-class movement in history, in its political programme simply rehearsed the old radical programme of political democracy published as long ago as 1780, but behind it was the whole drive for community of classes who felt alienated in the new society. A compound of social nostalgia and forward-looking politics, Chartism burned itself into the minds of a whole generation.*

Although most of their Six Points are now the British Way of Life, the optimism of the Chartists seems misplaced. In a very real sense, these movements failed to break through, to break out of a world which others created. In 1831 Bronterre O'Brien, later a Chartist leader, told an audience of co-operators that working people had no system of ideas of their own; they simply shouted middle-class slogans in a harsher accent. There was some truth in the charge; it was the contradiction implicit in Tom Paine's democracy; even the labour notes of the Owenite labour exchanges, which were meant to supersede the commercial system, simply translated current market prices.

But there is another truth about these passionate, frustrated movements. In this age of iron, when British society seems to grind apart like some clumsy cast-iron mechanism, when in a popular paper like The Poor Man's Guardian *the very language sometimes seems to break down from sheer inadequacy in social communication, in such a deadly, breaking time, working men and women, at great price, created for themselves a world of sensibility, aspiration and community which in some very real senses proved enduring. Apprentices to liberty, their master-piece is making yet.*

'Community! the joyful sound
That cheers the social band,
And spreads a holy zeal around
To dwell upon the land.
Community is labour blessed,
Redemption from the fall;
The good of all by each possessed,
The good of each by all.
Community does all possess
That can to man be given;
Community is happiness,
Community is heaven.'

(Owenite hymn, quoted in J. F. C. Harrison, *Robert Owen and the Owenites*, 1969.)

'JOHNSTON (Renfrew): We have now formed one union and I hope there will be no attempt to separate one district from another. It has been the practice in a certain district to exclude members of the district to which I belong. Even if they had in the past lowered prices in Glasgow, we are now united and I hope they will help to raise them and not turn their backs on us . . .

'GLASGOW DELEGATE: It has cost the spinners of Glasgow many hundred pounds to keep up the prices and the repeated sacrifice of some of our best men. The West have allowed their prices to sink so low shall they now come in and share Glasgow's benefits. The fact is they are not allowed to come into Glasgow now and I think we shall be more particular from this forward in this respect than ever . . .

'JOHNSTON: I hope Glasgow is not going to set up a barrier to the union we have come to form (applause) . . . The West sent £900 to Glasgow during the general strike (cries of Question! Question!).

'DOHERTY: I am extremely sorry to perceive the exclusive sort of spirit of Glasgow; they are surely not so weak and selfish. If they are, they had better break up at once (applause). The question before us is one on which the

very existence of our union depends. How can you form
a union when one set of men look upon another as inferior
(cries of Hear! Hear!) Our union card must admit all
(applause).'

(*Proceedings of a Delegate Meeting of the Operative Spinners of England,
Ireland and Scotland, Ramsay, Isle of Man, December 1829* (Man-
chester, 1830). John Doherty took the lead in efforts to form a
General Union and a National Association for the Protection of
Labour, 1830–31.)

'From the competition and the increase of machinery which
supersedes hand labour, combined with various other causes
over which, as yet, the labouring classes have no control, the
minds of thinking men are lost in a labyrinth . . . By the
increase of capital the working classes may better their
condition, if they only *unite* and set their shoulders to the
work; like men of one family, strive to begin to work for
themselves. The plan of co-operation which we are recommending to the public is not a visionary one, but is acted
upon in various parts of the kingdom.
'*Fundamental principles*. First, that labour is the source of all
wealth; consequently the working classes have created all
wealth . . .'

(Rules of Ripponden Co-operative Society, 1833 or 1839,
quoted in E. P. Thompson, op. cit.)

'A tailor will bring, say a waistcoat, or topcoat, say it cost
four shillings for the cloth etc. and six hours' labour; we give
him a note to this amount; he turns round and sees a pair of
shoes, they cost four shillings and six hours' labour; he gives
his labour note the same as we give a shilling over the
counter; the shoes are taken away and the note destroyed,
because it ceases to represent real wealth.'

(*Lancashire and Yorkshire Co-operator*, 1832, explaining the system
of Equitable Labour Exchanges by which the Owenites tried to
bypass and ultimately supersede the commercial market.)

'I now give you a short outline of the great changes which
are in contemplation and which shall come suddenly upon

society like a thief in the night ... It is intended that national arrangements shall be formed to include all the working classes in the great organisation and that each department shall become acquainted with what is going on in other departments; that all individual competition is to cease; that all manufactures are to be carried on by national companies. All trades must first form associations of lodges ...'

(*Crisis*, *1833*. Robert Owen urging the formation of a vast union federation, the Grand National Consolidated Trades Union, to institute co-operative socialism. It was during the campaign against this movement that six Dorchester labourers were transported, to become the Tolpuddle Martyrs of the trade unions.)

'And so, in deep perplexity, I took the bible in one hand and d'Holbach's System of Nature in the other and went into my bedroom and kneeled me down with the books open and prayed for that divine illumination of which I was so much in need.'

(Elijah Dixon of Manchester, milkman, who, when illumination came, joined the Owenite movement as a 'free-thinking Christian'.)

'London Zetetic Society, Spitalfields. Mr Thomas Pitts read a paper on Does Man have a Soul? The company devoted an evening to the Simian Theory, that men are descended from the apes ...'

'Nottingham Zetetic Society. Edward Sale, aged 55, a resolute Infidel, died on 24 October last. Tales spread by Christians that Sale at the last cried out for mercy and that one of his infidel friends present said "Damn you, you dont die tender" are completely without foundation. Mr Sale died perfectly tranquil.'

(From the free-thinking journals edited by Richard Carlile, the *Republican* of 1820 and the *Lion* of 1828, around which grew a network of Zetetic (free inquirer) societies and an 'infidel' book club, which nurtured a whole generation of working-class leaders and militants.)

'I acknowledge one omnipresent eternal and unchangeable Being, the primeval essence of all materiality and the Creator of all things visible and invisible whose revelations are written in the volume of his works and whose laws are manifest in the harmonies of nature. But of what cannot be known I am content to be ignorant and acknowledge no faith but what is grounded in knowledge or built upon the analogies of experience. I will not bind myself to my state of mind today because it is my duty to become wiser tomorrow.'

(From *A form of public worship on the principles of Pure Deism* at the Brinksway chapel, Stockport, 1827. A liturgy composed by Rowland Detrosier, a self-taught genius who from a wretched childhood made himself into one of the most influential working-class lecturers and teachers in the North. During the Reform Bill crisis he went over to the 'moderate' movement advocating collaboration with middle-class radicals.)

'BENCH: What have you to say in your defence?
'DEFENDANT: Well, sir, I have been out of employment for some time; neither can I obtain work; my family are all starving ... And for another reason, the weightiest of all; I sell them for the good of my fellow countrymen; to let them see how they are misrepresented in parliament ... I wish to let the people know how they are humbugged ...
'BENCH: Hold your tongue a moment.
'DEFENDANT: I shall not! for I wish every man to read these publications.
'BENCH: You are very insolent, therefore you are committed to three months' imprisonment in Knutsford House of Correction, to hard labour.
'DEFENDANT: I've nothing to thank you for; and whenever I come out I'll hawk them again. And *mind you*, the first that I hawk shall be to your house ...'

(*Poor Man's Guardian*, best known of the illegal, unstamped press, reporting the trial, in 1831, for selling unstamped newspapers of Joseph Swann, hatter of Macclesfield, who spent years in prison for his persistence.)

'Lift up your democratic heads, my friends! Look proud and

be merry. I was at a meeting on Tuesday night which does one's heart good to think on ... The arrangements of the committee were in every respect complete, and of the true democratic stamp. A working man was appointed to preside. The resolutions and petitions were severally proposed and seconded by working men. The principal speakers who supported them were working men. The petition itself, which is one of the very best of the kind ever submitted to Parliament, was drawn up by working men. In short, the whole proceedings were originated, conducted, and concluded by working men, and that in a style which would have done credit to any assembly in the world.'

(*London Mercury*, 1837, quoted in *The Early Chartists*, ed. Dorothy Thompson, 1971. Bronterre O'Brien reports on the radical meeting at the *Crown and Anchor* in February 1837, the clauses of whose petition, universal suffrage, annual parliaments, vote by ballot, equal representation, no property qualification and payment of members, became the Six Points of the People's Charter.)

' "Well, what do *you* want?" I fumbled for my *prize* ticket, and said, "Here's a ticket, sir – a gentleman gave me in Russell Square." "Well, well, what do you want, I say?" "If you please sir, I met this morning a man carrying a board on which was stated that I could get food, work, and clothing – but I only want work, sir." "Are you a beggar?" "Yes, sir." "How long?" "Eight days." "Only eight days – are you sure of that?" (with a cunning infidel leer) "Yes, sir, that is all." "Are you married?" "Yes sir." "Ah I thought so. How many children have you got?" "One sir." "O I wonder you didn't say a dozen – most beggars say a dozen. How do you beg?" "I sing hymns sir." "O, one of the pious chanters" – with a grin at the *gentlemen*, Who grinn'd, too, at his brilliant wit. "Have you applied to your parish?" "No, sir." *That* did it – that *truth* – if I had told a lie, the wrath of his worship the Chairman might in time have been assuaged, but telling the truth proved I was not "*up to snuff*" ... Now its some time before I break loose, but when I do, I never stay at a half-way house – all the way there and no stoppages – is my motto; so I retaliated, as every honest man ought to do when he's insulted and belied by a thing that feeds on him according to law. I retaliated, I say, with equal warmth, calling him a liar (a scriptural phrase by-the-bye) point-blank and all the *gentlemen*, too . . . I fired away bang, bang, till I was more than a match for the Chairman, who at last listened staring, without saying a word, but just a grunt now and then, like a pig as he was . . .

'Politics, my Lord, was with me just then, a bread and cheese question. Let me not, however, be mistaken; – I ever loved the idea of freedom – glorious freedom, and its inevitable consequences – and not only for what it will fetch but the *holy principle*; – a democrat in my Sunday School – everywhere – and whether the sun shines on my future pathway or the clouds look black as they have ever done, neither sun nor cloud shall alter my fixed principle.

> 'A boy I *dreamt* of liberty;
> A youth – I said, but I am free;
> A man – I felt that slavery
> Had bound me in her chain.
> But yet the *dream*, which, when a boy,
> Was wont my musings to employ,
> Fast rolling years *shall not* destroy,
> With all their grief and pain.'

('How I became a rebel. Dedicated to my Lord John Russell', *Christian Socialist*, 1851. The autobiography of a Chartist, printed in *The Early Chartists*, ed. Dorothy Thompson, 1971.)

4

The Two Nations: Industrialization and Its Discontents

GEORGE RUDÉ

The age of the Industrial Revolution was one of rapid technical change which, as has often been said, made Britain 'the workshop of the world'. But it was an age of major social change as well, in which some older classes tended to decline and new classes emerged or came to the fore. Among the latter were the masters and workmen of the new factory towns, whose habits and manner of living were moving ever further apart and who were beginning to confront one another as the main protagonists of a new industrial society. Something similar was taking place in the village, where the social status of the farmer had risen through the years of war and where, with the virtual extinction of the cottager and small peasant producer, society was now strictly divided into the trinity of landlords, farmers and agricultural labourers. It was this polarization of classes, this deepening chasm between masters and men, farmers and labourers, between the richer and poorer classes, that filled many observers of the 1830s and 1840s with evident alarm. Among them was Benjamin Disraeli who, in his novel Sybil, *expressed his concern in the theme of the 'Two Nations'.*

The Two Nations

' "Well, society may be in its infancy," said Egremont, slightly smiling; "but, say what you like, our Queen reigns over the greatest nation that ever existed." "Which nation?" asked the younger stranger, "for she reigns over two." "Yes," resumed the younger stranger after a moment's interval. "Two nations; between whom there is no intercourse, and no sympathy; who are as ignorant of each other's habits, thoughts, and feelings, as if they were dwellers in different zones, or inhabitants of different planets; who are formed by a different breeding, are fed by a different food, are ordered by different manners, and are governed by the same laws."

' "You speak of – ", said Egremont, hesitatingly.

' "THE RICH AND THE POOR." '

(Benjamin Disraeli, *Sybil: or The Two Nations*, first published in 1845. Disraeli, then a Young Tory, later became a Conservative Prime Minister.)

The Rich and the Poor

One way in which the social chasm expressed itself was in the increasing disparity in wealth between rich and poor. It may not be true that the poor were becoming poorer (though many have argued that they were); but it was undoubted that the rich were becoming richer and there was little sign that any substantial part of the new wealth being created was finding its way into the pockets of the poor. This and the squalor of living and working conditions and the tyranny of employers were the constant theme of the 'social' novelists of the day, men and women like Disraeli, Charles Kingsley and Mrs Gaskell. Some, however, dissented from this pessimistic view. One such dissenter was Francis Place, who, writing of London in the 1820s and 1830s, found it a more salubrious place to live in than the London he had known as a young tailor's apprentice and journeyman nearly half a century before. But Place's view was one-sided. For one thing, he was mainly concerned with London; for another, being a moralist, he was unduly influenced by the decline in 'low-lived and degrading pursuits'; moreover, he took little account of that 'quality of life' that historians like the Hammonds and Edward Thompson have stressed in our time and an awareness of which emerges so clearly from the address of the Bradford woolcombers in the last of the passages that follow.

'I stumbled after Mr Jones up a dark, narrow iron staircase till we emerged through a trap-door into a garret at the top of the house. I recoiled with disgust at the scene before me; and here I was to work – perhaps through life! A low lean-to room, stifling me with the combined odours of human breath and perspiration, stale beer, the sweet sickly smell of gin, and the sour and hardly less disgusting one of new cloth. On the floor, thick with dust and dirt, scraps of stuff and ends of thread, sat some dozen haggard, untidy, shoeless men, with a mingled look of care and recklessness that made me shudder. The windows were tight closed to keep out the cold winter air; and the condensed breath ran in streams down the panes, chequering the dreary outlook of chimney-pots and smoke. The conductor handed me over to one of the men. "Here, Crossthwaite, take this younker and make a tailor of him. Keep him next you, and prick him up with your needle if he shirks." '

(Charles Kingsley, *Alton Locke*, 1850. One of the most committed of the 'social' novelists of the day, Kingsley is describing a tailor's workroom of the early nineteenth century.)

'It is time for me now ... to speak of the state of *the people*, and of the manner in which their affairs are affected by the workings of the system. With regard to the labourers, they are, everywhere, miserable. The wages for those who are employed on the land are, through all the counties I have come, twelve shillings a week for married men, and less for single ones; but a large part of them are not even at this season employed on the land. The farmers, for want of means of profitable employment, suffer the men to fall upon the parish; and they are employed in digging and breaking stone for the roads ... None of the best meat, except by mere accident, is consumed here. Today (the 20th of April), we have seen hundreds upon hundreds of sheep, as fat as hogs, go by this inn-door, their toes, like those of the foot marks at the entrance of the lion's den, all pointing towards the Wen; and the landlord gave us for dinner a little skinny, hard leg of old ewe mutton! Where the man got it, I cannot imagine. Thus it is: every good thing is literally driven or carried away out of the country. In walking out yesterday, I saw three poor fellows digging stone for the roads, who told me that they never had anything but bread to eat, and water to wash it down. One of them was a widower with three children; and his pay was eighteenpence a day; that is to say, about three pounds of bread a day each, for six days in the week; nothing for Sunday, and nothing for lodging, washing, clothing, candle light, or fuel! Just such was the state of things in France at the eve of the Revolution! Precisely such; and precisely the same were the *causes*.'

(William Cobbett, *Rural Rides*, 1912 edition. Cobbett, a one-time Tory turned Radical, is in this passage relating his impressions of the lives of the farm-workers around Lincoln. The 'Wen' is the author's name for London.)

> 'How little can the rich man know
> Of what the poor man feels,
> When Want, like some dark demon foe,
> Nearer and nearer steals!
>
> He never tramp'd the weary round,
> A stroke of work to gain,
> And sicken'd at the dreaded sound
> Which tells he asks in vain.
>
> Foot-sore, heart-sore, *he* never came
> Back through the winter's wind
> To a dank cellar, there no flame
> No light, no food to find.
>
> He never saw his darlings lie
> Shivering, the flags their bed;
> *He* never heard that maddening cry,
> "Daddy, a bit of bread!" '

(Manchester Song, from Mrs Gaskell, *Mary Barton*, 1947 edition; first published in 1847.)

'The people are better dressed, better fed, cleanlier, better educated, in each class respectively, much more frugal, and much happier. Money which would have been spent at the tavern, the brothel, the tea garden, the skittleground, the bull-bait, and in numerous other low-lived and degrading pursuits, is now expended in comfort and conveniences, or saved for some useful purpose.'

(The voice of dissent: Francis Place, writing of the improvement in manners in London between the 1780s and 1820s. Cited by M. D. George, *London Life in the Eighteenth Century*, 1925.)

'Our homes, which were not many years ago the abodes of comfort and domestic enjoyment have now in consequence of the frequent reductions in our wages and other alterations of the sort, become the dwelling places of misery and receptacles of wretchedness . . . We are compelled to work from fourteen to sixteen hours per day, and with all this sweat and toil we are not able to procure sufficient of the necessities of life wherewith to subsist on. When we leave off work at night our sensorial power is worn out with fatigue; we are only fit for sleep or sensual indulgence, the only alternations our leisure knows; we have no moral elasticity to enable us to resist the seductions of appetite or sloth; no heart for regulating our households, superintending our family concerns, or enforcing economy in our domestic arrangements; no power or capability to rise above our circumstances or better our condition; we have no time to be wise, no leisure to be good: we are sunken, debilitated, depressed, emasculated, unnerved for effort; incapable of virtue, unfit for anything which is calculated to be of any benefit to us at present or any future period.'

(Address of Bradford woolcombers to the masters in 1840; cited by J. L. and B. Hammond, *The Skilled Labourer 1760–1832*, 1919.)

The Growth of Cities and the Loss of Community

Industrial revolution was accompanied – though the two were not always closely related – by the rapid growth of cities; and this, too, had a marked effect on the lives of the people. Long before, Daniel Defoe, when describing the London sprawl in the 1720s, had asked the anguished question 'Whither will this monstrous city then extend?' London had grown immeasurably since then: from 500,000

*in the 1750s to nearly a million in 1801, and nearly three times that
number in the half-century that followed. Among other great cities,
Leeds and Sheffield doubled their population between 1801 and 1851,
while the population of Birmingham, Manchester and Glasgow, like
London's, trebled in that time. For the new arrivals, many of whom
were poor Irish or men and women recently uprooted from the villages
and market towns, it was often a traumatic, even a tragic, experience
to have to learn to adapt to the new ways of large-city life. For with
change came a sense of 'alienation' and a loss of old values and
communal ties. Contemporaries were acutely aware of this problem;
and it is this aspect of urban growth and urbanization that is
stressed in the passages that follow.*

' "As for community," said a voice which proceeded neither
from Egremont nor the stranger, "with the monasteries
expired the only type that we ever had in England of such an
intercourse. There is no community in England; there is
aggregation, but aggregation under circumstances which
make it rather a dissociating than a uniting principle . . ."

' "It is a community of purpose that constitutes society,"
continued the younger stranger; "without that, men may be
drawn into contiguity, but they still continue virtually
isolated."

' "And is that their condition in cities?"

' "It is their condition everywhere; but in cities that
condition is aggravated. A density of population implies a
severer struggle for existence, and a consequent repulsion of
elements brought into too close contact. In great cities men
are brought together by the desire of gain. They are not in a
state of co-operation, but of isolation, as to the making of
fortunes; and for all the rest they are careless of neighbours.
Christianity teaches us to love our neighbour as ourself;
modern society acknowledges no neighbour." '

(Benjamin Disraeli, op. cit.)

'The dispersion of the Wen is the only real difficulty that I
see in settling the affairs of the nation and restoring it to a
happy state. But dispersed it *must* be; and if there be half a

million, or more, of people to suffer, the consolation is, that the suffering will be divided into a half a million parts. As if the swelling out of London, naturally produced by the funding system, were not sufficient; as if the evil were not sufficiently great from the inevitable tendency of the system of loans and funds, our pretty gentlemen must resort to positive institutions to augment the population of the Wen. They found that the increase of the Wen produced an increase of thieves and prostitutes, an increase of all sorts of diseases, an increase of miseries of all sorts; they saw that taxes drawn up to one point produced these effects; they must have a "*penitentiary*", for instance, to check the evil, and that they must needs have in the Wen! So that here were a million pounds, drawn up in taxes, employed not only to keep the thieves and prostitutes still in the *Wen*, but to bring up the Wen workmen to build the penitentiary, who and whose families, amounting perhaps to thousands, make an addition to the cause of that crime and misery to check which is the object of the penitentiary! People would follow, they must follow, the million of money. However, this is of a piece with all the rest of their goings on. They and their predecessors, ministers and *House*, have been collecting together all the materials for a dreadful explosion; and if the explosion be not dreadful, other heads must point out the means of prevention.'

(William Cobbett, *Rural Rides*.)

'After roaming the streets of the capital a day or two, making headway with difficulty through the human turmoil and the endless lines of vehicles, after visiting the slums of the metropolis, one realises for the first time that these Londoners have been forced to sacrifice the best qualities of their human nature, to bring to pass all the marvels of civilisation which crowd their city; that a hundred powers which slumbered within them have remained inactive, have been suppressed in order that a few might be developed more fully and multiply through union with those of others . . . The brutal indifference, the unfeeling isolation of each in his private interests becomes the more repellent and offensive, the more these individuals are crowded together, within a limited space. And, however much one may be aware that this isolation of the individual, this narrow self-seeking is the fundamental principle of our society everywhere, it is nowhere so shamelessly barefaced, so self-conscious as just here in the crowding of the great city. The dissolution of mankind into monads, of which each one has a separate principle, the world of atoms, is here carried out to its utmost extreme. Hence it comes, too, that the social war, the war of each against all, is here openly declared ... What is true of London is true of Manchester, Birmingham, Leeds, is true of all great towns. Everywhere barbarous indifference, hard egotism on one hand, and nameless misery on the other, everywhere social welfare, every man's house in a state of siege, everywhere reciprocal plundering under the protection of the law, all so shameless, so openly avowed that one shrinks before the consequences of our social state as they manifest themselves here undisguised, and can only wonder that the whole crazy fabric still hangs together.'

(Friedrich Engels, *The Condition of the Working Class in England in 1844* (1845), 1892 edition.)

The Idyllic Past

People thus alienated or uprooted reacted to the new conditions in a variety of ways. Some remained passive; some took them in their stride; others sought consolation in drink or in the comforts of religion; some reacted violently through crime or social protest; others again looked back with yearning to a past which now, in retrospect, appeared more 'golden' than in fact it ever was. One of the commentaries that follow, however, brings out another side as well – Engels, while conceding that the workers had had to pay a heavy price in loss of freedom and in worsened material conditions, argues that they were nevertheless becoming intellectually enriched through their experience by gaining an understanding of society and the role they were called upon to play in it which they had lacked before.

'Would such atrocious acts have been suffered in the days of Alfred? Is this the land so famed for liberty? Did Sydney and Russel bleed for this? Oh, my poor country!'

(From a handbill circulating in London at the time of the riots against 'crimping' houses, or barracks used to house men impressed for the French Wars, Old Bailey *Proceedings*, 1794, p. 1327.)

'Many warm-hearted philanthropists have charmed you with the assurance that the land is man's rightful inheritance, but not one has ever attempted to put you in possession of it . . . A foolish reliance upon those fascinating principles has diverted your mind from the reality – THE ACTUAL POSSESSION OF THE THING ITSELF.'

(Feargus O'Connor at the opening of O'Connorville, near Watford, May Day 1847. O'Connor was one of the principal Chartist leaders and the author of the Land Plan launched in 1845.)

'Before the introduction of machinery, the spinning and weaving of raw materials was carried on in the working-man's home . . . So the workers vegetated throughout a passably comfortable existence, leading a righteous and peaceful life in all piety and probity; and their material position was far better than that of their successors. They did not need to overwork; they did no more than they chose to, and yet earned what they needed. They had leisure for healthful work in garden or field, work which in itself was recreation for them, and they could take part besides in the recreations and games of their neighbours, and all these games – bowling, cricket, football, etc., contributed to their physical health and vigour. They were, for the most part, strong, well-built people, in whose physique little or no difference from that of their peasant neighbours was discoverable. Their children grew up in the fresh country air, and, if they could help their parents at work, it was only occasionally; while of eight or twelve hours work for them there was no question . . .

'But intellectually, they were dead; lived only for their petty, private interest, for their looms and gardens, and knew nothing of the mighty movement which, beyond their horizon, was sweeping through mankind. They were comfortable in their silent vegetation, and but for the industrial revolution they would never have emerged from this existence, which, cosily romantic as it was, was nevertheless not worthy of human beings. In truth, they were not human beings; they were merely toiling machines in the service of the few aristocrats who had guided history down to that time. The industrial revolution has simply carried this out to its logical end by making the workers machines pure and simple, taking from them the last trace of independent activity, and so forcing them to think and demand a position worthy of men. As in France politics, so in England manufacture, and the movement of civil society in general drew into the whirl of history the last classes which had remained sunk in apathetic indifference to the universal interests of mankind.'

(Friedrich Engels, op. cit.)

Popular Protest

Popular reaction might, as we have seen, take a less muted form and express itself in violent protest. In fact, the thirty-five years after 1812 were among the most troubled in the whole of British history. It was the period of Luddism, of trade union activity in the new factory towns, of the 'last labourers' revolt' in the southern counties, of the Rebecca riots in Wales, of renewed peasant rebellion in Ireland, of Chartism and the great Reform Bill agitation of the early 1830s. Protest might be peaceful; but, more typically, it assumed the form of violent assaults on property. Though the old-style food riot was dying out, arson was on the increase in country districts; threatening letters continued to be sent to landlords, employers and parsons; machine-breaking survived in both urban and rural centres until the 1830s; and toll-gates were smashed in Wales and houses were 'pulled down' in the Potteries towns as late as 1842. In short, protest still generally bore the mark of a pre-industrial age.

'Our complaint is that we have not sauficient maintance to suport our famleys, and as theare a geving more wages in the joining Parishes we do request that you will consent and sine your hands to this Paper that all labering men mairred and singel abel to do a day's work to have 2s. per day, and all lads over 16 yers of age to have 6d. per day, and refuse to pay tythes and taxes, and we will stand your frends and asist you old men that have a wife to Ceep to have 1s. 6d. per day.'

(The Hampshire labourers of 1830 demand a living wage. *The Times*, 30 November 1830.)

'To the Divil of Hollow's-miln –
'Your hellish marchinery is shivered to smash on Stilbro' Moor, and your men are lying bound hand and foot in a ditch by the roadside. Take this as a warning from men that are starving, and have starving wives and children to go home to when they have done this deed. If you get new machines, or if otherwise go on as you have done, you shall hear from us again. Beware!'

(Charlotte Bronte, *Shirley*, 1849. Robert Moore, the mill-owner, reads a letter left for him by his employees. The time is towards the close of the Napoleonic Wars.)

'Sir,
'Your name is down amongst the Black hearts in the Black Book and this is to advise you and the like of you, who are Parson Justasses, to make your Wills. Ye have been the Blackguard Enemies of the People on all occasions, Ye have not done
as ye ought
                    Swing'

(Threatening note addressed to a Church of England magistrate during the 'Swing' riots of November-December 1830. From E. J. Hobsbawm and G. Rudé, *Captain Swing*, 1969.)

'Among all the crimes that men committed against their neighbours, that which the law calls ARSON, and which is *a malicious setting fire to their buildings or their stacks*, is a crime always held in great and just abhorrence, and always punished *with death* . . .

'When therefore, we hear of acts of this description being almost nightly committed *in England*, our first feeling is that of *resentment against the parties*; but, when we have had a little time to reflect, we are, if we be not devourers of the fruit of the people's labours, led to ask What can have been *the cause* of a state of things so unnatural as that in which crimes of this horrid sort are committed by hundreds of men going in a body, and deemed by them to be a sort of *duty* instead of *crimes*? When we put this question we are not to be answered with the assertion, that the crimes arise from the *vicious disposition* of the working people; because then we ask, *what it is* that has made them so vicious? No; this cannot be the cause. The people are of the same make and maker that they always were; the land is the same, the climate the same, the language and religion the same; and, it is very well known that schools and places of worship and the circulation of the Bible and of religious books have all been prodigiously increasing for many years, and are now more on the increase than ever. There must, therefore, be some *other cause*, or causes, to produce these dreadful acts in a people the most just, the most good-natured, and the most patient, in the world. I know this *cause*, or, rather these causes; I know also that there is an effectual *remedy* of this great and melancholy evil; and I need not say, that it is my duty to state them both with perfect frankness; a duty I shall perform as briefly and with as much clearness as I am able.'

(Rural incendiarism in 1830. From Cobbett's *Twopenny Trash*, November 1830.)

'On Friday afternoon, about four o'clock, a large body of rioters suddenly attacked the weaving factory belonging to Messrs Wroe and Duncroft, at West Houghton, about thirteen miles from this town; of which, being unprotected, they soon got possession. They instantly set it on fire, and the whole of the building with its valuable machinery, cambrics,

&c were entirely destroyed. The damage sustained is immense, the factory alone having cost 6,000 l. The reason assigned for this horrid act is, as at Middleton, "weaving by steam". By this dreadful event, two worthy families have sustained a heavy and irreparable injury, and a very considerable number of poor are thrown out of employment. The rioters appear to level their vengeance against all species of improvement in machinery. Mistaken men! – what would this country have been without such improvements?'

(Machine-breaking in Lancashire; from the *Annual Register*, April 1812.)

> 'Come all ye croppers stout and bold,
> Let your faith grow stronger still,
> Oh, the cropper lads in the county of York
> Broke the shears at Forster's mill.
>> The wind it blew
>> The sparks they flew
> Which alarmed the town full soon.

> 'Around and around we all will stand,
> And sternly swear we will,
> We'll break the shears and windows too,
> And set fire to the Tazzling mill.'

(Yorkshire croppers' song of 1812.)

'I live with my father in Ashampstead Street: my younger brother George . . . lives at home also. About three o'clock in the morning of yesterday week I was awakened by the blowing of a horn. Stephen Davies of Ashampstead Common came and called us and said the Press Gang was coming; he is a cripple and rides on a donkey. Myself and brother got out of bed. I looked through the window: we had no upstairs. A great many persons came before the house and holloed to us to unlock the door or they would beat it open. I opened the door. Three or four came in. They said if we did not go with them they would draw us out. My brother

and I went out with them into the street. They stopped at
Hunt's the next door, but the gate was locked and he did not
go up . . . They would not let my brother stay in doors to do
up his shoes. One catched him by the arms and pulled him
out and I went out and did up my shoes beyond the gate . . .
They waited for my father and then went on to Farmer
Taylor's . . . A horn was blown sometimes by one and sometimes by another . . . All the houses were visited and the men
in them pressed.'

(A machine-breakers' 'press-gang' at work in Berkshire in the
riots of 1830. Public Record Office, Treasury Solicitor's Papers,
T.S. 11/849 (Berks. 1830).)

'As we are here, we will have £5 before we go out of the
place or be damned if we don't smash it. You and the gentlemen have been living upon all the good things for the last
ten years. We have suffered enough, and now is our time,
and we will now have it. You only speak to us now because
you are afraid and intimidated.'

(William Oakley, a twenty-four-year-old wheelwright of Kint-
bury, threatens the Berkshire magistrates in Hungerford Town
Hall. H.O. 52/6 (letter of 28 November 1830).)

'When I saw the house on fire, [George Bailey, a bricklayer,
is speaking] I went to fetch the engine, and helped to work it
and put out the fire . . . Williams came to stop us from working the engine. He first set his foot on the hose, and then he
borrowed a knife from Cartledge to cut the hose; but he was
taken into custody before he could do it by Mr Richard
Cyples . . . I saw Wright put a bed upon the fire in front of
the house. I had known him before. I also saw Joseph
Whiston, who was known by the name of Joco. I saw him
take a piano and put it on the fire. He said the Lord was at
his side, and the flames would not hurt him . . .

'At this time there were about four or five hundred persons
present. One of the prisoners was detected in pilfering small
articles, caps, scissors, and the like, and putting them in his
pocket. The people who had brought the engine were

putting out the fire, when the military came to the spot, and several of the rioters were taken into custody.'

(An urban riot: the assault on the Rev. Benjamin Vale's house at Longton, by Stoke-on-Trent, during the 'Plug-Plot' disturbances of 1842. From the *Annual Register*, 1842, pp. 157–9.)

The Response of Authority: Law and Order

The violent response of the poor was matched by the violent counter-response of those in authority. Employers and landlords were appalled by the threats and damage to property; since the beginning of George III's reign the penal code had become more severe; and, as Fowell Buxton reminded the Commons in a memorable debate of 1819, 'more crimes have been denounced as capital in the reign of his present majesty than in the reigns of the Plantagenets, the Tudors, and the Stuarts combined'. Juries were, it is true, in reaction against the severity of the law, inclined to hesitate to return verdicts of guilty in capital cases and executions were more often respited than in the past. Nevertheless, protest was often met with savage retribution. The most notorious case of all was the punishment meted out to the rebellious country labourers of 1830, when nineteen men were hanged, 644 were jailed and over 480 were transported to the Australian colonies.

'The contempt for the existing social order is most conspicuous in its extreme form – that of offences against the law. If the influences demoralising to the working-man act more powerfully, more concentratedly than usual, he becomes an offender ... Under the brutal and brutalising treatment of the bourgeoisie, the working-man becomes precisely as much a thing without volition as water, and is subject to the laws of nature with precisely the same necessity; at a certain point all freedom ceases. Hence with the extension of the proletariat, crime has increased in England, and the British nation has become the most criminal in the world. From the annual criminal tables of the Home Secretary, it is evident that the increase of crime in England has proceeded with incomprehensible rapidity. The number of arrests for *criminal* offences reached in the years: 1805,

4,605; 1810, 5,146; 1815, 7,898; 1820, 13,710; 1825, 14,437; 1830, 18,107; 1835, 20,731; 1840, 27,187; 1841, 27,760; 1842, 31,309 in England and Wales alone. That is to say they increased seven fold in thirty-seven years. Of these arrests, in 1842, 4,907 were made in Lancashire alone, or more than 14 per cent of the whole; and 4,094 in Middlesex, including London, or more than 13 per cent. So that two districts which include great cities with large proletarian populations, produced one-fourth of the total amount of crime . . . Moreover, the criminal tables prove directly that nearly all crime arises within the proletariat . . . The offences . . . are, in the great majority of cases, against property, and have, therefore, arisen from want in some form; for what a man has, he does not steal . . .

' . . . In this country, social war is under full headway . . . And this war grows from year to year, as the criminal tables show, more violent, passionate, irreconcilable.'

(Friedrich Engels, op. cit.)

'[Mr F. Buxton said] . . . Descending then from common law to statute law, I hold in my hand a list of those offences, which, at this moment are capital, in number 223 . . .

' . . . It is a fact, and a very melancholy fact, that there are persons living in this kingdom at whose birth the criminal code contained less than sixty capital offences, and who, in the short space permitted to the life of man, have seen that number quadrupled – who have seen an act pass, making offences capital by the dozen and by the score; and, what is worse, bundling up together offences, trivial and atrocious, some nothing short of murder in malignity of intention, and others nothing beyond a civil trespass . . .'

(*Parliamentary Debates*, 1/xxxix/808/810, 2 March 1819, H. of C.; cited in Evans and Pledger, *Contemporary Sources and Opinions in Modern British History*, vol. 2, 1967.)

'I induced the magistrates to put themselves on horseback, each at the head of his own servants and retainers, grooms, huntsmen, game-keepers, armed with horsewhips, pistols, fowling pieces and what they could get, and to attack in concert, if necessary, or singly, these mobs, disperse them, and take and put in confinement those who could not escape. This was done in a spirited manner, in many instances, and it is astonishing how soon the country was tranquillised, and that in the best way, by the activity and spirit of the gentlemen.'

(The Duke of Wellington relates how he rounded up riotous labourers in Hampshire in the disturbances of 1830. From Wellington's *Despatches*; cited by David Williams, *John Frost*, 1939.)

'These machines are as much entitled to the Protection of the Law as any other Description of Property, and . . . the course which has been taken of presenting or recommending the Discontinuance of them is, in fact, to connive at, or rather to assist in the Establishment of a Tyranny of the most oppressive Character . . . It is my duty therefore to recommend in the strongest Manner, that for the future all Justices of Peace, and other Magistrates, will oppose a firm Resistance to all demands of the Nature above described, more especially when accompanied with Violence and Menace; and that they will deem it their Duty to maintain and uphold the Rights of Property, of every Description, against Violence and Aggression.'

(*The Times*, 9 December 1830. Viscount Melbourne, Whig Home Secretary, is urging magistrates to be more resolute in defence of threshing machines.)

'I hope that your fate will be a warning to others. You will leave the country, all of you: you will see your friends and relatives no more; for though you will be transported for seven years only, it is not likely that at the expiration of that term you will find yourselves in a situation to return. You will be in a distant land at the expiration of your sentence. The land which you have disgraced will see you no more: the friends with whom you are connected will be parted from you for ever in this world.'

(Words of comfort from the Bench: Mr Justice Alderson

sentencing machine-breakers to transportation at Salisbury on 2 January 1831. *The Times*, 3 January 1831.)

'At four o'clock in the morning [June 21, 1809], myself and eleven others were conveyed by water on board the Retribution hulk at Woolwich. I had now a new scene of misery to contemplate; and, of all the shocking scenes I had ever beheld, this was the most distressing. There were confined in this floating dungeon nearly six hundred men, most of them double-ironed; and the reader may conceive the horrible effects arising from the continual rattling of chains, the filth and vermin naturally produced by such a crowd of miserable inhabitants, the oaths and execrations constantly heard among them; and above all, from the shocking necessity of associating . . . with so depraved a set of beings . . . On descending the hatchway, no conception can be formed of the scene which presented itself . . . nothing short of a descent into the infernal regions can be at all worthy of a comparison with it.'

(James Hardy Vaux, *Memoirs*, 1819; cited by Evans and Pledger, *Contemp. Sources*, op. cit. The author, a convicted felon, is describing the scene on board the transport that will take him to Botany Bay.)

'To D. Thompson, Secretary, Sydney.
'Mr Thompson, Sir, pardon me for taking the Liberty of a Drass you but mi trobles calls me to do so. I rived by the Ship Captain Cook in the Year 1833 Santanse Life for Riating & Meshan Braking. I saw the newspaper with menn that was triad with me the have goot ther Liberty. I have been in no troble since mi arivale. I hope you will be so kind as to in form me if theires anthing against me mi name Is Jacob Wilsher and it so far up the contry I have no ways of guting Down to make in qury I have a sined Sarvent to Mr Thos BEATTS of Paramatta and is at Molong[y?] in the Districk of Willington . . .

Your humble sarvent & &
Jacob Wilsher.'

(A Hampshire farm-worker petitions for his release from penal servitude in Australia, 1838. Archives of New South Wales, MS 4/1123.1.)

The Changing Face of Protest

As industrial society developed, the old modes of protest, like the old nostalgic illusions, began to disappear. It was not that the divisions within society became healed, but that the workers and the poor sought other means to secure themselves a larger share of the cake or a place in the sun. Here Chartism served as a kind of watershed or transition between the old and the new. On the one hand, it saw such archaic solutions for industrial ills as Feargus O'Connor's plan to resettle urban workers on the land and the old-style attacks on property in the Potteries towns. On the other hand, it witnessed the first attempt made to set up a national workers' party in the National Charter Association of the 1840s. Meanwhile, trade unions were acquiring greater durability and more stable organizations; and new working-class leaders were emerging from the ranks of the workers themselves, men who were willing to come to grips with the new industrial society rather than seek solutions in a past that had gone. Such a man was George Loveless, the Tolpuddle Martyr, who, on returning from transportation to Australia in 1837, wrote:

'I believe that nothing will ever be done to relieve the distress of the working classes, unless they take it into their own hands. With these views I left England, and with these views I am returned.'

(George Loveless, *The Victims of Whiggery*, 1837.)

5

The Early Railway Age

THEO BARKER

Industrialization, as the previous chapters have shown, was accompanied by a great deal of social discontent, particularly when food prices were high and when new labour-saving machines were being introduced. And the shift in emphasis from habit and tradition in the countryside to rough and tumble in the town, and the too rapid growth of these places to accommodate both the immigrants and the larger numbers actually born there, were also circumstances which helped to breed discontent. The youthfulness of the population, a result of the rapid population increase, also deserves to be stressed. At the census of 1821, for instance, more than a fifth of the inhabitants of Great Britain were aged between ten and twenty. This strong teenage element, wage-earning and to a considerable extent independent, needs to be borne in mind.

The spread of steam power, not extensively used until the advent of precision engineering in the 1830s, did not quickly improve Everyman's lot, for it often inflicted new hardships. It is true that it took the drudgery out of a few tasks which had previously been laborious and back-breaking; but by imposing discipline and strict time-keeping and fines for lateness, it deprived men and women of the right to work when they pleased, and by creating larger production units it gave rise to new social problems, particularly the break-up of the family work group.

Similarly, when the steam engine was put on wheels and ran, travelling about became easier, cheaper and more rapid. Railway trains became objects of wonder. In the days of stage-coaches few people could afford to travel and the postal services were limited and expensive. Railways made the penny post possible, encouraged the more rapid dissemination of ideas and popularized the day excursion.

'Within the last two or three years,' noted the *Illustrated London News* in September 1850, 'the "people", popularly so called, have been enabled, thanks to the railways and to the organisation of cheap pleasure-trips, to indulge in travel to distances which their forefathers had neither time nor money to undertake. The working class of 30, or even 15, years ago did not know their own country. Very few travelled for pleasure beyond a small circle around the place which they inhabited ... Now travelling bids fair to become not only the necessity of the rich, but the luxury of the poor. The great lines of railways in England, by granting facilities for "monster" or excursion trains at cheaper rates, have conferred a boon upon the public ...'

Statistics support this opinion. The number of railway travellers booked on the railways of the United Kingdom rose from 64,000 during the year ended 30 June 1843 to 174,000 a mere five years later; the third-class element in those totals grew from 19,000 to no fewer than 86,000.

Yet railways, with their strict emphasis on first, second and third-class compartments, were perpetuating and underlining the divisions within society. The railway companies even employed first, second and third-class moppers to clean out carriages. And the trains placed more people at risk of accident, particularly in the very early days when the dangers of the new locomotives were not properly understood and passengers rode on the front of the engine or alighted from their trains on to the open track. Breakdowns were frequent, and fixed signals late on the scene. Huskisson was far from being the only railway passenger to lose his life in the railways' early years.

While steam was a mixed blessing to those who came under its direct influence, there were many others whom, so far as their work was concerned, it passed by entirely. Many industries still lacked steam power even in the 1860s; and the vast range of service occupations, such as retailing or domestic service or portering, were completely unaffected by it. A much worse fate, however, befell those in occupations which came into direct competition with steam: the hand-loom weavers, for instance, when directly confronted by the weaving mill, or those working in road transport when confronted by the railway. Many of the greatest hardships of this period were suffered not by workers in the factories or on the railways but by others who were deprived of their very livelihood by steam power.

The other most notable examples of hardship occurred, as in previous periods, in particular years, during cyclical depressions when trade was bad and unemployment high. The early railway age saw one of the worst of these slumps, in the early 1840s, perhaps the worst spell of misery and distress in the whole of the nineteenth century. Political historians remember it as the age of the Chartists; but behind Chartism lay want, want made all the worse by the better times that had been enjoyed during the preceding boom years. The peaks should not be overlooked when considering the troughs, for the peaks to a large degree determined their extent.

Steam was of little help to the course of urbanization until, about the middle of the century, water supply and sewerage systems increasingly invoked its aid. The early railway age witnessed that particularly unsatisfactory interval when more towns had to accommodate greater swarms of people than ever, but before local government, sanitary engineering or the art of medicine had developed to the point of being able to cope with the grave public health and medical problems to which these huge settlements gave rise. The sanitary shortcomings are well-known; medical ignorance, in the year before Pasteur and knowledge of germs, perhaps less so.

The old — old ideas, old techniques and old customs — resisted surprisingly well the challenge of the new steam age. A greater measure of restraint and more emphasis on temperance there may have been among certain sections in all walks of life; yet the unruly gaiety of the fair, the cruel sport of fighting with cocks, dogs and cats — or the sheer brutality of naked men fighting together — and the gruesome spectacle of a public hanging, all of which still flourished in the 1850s and 1860s, take us backwards to the eighteenth century rather than forwards to the twentieth. The British people seem to have been remarkably resistant to physical and environmental change.

The Drudgery of Work without the Aid of Power-Driven Machines

'The position in which the weaver sits is not the best for muscular exertion, having no firm support for his feet, which are alternately raised and depressed in working the treddles. He has thus to depend for a fulcrum chiefly on the muscles of his back.'

(Peter Gaskell, *The Manufacturing Population of England*, 1833. The writer was a doctor in the Manchester area.)

'A Member of Parliament: Do you think that he [a miner] could not work as much every day for seven days as every day for three days?

'James Philip Baker, Mines Inspector for the South Staffordshire and East Worcestershire area: It would be an utter impossibility. A man works until he can scarcely stand. The pikeman works by stint and ... a good workman, healthy and that understands his work, can do something like two days work in about eight hours or nine hours; but generally eight ... In order to do that, his hands and arms are going like a machine, while his contorted body is in various shapes; therefore I contend that it would be impossible for any man to follow it up day by day.'

(Evidence to the Select Committee on Coal, 31 March 1873.)

'My appointed station in life was that of a basketmaker, and straightaway I was set to work at the elementary stages, as an informal apprentice at eightpence a week with dinner and tea – a welcome addition to the family budget. Hours were long: a day of twelve hours for us boys. For men, the workshop hours, before the general swarming of the working classes to the suburbs, were from 6 a.m. to 9 p.m. except for a brief period at the spring or autumn equinoxes, when lighting-up time ended or began: the latter event being celebrated by the men with a sing-song held in the workshop to the stimulus of beer and tobacco ... leaving-off time on Saturday was five o'clock. The workman paid for his light, and gas money was deducted from his wages. Devotion to St Monday, with greater or less piety, was general, but on Fridays the nose-bag was put on in compensation ...

'Men lived near their employment. Wife or child brought the breakfast and other meals to the shop; the master knew the womenfolk and children of his men; he was the deliverer of his people and advanced money for confinements, which was paid back in instalments.'

(Thomas Okey, *A Basketful of Memories*, 1930. The writer was born in 1852, the son of a journeyman basketmaker. He himself became a basketmaker, taught himself languages and, in 1919, at the age of sixty-seven, was elected to the newly-created Chair of Italian Studies at Cambridge. As Professor Harrison has noted in his introduction to Chapter 1, 'St Monday' refers to the habit of taking Monday off.)

'I remember one day at Liverpool when walking on the Docks, stopping to observe the mode in which the labourers, employed to carry sacks of oats from the adjoining store-houses to a vessel lying at the waterside, conducted the operation. These men (chiefly Irishmen) received the full sacks as they were lowered by the crane off the hitch on their shoulders and carried them across the road. They pursued their heavy task during the working hours of a summer's day at a uniform, unremitting pace, a trot of at least five miles an hour, the distance from the vessel to the storehouse being a full fifty yards ... It was said that at this work a good labourer earned, at 16d. per 100 sacks, ten shillings a day; so that consequently he made 750 trips from the storehouse to the vessel, carrying for half the distance a full sack of oats on his shoulder, thus performing a distance of ... 43 miles nearly ...'

(Sir George Head, *A Home Tour Through the Manufacturing Districts of England in the Summer of 1835*, 1836.)

'Standing behind the counter all day, or sitting in a small back parlour, with eyes directed through an inner window, to watch for customers – taking their meals at broken times – all day on the move, yet never in exercise – closing their shutters at 9, and often sorting and replacing their goods till 11 or 12, they present a sad picture of an unnatural life.'

(C. Turner Thackrah, *The Effects of Arts, Trades and Professions on Health and Longevity*, 2nd edition, 1832.)

'Little children here begin to work at stitching gloves when very young. My little sister, now 5½ years old, can stitch a good many little fingers and is very clever, having been at it for two years . . . She used to stand on a stool so as to be able to see up to the candle on the table. I have seen many begin as young as that, and they do so still, because it makes them cleverer if they begin young. Parents are not particular about the age if they have work as they must do it.

'Little children are kept up shamefully late if there is work, especially on Thursday and Friday nights when it is often till 11 and 12. Children younger than 7, but not younger than 6, are kept up as late as that. Mothers will pin them to their knee to keep them to their work, and if they are sleepy give them a slap on their head to keep them awake. If the children are pinned up so, they cannot fall when they are slapped, or if they go to sleep. I have often seen the children slapped in this way and cry. The child has so many fingers set for it to stitch before it goes to bed and it must do them.

'What makes the work come so heavy at the end of the week is that the men are slacking at the beginning. On St Monday they will go pigeoning or on some other amusement, and do but little on Tuesday beyond setting the winders to work and much do not begin regularly till Wednesday . . . It would be much better for all to make Monday like any other day. As it is, the work is always behind, and comes in to the stitchers at all times on Friday night up to 12, and 1 and 2. They must sit up to do the work then as the gloves have to be finished and taken into Nottingham in the morning.'

(Evidence of Mary Thorpe (aged twenty-five) of Bulwell, Nottingham, to the Children's Employment Commission, 1862.)

'. . . I go about the streets with water-creases, crying, "Four bunches a penny, water-creases". I am just eight years old – that's all and I've a big sister and a brother and sister younger than I am. On and off I've been near a twelve-month in the streets. Before that I had to take care of a baby for my aunt . . . Before I had the baby I used to help my mother, who was in the fur trade; and if there were any slits in the fur, I'd sew tham up. My mother learned me to needle-work and to knit when I was about five. I used to go to school, too, but I wasn't there long . . . It's very cold before winter comes on reg'lar – specially getting up of a morning. I gets up in the dark by the light of the lamp in the court . . . I bears the cold – you must; so I puts my hands under my shawl, though it hurts 'em to take hold of the creases, especially when we take 'em to the pump to wash 'em. No; I never see any children crying – it's no use.'

(A London watercress girl, aged eight, reported in Henry Mayhew, *London Labour and the London Poor*, 1861/2.)

The Advantages and Disadvantages of Steam Power

'In my recent tour, continued during several months, through the manufacturing districts, I have seen tens of thousands of old, young and middle-aged of both sexes, many of them too feeble to get their daily bread by any of the former modes of industry, earning abundant food, raiment, and domestic accommodation, without perspiring at a single pore, screened meanwhile from the summer's sun and the winter's frost, in apartments more airy and salubrious than those of the metropolis . . . In the spacious halls, the benignant power of steam summons around him his myriads of willing menials, and assigns to each the regulated task, substituting for painful muscular effort on their part the energies of his own gigantic arm, and demanding in return only attention and dexterity to correct such little aberrations as casually occur in his workmanship . . .

'The main difficulty did not, to my apprehension, lie so much in the invention of a proper self-acting mechanism for drawing out and twisting cotton into a continuous thread as in the distribution of the different members of the apparatus into one co-operative body, in impelling each organ with its appropriate delicacy and speed, and above all, in training human beings to renounce their desultory habits of work, and to identify themselves with the unvarying regularity of the complex automaton. To devise and administer a successful code of factory discipline, suited to the necessities of factory diligence, was the herculean enterprise, the noble achievement, of Arkwright . . .

'Even at the present day, when the system is perfectly organised, and its labour lightened to the utmost, it is found nearly impossible to convert people past the age of puberty, whether drawn from rural or from handicraft occupations, into useful factory hands. After struggling for a while to conquer their listless or restless habits, they either renounce the employment spontaneously, or are dismissed by the overlookers on account of inattention.'

(Andrew Ure, *Philosophy of Manufactures*, 1835. The writer, who was also author of a *Dictionary of Chemistry* and other works, became analytical chemist to the Board of Customs in 1834.)

'. . . I saw a machine at work for the purpose of sawing blocks of stone. It was driven by a steam-engine, apparently of small power, although by it were set in motion upwards of three dozen saws . . . One boy attended all the saws with sand and water, adjusting at the same time by a screw purchase, their contact and pressure on the stone.

'It was agreeable to see, in this instance above all others, the steam engine substituted for human labour. Nothing can be less gratifying to the mind than to watch the patient endurance and almost imperceptible progress of a mason employed in cutting through a large stone . . . Pass on . . . in three, four or five hours return to the same spot, and there appears the same man and the same stone . . .'

(Sir George Head, op. cit.)

'The great curse of the factory system is to be found, not in the protracted hours of labour, nor in the slightly unhealthy influences to which those engaged in it are exposed. It is in the breaking up of all home and social affections: the father, the mother and the child are alike occupied and never meet under the common roof except during the evenings.'

(Peter Gaskell, *Prospects of Industry*, 1835.)

The Impact of Railways

'All sights which I had seen, in London and elsewhere . . . shrank into comparative nothingness, when, after reaching Liverpool, I went into the country for a week, in the neighbourhood of Prescot, and saw (each day I sought to see it, each hour of the day I could have stood to see it again) the white steam shooting through the landscape of trees, meadows and villages, and the long train, loaded with merchandise, men and women, and human enterprise, rolling along under the steam. I had seen no sight like that; I have seen nothing to excel it since. In beauty and grandeur, the world has nothing beyond it.'

(*The Autobiography of a Working Man* by 'One Who Has Whistled at the Plough' [Alexander Somerville], 1848.)

'The sensation created by our transit . . . was particularly striking. Had the double-tailed comet passed that way, the country people could hardly have been more interested by the spectacle; the men at work in the fields and quarries stood like statues, their pickaxes in their hands, in attitudes of fixed attention . . . and women in troops, in their best gowns and bonnets, fled from the villages and congregated at the corner of every intersecting lane. Neither were the brute creation less animated on every occasion . . . every horse was on the alert, viewing the huge moving body as it approached with a mixture of fear and surprise, stamping, pointing forward his ears, snorting, and evincing a degree of curiosity so intense that it appeared as if to the instinctive faculty was added reason and the desire of knowledge. Even the cows, as they cocked and twisted their tails, spit out mouthfulls of unchewed grass and tried to gallop . . .'

(Sir George Head, op. cit. He had been travelling upon the Leeds & Selby Railway.)

'The Irish and other labourers, on seeking work, inevitably walk their journeys, if ever so long; in this practice there is no alteration; it was the custom before the railways were established, and it is still followed: in the season you may see hundreds of these industrious men on their journeys walking barefooted, with their shoes under their arms, to lessen as much as possible the cost of their journeys.'

(John Hewitt, a Removing Officer in Liverpool, in a report to the Assistant Poor Law Commissioner in Manchester, 9 February 1842, printed as part of an appendix in the Report of the Select Committee on Railways, 1844.)

'. . . the sides and ends being only two feet high . . . a moderate shock is enough to throw the passengers out of the carriage. The object of this no doubt is partly to save expense, but mainly to deter second-class passengers from travelling by the third class by a fear of the exposure for eight or ten hours, without any shelter, to the cold.'

(Comment by Samuel Laing, then a Board of Trade Official, on third-class carriages, following a railway accident on Christmas Eve 1841, quoted in Henry Parris, *Government and Railways in Nineteenth Century Britain*, 1965. Laing was later to become Chairman of the London, Brighton & South Coast Railway and an M.P.)

'[On a Friday in the summer of 1845] I walked to Hebden Bridge and took a train to Rochdale, my first railway ride. We were put into a truck worse and more exposed than cattle trucks now are. There were seats, or forms, to sit on, but they were swimming with rain. Not a bit of shelter from the driving rain, or sparks from the engine chimney, which then were very plentiful and had a peculiar knack of falling down the back of your neck.'

(Autobiography of Thomas Wood, privately printed by Miss J. D. Wood, 20 Maidstone Road, Heaton Mersey, Stockport, about 1955. The writer was born at Bingley in January 1822. That particular railway company had evidently not yet put into force the provision of the Act, passed in the previous year, which laid down that adequate protection against the weather had to be provided on all time-tabled trains (but not necessarily on excursions). This Act also laid down that at least one train per day in each direction, stopping at every station on the line, should provide third-class accommodation at a fare not exceeding 1d per mile. No historian has, however, so far considered to what extent the working classes could afford to pay even this low fare.)

'In these [third-class carriages] there was a general feeling of bare boards and cheerlessness as you entered them and if you were travelling in the winter time they gave you a kind of cold shiver. Even the windows were but small square apertures giving the most limited view possible of the outside world. The seats were cushionless and the longer you sat on them the harder and more unyielding they seemed to grow . . . Trains stopped at every little place on the way; you were shunted here and shunted there, or you found yourself resting in some lonely siding for what seemed an age. At other times you were kept whistling and letting off steam in a very angry fashion just outside some station when you had at last reached some point in your journey where you could stretch your aching, weary limbs and refresh the inner man.'

(Louis M. Hayes, *Reminiscences of Manchester and Some of Its Local Surroundings from the Year 1840*, Manchester, 1905.)

'The refreshment establishment at Wolverton is composed of –
  '1. A matron or Generallissima
  '2. Seven very young ladies to wait upon the passengers
  '3. Four men and three boys to wait upon the passengers
  '4. One man-cook, his kitchen-maid, and his two scullery maids
  '5. Two housemaids
  '6. One still-room maid, employed solely in the liquid duty of making tea and coffee
  '7. Two laundry maids
  '8. One baker and one baker's boy
  '9. One garden boy . . .
  '10. An odd man . . .

'Very early in the morning . . . the odd-man wakens the two house-maids, to one of whom is entrusted the confidential duty of awakening the seven young ladies exactly at seven o'clock . . . in time for them to receive the passengers of the first train which reaches Wolverton at 7.30 a.m. From that time until the departure of the passengers by the York mail, which arrives opposite the refreshment room at about eleven o'clock at night, these young persons remain on duty . . .'

(Sir Francis Bond Head, *Stokers and Pokers: Or the London & North-Western Railway*, 1849. In days before corridor coaches, regular stops on long journeys were obviously essential.)

'[After passenger trains have been taken from Euston to the sidings] a large gang of he-housemaids, clattering towards them in wooden shoes and leggings . . . are seen advancing; some with mops in their hands, others with large chamois leathers, while others are carrying on their shoulders a yoke, from which are suspended *in equilibrio* two pails . . . Among "moppers" there exist the same gradations which so distinctly separate other classes of society. A "first-class mopper" would on no account demean himself by mopping a second-class carriage, and in like manner a "second-class mopper" only attains that distinction after he has for a sufficient length of time been commissioned to mop horse-boxes and common luggage trains.'

(ibid.)

' . . . I was brought up in stablework. I was employed in a large coaching inn in Lancashire when I was last employed in that way, but about ten years ago a railway line was opened, and the coaching was no go any longer; it hadn't a chance to pay, so the horses and all was sold and I was discharged with a lot of others. I walked from Manchester to London – for I think most men when they don't know what in the world to do come to London – and I lived for a few months on what little money I had, and what I could pick up in an odd job about horses . . . I was beat out three or

four times, and didn't know what to do, but somehow or
other I got over it . . .'

(Henry Mayhew, op. cit.)

'Leeds, 6 November 1845. Rail, rail, nothing but the railway uppermost! What a different aspect the business world
now wears, compared to former times! . . . Men of business,
steady to their trade originally, are now anxious and beside
themselves about these apparently money-making, fluctuat-
ing, speculative railways . . . And the comforts at hotels are
so infringed upon by the latitudinarian principle carried out
by the swarm of architects and attorneys, engineers, civil and
otherwise, surveyors and levellers . . . as to give the inns,
and in many instances the commercial room itself, the
semblance of a fair, or bear-garden, rather than the usual
residence of the plodding sons of commerce . . .'

(Throne Crick, *Sketches from the Diary of a Commercial Traveller*,
1847.)

'The effects of this extraordinary improvement in the means
of travelling, especially since the introduction of railways,
have been as striking on the manners as on the industry of all
classes . . . During the spring the metropolis is crowded with
visitors of all ranks and orders from the remotest provinces,
and during summer and autumn vast numbers of the
citizens are spread over the country. Hence it is that manners, as well as prices, are reduced to nearly the same
standard. A respectable family in Penzance or Inverness
live very much in the same way as a respectable family in
London. Peculiarities of all sorts have disappeared . . .'

(J. R. McCulloch, *Dictionary of Commerce*, 2nd edition, 1850.
McCulloch had been the first Professor of Political Economy at
London University and later (1838) Comptroller of the
Stationery Office.)

'The first real event of my life came in 1851, when I was six
years old. My mother then took me up to town to see the
Great Exhibition. Our special Exhibition train from Thirsk
to King's Cross was a wonder to me . . . The train was of

enormous length and drawn by six locomotives. Every seat was occupied; the first-class return fare from Thirsk to King's Cross being only 16s.'

(R. E. Crompton, *Reminiscences*, 1928. The little boy who went up to the Exhibition later became a notable electrical engineer. Third-class returns to the Exhibition from Leeds cost only 5s. The London & North Western Railway alone carried 750,000 passengers up to London to see it.)

'Between Keith and Aberdeen I came across a cheap excursion train, its carriages crammed with people. They were all on their way to a religious meeting, a "revival" at which a number of famous preachers would be speaking. The crowd of people wishing to attend was so great that the railway company had to telegraph for extra carriages, and even so girls had to sit on the young men's knees in many of the compartments. My neighbour told me there would be twenty thousand people at the meeting, some of them coming great distances, fifty or sixty miles . . . The carriages were all third-class, and the people shopkeepers, working folk and small farmers . . .'

(*Taine's Notes on England*, trans. Edward Hyams, 1957. The French philosopher and writer, Hippolyte Taine, visited Britain in the 1860s.)

The Operation of the Trade Cycle and the Sharp Contrast between Good Times and Bad

'When trade is in a good state, the earnings of the "thick-coal collier" are from 20s to 30s per week, and those of his family often 10s to 20s in addition . . . the recklessness and extravagance with which these sums are spent have been commented on in all the reports of the habits of the mining population yet published. Poultry, especially geese and ducks, the earliest and choicest vegetables (e.g. asparagus, green peas and new potatoes when they first appear in the market); occasionally even port wine, drunk out of tumblers and basins; beer and spirits in great quantities, meat in abundance, extravagantly cooked; excursions in carts and cars, gambling etc. are the well-known objects upon which their money is squandered.'

(Report of H. Seymour Tremenheere, a mining inspector, dated December 1849 and published in the Report on the Mining Districts, 1850.)

'When I first became acquainted with the town [Stockport], about five years ago, I believed that there was no place in the world better assured of a long and continuous career of commercial prosperity. The incomes of operative families varied from one to three pounds per week; they lived in comfortable tenements and exhibited much pride of station, rarely mixed with the mere hand-labourers and excavators employed on the railways and other public works . . . The prosperity of Stockport is no more . . . It is now a town in a state of social dissolution . . .

'I have visited Manchester at seasons when trade was pre-eminently prosperous: I see it now suffering under severe and unprecedented distress; and I have been forcibly struck by observing the little change which the altered circumstances have produced in the moral aspect of the population. Agricultural distress soon makes itself known . . . But suffering here has not loosened the bands of confidence . . . This very crisis has been a rigid test of the strength of the Factory system, and precludes the necessity of any further argument to show it cannot be overthrown.'

(W. Cooke Taylor, *Notes on a Tour in the Manufacturing Districts of Lancashire*, 1842 edition.)

' . . . I started early this morning for Colne. On the road I was stopped by a group of seven operatives, who stated their distress in firm but respectful terms, and asked for relief. One of the men particularly struck my attention; he was the living skeleton of a giant . . . He had been a weaver of mousselines de laine, and in prosperous times he had earned from thirty to forty shillings per week; he had a wife and four children . . . work began to grow slack, he hoped that times would mend, and was unwilling that his family should lose the comforts to which they had been accustomed; he drew the little fund he had placed in the savings-bank; it was soon exhausted and work was slacker than ever. He began to retrench, to sell part of his furniture . . . Before last Christmas everything had disappeared . . . Since that time he had been for seven weeks without work of any kind, and had been principally supported by the charity of neighbours little better off than himself. When I offered him a shilling, he refused to receive it until I had given him my name and address, that he might repay it if ever an opportunity offered . . .'

(ibid.)

'There were other print works in the neighbourhood – the Oakenshaw works, superintended by Mr Mercer, a man who would have been a Dalton or a Faraday had he been differently placed. He had been a handloom weaver, but taught himself chemistry and revolutionised the calico printing trade by his practical discoveries. Already he was an old man . . . In August 1842 the great labour riots were passing over Lancashire. Almost every mill had been forcibly closed by the rioters. The only two which remained open were those at Primrose and Oakenshaw . . . We had scouts on horseback over the country to watch the movement of the rioters. One of these reported that many thousands were marching on Mercer's mill at Oakenshaw, so I drove over to join my friend, and had scarcely reached his house when the mob appeared in irresistible numbers . . . I told the rioters that though we had shut the gates of the mill, we knew their forces were irresistible . . . Instead of going down in crowds, and doing much mischief by their large numbers, they might send a deputation to remove the plugs from the boilers, and thus secure the stoppage of the works with the least damage. They had no objection to this proposal if it did not mean treachery. I offered myself as a hostage and walked into their midst, whilst they sent a few of their number to secure the stoppage of the works, and this they did without permanent damage. During my detention the leaders explained the nature of their demands, many of which were reasonable, and were afterwards conceded. After receiving a couple of sovereigns to buy food, the rioters went away cheering heartily . . .'

(Wemyss Reid, *Memoirs of the Correspondence of Lyon Playfair*, 1899. Playfair, later to become well known as a leading advocate of technical education, was at that time beginning to learn about applied chemistry at the calico printing works at Primrose, near Clitheroe.)

'No change here yet – The folks are gone at 5 this morning to Bacup – 3,000 of them to turn the hands out there and on the way we have an invasion of the Town at 11 by 2,000 women and girls who passed through the streets singing hymns – it was a very singular and striking spectacle – approaching the sublime – they are dreadfully hungry – a loaf is devoured with a greediness indescribable, and if the bread is nearly covered with mud it is eagerly devoured . . .'

(Letter written from Rochdale by John Bright, 12 August 1842, and quoted in Norman McCord, *The Anti-Corn Law League, 1838–1846* (1958).)

Some Glimpses of, and Comments upon, Life in Towns

SUNDAY MORNING IN WOLVERHAMPTON IN THE EARLY 1840s

'Walked about the town, streets and outskirts during church-time. Met men, singly and in groups, wandering about in their working aprons and caps, or with dirty shirt-sleeves tucked up, and black, smithy-smutted arms and grimed faces. Some appeared to have been up all night – probably at work to recover the time lost by their idleness in the early part of the week; perhaps drinking. Lots of children seen in groups at the end of courts, alleys and narrow streets – playing or sitting on the edge of the common dirt-heap of the place, like a row of sparrows and very much of that colour, all chirruping away . . . Boys fighting; bad language

and bloody noses. Women, in their working dresses, standing at doors or at the ends of passages, with folded arms . . .
Adults seated smoking, or with folded arms, on the threshold
of the door, or inside the houses, evidently not intending to
wash or shave. Many of them sitting or standing in the
house, with an air of lazy vacancy – they do not know what
to do with their leisure or with themselves . . . No merriment
– no laughter – no smiles. All dullness and vacuity. No signs
of joyous animal spirits, except with the girls on the dirt-
heaps.'

('Copied verbatim from my notebook' by R. H. Horne, a sub-
commissioner working for the Children's Employment Commission, and published in its Report in 1843.)

LIVERPOOL IN THE 1860s

'At six o'clock we made our way back through the poor
quarters of the city. What a spectacle! In the neighbourhood
of Leeds Street there are fifteen or twenty streets with ropes
stretched across them where rags and underwear were hung
out to dry. Every stairway swarms with children, five or six
to a step, the eldest nursing the baby; their faces are pale,
their hair whitish and tousled, the rags they wear are full of
holes, they have neither shoes nor stockings and they are
vilely dirty. Their faces and limbs seemed to be encrusted
with dust and soot. In one street there must have been about
two hundred children sprawling and fighting . . . Livid,
bearded old women came out of gin-shops: their reeling gait,
dismal eyes and fixed, idiot grin are indescribable. They look
as if their features had been slowly corroded by vitriol.
Their rags hardly hold together and here and there reveal
glimpses of their filthy bodies: and these rags are old
fashionable clothes, their hats once ladies' hats . . . Rem-
brandt's beggars were happier and better off in their
picturesque hovels. And I have not seen the Irish quarter!'

(*Taine's Notes on England*, op. cit.)

MANCHESTER IN THE 1860s

'. . . What dreary streets. Through half-open windows we could see wretched rooms at ground level, or often below the damp earth's surface. Masses of livid children, dirty and flabby of flesh, crowd each threshold and breathe the vile air of the street, less vile than that within. You catch glimpses of a vestige of carpet and washing hung to dry. We pushed on towards the suburbs, coming to a more open space where rows of cheap houses have been built by speculators. The black streets were paved with ironstone slag. Lines of red roofs were ruled against the universal grey of the sky. But at least each family has its own home, and the fog they breathe there is not so contaminated. They are the privileged, the fortunate ones . . .'

(ibid.)

'And what a scene of noise and bustle it was as you passed along Deansgate to the Fair proper. The street was plenti-fully lined with stalls, laden with all manner of temptations for the young. Apples, oranges, nuts, cocoanut, toffee and gingerbreads of all shapes and varieties, met your longing gaze on all sides. There were gingerbread men and toffee built up in huge pyramids and in all the colours of the rainbow. At night the stalls were illuminated by cans of flaring naptha . . . But this was merely the introduction to Fairyland, as the real Fair only commenced as you turned out of Deansgate into Campfield, where the stalls and booths were almost bursting out with toys of every possible des-cription, all of them brilliantly laden with new paint . . . Here the crowds of useful purchasers formed their undrilled forces into a series of unpremeditated German bands, causing a concentration of discord which it was delightful to listen to. You would hear the sound of the drum, whistle, fiddle, accordion, Jew's harp and all manner of squeaking things in the shape of dogs, cats, beasts, birds and reptiles, the whole making a strange medley of sound . . . And so you would pass through the avenues of booths with an ever-increasing toy-hunger upon you which would never be satisfied. Then you would be hurried along so that the temptations surrounding you might not be too much for you, when suddenly you would find yourself round the corner and in the full whirl of the Fair.

'What a delightful racket there is, as you gaze round the sea of faces and listen to the bands of the various shows, trying to drown each other in their efforts to attract the people to their various entertainments. You begin to distinguish the voices of the showmen shouting hoarsely, the thumping energetically on big drums or the sudden shrill blast of a long brass trumpet, nearly cracking the drum of your ear in its determination to be heard. Mingling with it there is the clanging of cymbals, the firing of guns, the cracking of whips and the distant roar of the wild animals in the far-famed Wombwell's Menagerie . . .'

(Louis M. Hayes, op. cit. The writer is writing about his child-hood, presumably the later 1840s and early 1850s.)

LONDON

'A MEMBER OF A PARLIAMENTARY SELECT COMMITTEE: Can you give the Committee any instances of the improvement of their [working-class] habits which you have observed [since coming to London twenty-eight years before, in 1821]?

'WILLIAM LOVETT: In the first place they are not so drunken and dissipated in their habits as they were at that period; which beneficial change I attribute to the great increase of coffee-houses and reading rooms . . . I should say that they [coffee-houses] have increased five-fold within the last 17 or 18 years . . . You can go into those places and see a great number of the working classes reading; I am told that somewhere about 500 of them have libraries connected to them . . . I may mention further, as regards the improvement of the working classes, that they are not so eager after brutal sports and pastimes as they were when I came to London. At that period you might see the working classes of

London flocking out into the fields on a Sunday morning, or during a holiday, in their dirt and dishabillé, deciding their contests and challenges by pugilistic combats. It was no uncommon thing, at that time, on taking a Sunday morning's walk, to see about twenty such fights. Dog fights and cock fights were equally common at that time; and at that time what were called "Cock and Hen Clubs" and "Free and Easies" were very common among the working classes.

'What were "Cock and Hen Clubs"?: Males and females meeting together at a public house and hearing songs sung; indeed, every species of debauchery, in some instances. Now, they have singing, and something that may be called "Free and Easies" at public houses; but they are comparatively few and these are also confined to the lowest class. And in the work-shop, too, a great improvement has taken place among the working classes; their bookings, fines and drinking bouts are now almost done away with.'

(Evidence to the Select Committee on Public Libraries, 1849, of William Lovett, the Owenite, Co-operator and Chartist. Cruel sports did, however, survive, as may be seen from the next extract.)

'Witnessed something fresh in the way of sport – cock-fighting. The spectators sit on benches round the room, the centre of which is covered with carpet and surrounded by an upright board to enclose the space for the birds ... Several cocks were fought, the finale always resulting in death – on one or both sides. The pugnacity of these small creatures is something surprising. No sign of flinching – not a whit. Game to the last breath, giving and taking punishment inflicted by their long steel spurs with the greatest of heroism ... We then adjourned to "the Pit", a crib up-stairs, boarded high all round, in which the amusements of dogfighting, ratting and badger hunting were accustomed to be held. Two huge dogs were first brought in ... and a struggle ensued which a couple of lions could not have equalled. Frightful were the bites given and received on both sides, and blood streamed in all directions. 'Tis a brutal sport. The spectacle made me sick . . . Several other fights followed and then a badger-bait . . . After the badger-baiting some rats were turned in and killed . . . A complete slaughterhouse the room became, and none of us was sorry when the last part of the entertainment was brought in, which was of the novelest and cruellest I ever beheld. Two cats were unbagged and set a-fighting; afterwards dogs were set on them to finish them, and this took an immense time to do, the struggles made by the poor cats being something fearful.'

(J. O. Thompson (compiler), *Diary and Reminiscences of Dr. Salter*, 1933. The writer was born in Arundel in 1841 and this extract from his diary is dated 18 February 1863. The events seem to have taken place in central London.)

A Public Hanging in 1864

'Yesterday morning Muller was hung in front of Newgate. He died before such a concourse as we may hope may never be again assembled either for the spectacle which they had on view or for the gratification of such lawless ruffianism as yesterday found its scope around the gallows . . . Until about 3 o'clock not more than some 4,000, or at most 5,000, were assembled . . . Then, as every minute the day broke more and more clear, the crowd could be seen in all the horrible reality in which it had been heard throughout the long wet night . . . Among the throng were very few women; and even these were generally of the lowest and poorest class, and almost as abandoned in behaviour as their few better dressed exceptions. The rest of the crowd was, as a rule, made up of young men, but such young men as only such a scene could bring together – sharpers, thieves, gamblers, betting men, the outsiders of the boxing ring, bricklayers' labourers, dock workmen, German artisans and sugar bakers, with a fair sprinkling of what may be almost called as low a grade as any of the worst there met – the rakings of cheap singing-halls and billiard rooms, the fast young "gents" of London. But all, whether young or old, men or women, seemed to know nothing, feel nothing, to have no object but the gallows and to laugh, curse and shout as in this heaving and struggling forward they gained or lost in their strong efforts to get nearer to where Muller was to die . . .

'Then and then only, as the sun rose clearer did the mysterious, dull sound so often mentioned explain itself with all its noises of laughter and of fighting. It was literally and absolutely nothing more than the sound caused by knocking the hats over the eyes of those well-dressed persons who had ventured among the crowd, and while so "bonneted" stripping them and robbing them of everything . . .

'At last, when it was near towards 8 o'clock, there came shouts of "Hats off!" and the whole mass commenced, amidst cries and struggles, to wriggle to and fro as the bell of Newgate began to toll . . . A signal having been given by the Governor, the prisoner was escorted by the sheriffs and under-sheriffs to the foot of the scaffold, the Rev Mr Davis, the ordinary, leading the way and reading as he went some of the opening verses of the burial service . . . [Muller's] arms were pinioned close behind him . . . Like a soldier falling into the ranks, he took with a steady step his place beneath the beam . . . Following him close came the common hangman, who at once pulling a white cap over the condemned man's face, fastened his feet with a strap and shambled off the scaffold amid low hisses . . . [The prisoner uttered some final words.] Almost as soon as these words had left his lips, his kind spiritual guides quitted the platform and the drop fell. Those who stood close to the apparatus could just detect a movement twice, so slight indeed that it could scarcely be called a movement but rather an imperceptible muscular flicker that passed through the frame. That was all; and before the peculiar humming of the crowd was over, Muller had ceased to live, though as he hung his features seemed to swell and sharpen so under the thin white cap that the dead man's face stood like a cast in plaster. For five or ten minutes the crowd . . . were awed and stilled by this quiet, rapid passage from life to death. The impression, however, ... did not last for long, and before the slight, slow vibrations of the body were well ended, robbery and violence, loud laughing, oaths, fighting, obscene conduct, and still more filthy language reigned round the gallows far and near. Such, too, the scene remained, till the old hangman slunk again along the drop amid hisses and sneering enquiries of what he had had to drink that morning. He after failing once to cut the rope made a second attempt more successfully and the body of Muller disappeared from view ...'

(*The Times*, Tuesday, 15 November 1864.)

The Penalties of Medical Ignorance

'I used to go sick when I met the cholera vans carrying the people to the hospitals or taking the dead away; it made me think of the plague in London in the olden time. Mr Gardner came to see us to tell us all to be more careful and not to eat unripe fruit or vegetables, and to wear flannel belts over the stomach, which we did, and fortunately we all escaped taking it ... It did not go away until the winter, when the cold winds and frosts purified the air, then it gradually disappeared.'

(Mrs John Carver (Anne Rickards), *Recollections of My Old Homes*, privately printed, Liverpool, 1908. The writer (1817–83) is referring to the Manchester area, where her father was in business.)

'At last I was one morning summoned to attend a poor Irishwoman in a crowded court. She was in the middle of fever, although near her confinement ... The room in which we were immured was no better than a London coal-cellar; it was like a room in "darkness visible". Fortunately it was not overcrowded; there was the patient herself on a kind of straw couch in the centre; there was her husband [also with fever] on a straw crib in one corner; there was an old haggish-looking woman acting as a kind of nurse, probably the mother ... The air was terribly close, and by my occupation I was held there for at least two hours . . . The puerperal woman did not seem to me to be conscious of her condition, and her child was born dead. The old woman, as she took it from me leered horribly, as if she thought it was a happy release.'

(Sir Benjamin Ward Richardson, *Vita Medica: Chapters of Medical Life and Work*, 1897.)

'. . . and I remember, still even with sorrow, what operating day meant as each week came round . . . "The quicker the surgeon, the greater the surgeon" was the order of the day and such was the rapidity in this case the operation was actually over, in so far as the major part of it was concerned, before the patient uttered a single cry. If all had stopped there, all had been well; but just at that moment, as if giving vent to a long-suppressed agony, the patient uttered a scream, and, in spite of the tenderness and firmness with which the nurses assured him it was all over, continued to scream and struggle, so that he had to be securely held whilst the final steps of the operation were performed. Some of my comrades, neophytes like myself, became faint, and some left the theatre . . . I heard many [patients] express that if they had known beforehand what the suffering was, and the effects subsequently endured, they would rather have faced death than such a fearful struggle for continued existence.'

(ibid.)

6

High Imperial Noon

V. G. KIERNAN

The British Empire, unlike some later modern ones, came into being haphazardly over a very long period; it was as gradual and unplanned a growth as Britain's industrial revolution. This gave it time to entwine itself with nearly every element in the national life, but in very diverse, often discordant ways. Aggressive patriotism had old beginnings in England, by comparison with most other countries, stretching back to Agincourt and Shakespeare, the colonial wars with Dutch and French, the duel with Napoleon. It could go on smouldering under the surface even in the mid-nineteenth-century period when trends of thought in the ascendant were opposed to policies of expansion abroad as useless and wasteful. When Toryism led by Disraeli set itself to fan the glow into a blaze it had an easy task.

Empire-building had never stopped, and now went ahead more rapidly. But there were always two distinct empires. One, with India its central bastion, was made up of populous, mainly tropical possessions. It was these that had most attractions for the upper classes, the gentry who provided governors and officers, the businessmen profiting by cheap labour. Of far more interest to the working masses were the lands lying empty, awaiting emigrants. Both kinds of territory were called, misleadingly, 'colonies'. In southern Africa the two magnetic pulls came nearest to converging. For Englishmen at large, however, a growing retinue of dependencies helped to bolster an old ingrained feeling of superiority to other European nations. Imperial psychology included a strong if illusory sense of collective ownership of vast territories, in which every Englishman had his part. Conquest fostered a cult of strength, of the martial and virile virtues, along with racialist infusions of Darwinian and other scientific or pseudo-scientific theories about inferior races and the survival of the fittest. But with these harsher features went an often authentic belief in a civilizing mission, a duty to go out into the world and spread the blessings of order and progress among backward peoples. Virgilian or Horatian tags expressed this for the educated; the figure of Gordon, the idealized 'Christian General', the martyr of Khartoum, embodied it for the nation.

Criticism and protest never disappeared, but in any active form they were confined to limited groups. Men of the school of Cobden and Bright, faithful to the Liberal tradition, could not appeal to the masses when their own class moved away from them towards 'Liberal Imperialism', and they were left isolated. The propertied classes in general had so much to gain, directly or indirectly, financially or politically, that faith in the civilizing mission came easily to them. The monarchy presided over both the empires, the 'black' and the 'white', and gave them a deceptive unity, while in return they provided it with a fresh purpose, and thereby with a renewal of the popularity lost by Victoria's long retirement. Churches could establish themselves more firmly as national institutions by falling in with the prevailing doctrine; missionaries helped to invest empire with an ideal glow. The aristocracy, in danger of being elbowed aside by the new millocracy, found in the colonies a congenial sphere of action; the landed gentry, with falling rentals after about 1870, found employment there for its sons, and a function or duty for Kipling to exalt into a gospel of service. The cult of British self-admiration of which he was priest was in reality a cult of the qualities claimed by these higher social groups – courage, character, leadership, and the rest; but demagogy allowed Demos to flatter himself with the notion that these were his virtues too, that every Briton was a born hero and leader of men.

It is only too easy to discover what the literate classes thought. Victorians were not men of few words; Carlyle was only the most voluble of them. They made speeches, kept diaries, wrote to the press, delivered sermons, and plied one another with letters; and in all this chorus the theme of dominion over palm and pine can be heard. With the unlettered mass it is very different. In this as in all other ways England was, as Disraeli said, two nations, which no heat of patriotic eloquence could fuse together. Some opinions, or prejudices, were bound to filter down from the one to the other. Cheap newspapers, election rhetoric, school textbooks, all assisted this process. Workmen *were getting votes, a labour movement was growing, and patriotic fervour would be a wholesome corrective. It would work best where labour was least organized or militant; most effectively of all in the countryside, where squire and rector still held firm sway. In big towns regimental bands, jingo music-hall songs, Jubilee festivities, supplied pleasurable thrills for the man in the street. Hearing about the frontier wars that were always going on, all the more enjoyable for being far away and inexpensive, white-collar workers could feel that they were sharing in the sport of kings. With no identity of their own as a class, by participating in Britain's glory they gained a reassuring sense of being part of the nation, belonging to a great family. All this could mean more still to the semi-pauperized casual labour that abounded in big towns, especially in London where the supply of fanfares and flourishes was most plentiful. G. S. Jones's book on* Outcast London *has lately shown how the wretched populace of the inner districts, where there was no big industry, went on voting for flag-waving, anti-foreign Tories.*

The solid industrial working class of the north was another species, with a collective life and self-respect of its own. It too might be touched now and then by fits of martial excitement, but the contagion reached it in far milder form. Its chapel-going minority, bigger than in London, was often conscientiously against war; though on the other hand it would be more open than the rest to the missionary theme of the duty of reclaiming and Christianizing benighted races. In general, millworkers and miners were absorbed in their economic struggle for better wages and conditions. Again, this could no doubt lay some of them open to the argument used by politicians like Chamberlain to divert them away from socialism: the bread-and-butter argument that a Britain faced with stiffening foreign competition and tariffs could only hold on to or improve its prosperity by having more and more colonies. Such reasoning might be fallacious, but it had at least a rational flavour, and it would seem that when trade was good most workers were prepared to give it a hearing. When trade was bad, or capital and labour more at odds than usual, it fell into the background, and the instinctive assumptions and loyalties of the class struggle took its place. Even in loyal London the Jubilee year 1887 saw the 'Bloody Sunday' of 13 November, when troops were used to clear Trafalgar Square – while other British troops were pacifying Upper Burma. The years before 1914 were a time of sharply rising labour militancy.

Suez and Singapore were after all very remote; ordinary Englishmen had nothing whatever to do with how they were run, and scarcely knew where they were. Even among the fervently Empire-minded middle classes there was at all times a monumental ignorance about everything connected with the Empire, except the balance-sheets of companies operating in it. India was the brightest jewel in Britain's crown, but the dullest clown in Britain knew scarcely less about it than the average M.P. As for the manual worker, apart from a sprinkling of technicians, railwaymen, and the like, he made the acquaintance of the 'black' colonies only when he joined the army and found himself doing duty there. What private soldiers could learn about the alien people around them was very little, and they were not in any case a faithful cross-section of the working class. Men enlisted when employment was slack, as a last resort; a great many other recruits were Irish or Highland peasants whom their own countries — or landlords — had nothing to offer.

It was the other empire, the colonies of white settlement, that the working masses could come by real knowledge of; their friends and neighbours and relatives were emigrating there (and of course to the U.S.A.) in multitudes, and were finding there an economic and social status denied them in the land of hope and glory of the well-to-do. A friendly interest in Canada or Australia would help to form a confusedly rosy image of the Empire as a whole, and Suez and Singapore would be taken for granted. But imperialism never became for the working class what it was for those higher up, a definite creed, a philosophy of life, a new evangel. As Richard Price's recent study brings out, the hysteria of the Boer War was a middle-class hysteria: even then the workers, by and large, if they were not firmly against the war were not passionately for it. Most of the time they were simply shut in on their own world and its affairs, trade union and Co-operative activities, the club-life of the public house, the football ground, the chapel.

If a long-sustained effort to indoctrinate them with jingoism was rewarded with acquiescence rather than with wholehearted assent, this partial failure was due more to their retreat from the national arena than to any resistance of principle. This meant equally that socialist or labour leaders who tried to transform indifference into anti-imperialism met with even smaller success. While 'spirited foreign policies' won the easy applause of the lower middle classes, attacks however spirited on these policies fell on deaf working-class ears. Flag-waving is elementary and euphoric, criticism of it complex, arduous, disagreeable. Of all imperial issues the one that roused most interest, because it was nearest home and mixed with religious prejudices, was Irish Home Rule, and this divided the workers as well as the Liberal party. There was widespread disillusion after the protracted later stages of the Boer War, and a renewal of Liberal opposition to imperialism by men like the economist Hobson and the humanist Gilbert Murray. Some trade union and Socialist spokesmen were reviving an opposition to it that had been voiced by Ernest Jones the Chartist. But between the active anti-imperialism of intellectuals or groups, and the apathy of the working masses, no positive alternative course for Britain emerged. Empire rolled on, for better or worse, by its own now immense momentum.

Throne and Empire

'. . . Look left, look right, the hills are bright,
  The dales are light between,
Because 'tis fifty years to-night
  That God has saved the Queen.

Now, when the flame they watch not towers
  About the soil they trod,
Lads, we'll remember friends of ours
  Who shared the work with God.

. . . It dawns in Asia, tombstones show
  And Shropshire names are read;
And the Nile spills his overflow
  Beside the Severn's dead . . .'

(A. E. Housman, *A Shropshire Lad*, 1896. This poem was written for the 1887 Jubilee.)

' "Native races", he laid down, "understood personal rule, and the great thing was to make the Queen vivid, a reality, to them. England? Yes, it was a place far distant, where there were no dark-skinned peoples. The Queen of England? Ah, yes, they could comprehend her! She sat on a throne, so beautiful that its place must be where all was beautiful and good. Her heart beat for her folk, irrespective of their colour; she would minister to their happiness. Nothing could more delight her, than to secure the well-being of those who claimed her powerful protection. That was intelligible!"'

(Sir George Grey, reported by James Milne in *The Romance of a Pro-Consul*, 1911. Grey served as colonial governor in South Africa and New Zealand, and was a champion of imperial federation.)

'I was for some time Chaplain to the 1st West Indian Regiment, which was stationed in my parish. They were men of magnificent physique and in their Zouave uniform . . . their appearance was most picturesque . . . They were very religious, and spent their leisure in playing cards and reading the Bible. They were as fond of theological discussions as a Scotchman . . . The most touching thing about them was their intense loyalty. Every one of them wore a locket round his neck in which was a photograph of Queen Victoria. It was a great grief to them that they were not allowed to take part in the South African War, but I believe it was not thought prudent to let them fight against white men.'

(Arthur Goldring, *Some Reminiscences of an Unclerical Cleric*, 1926. His parish at this time was in Bermuda.)

'Please let me know what steps you intend to take to protect the Zulus from being attacked by the Boers. Feel certain you agree with me that we are bound in honour to stand by my native subjects.'

(Telegram from the Queen to the Colonial Secretary, Joseph Chamberlain, 14 February 1900, in *The Letters of Queen Victoria*, 3rd Series, vol. III. She really did feel a responsibility for her 'native subjects'. This was early in the Boer War, when her ministers had very little attention to spare for Zulus or any other Africans.)

'I inspected about one hundred of the Colonial troops, who had been invalided. There were Canadians, Australians, Tasmanians, New Zealanders, and men from the Cape and Ceylon, representing forty-five regiments. Some of the men were very fine-looking, all in khaki with felt hats ... An old Australian Chaplain, who lost his leg by the bite of a mad horse, named the different regiments the men belonged to, as they came by ... They then gave three cheers, and a sergeant called for "One more Colonial", which apparently was a particular way of cheering in Australia.'

(Queen Victoria's Journal, Windsor, 16 November 1900, in *The Letters of Queen Victoria*, 3rd Series, Vol. III.)

The Intoxication of Imperial Expansion

'It is, of course, well-nigh impossible to form estimates of returns in a country that is absolutely stagnant, reposing in abysmal depths of barbarism; but the soil is there, the climate is there, the ... labour is there ... The day is not far distant when Africa will pour out her wealth of cattle, grain, minerals, rubber, cotton, sugar, copra, spices, and a thousand other products to a grateful world. And over and above this, will give a home of comfort to millions of Europeans now suffocated by lack of breathing-space, and afford a field of investment for the pent-up millions of capital that are crowding returns down to an impossible minimum.'

(E. S. Grogan and A. H. Sharp, *From the Cape to Cairo*, 1900. Grogan, a great admirer of Cecil Rhodes, was the first explorer to cross Africa from south to north.)

'Beyond the launches lie more steamers than the eye can count, and four out of five of these belong to Us. I was proud when I saw the shipping at Singapore, but I swell with patriotism as I watch the fleets of Hong-Kong from the balcony of the Victoria Hotel.'

(Rudyard Kipling, *From Sea to Sea*, 1900. He was making a round-the-world tour in 1887–8.)

'. . . For of pluck he's brimming full is young John Bull,
And he's happy when we let him have his head,
   It's a feather in his cap
   When he's helped to paint the map
With another little patch of red.'

(Music-hall song, cited in W. S. Adams, *Edwardian Heritage*, 1949.)

   'Britannia rules the waves,
     As I have heard her say;
   She frees whatever slaves
     She meets upon her way.

   . . . The Saxon and the Celt
     She equitably rules;
   Her iron rod is felt
     By countless knaves and fools.

   In fact, mankind at large,
     Black, yellow, white and red,
   Is given to her in charge,
     And owns her as a head . . .'

(J. K. Stephen (1859–92), *On a Parisian Boulevard*. He goes on to
regret that some Britons look 'Unspeakably obtuse, abominably
vain'. England's sense of humour was not completely drowned
in self-admiration.)

'In 1896 I come upon a passage too long to quote, in which
he is shaking his head over certain school-books which had
come into his hands, and which taught that the British
Empire was irresistible and all-powerful . . . "It is absurd
that the present generation should be taught out of books
which assume the state of Europe to be the same as it was
after the battle of Waterloo." '

(J. A. Spender, *The Comments of Bagshot*, 1907 – an imaginary
character whose jottings Spender purports to be editing.)

'[Little Englanders are] trying their little best to retard the
advancement of trade, commerce, civilization and religion
. . . I say, without any fear of contradiction, the more

Britain rules of the world, the better for the world . . . This is true to the letter, notwithstanding the carping, the railing, and the squealing of Little Englanders and traitors known and unknown.'

(Letter to *The Scotsman*, 6 November 1899, from 'A True Briton' of Inverness.)

'THE DEAN OF STOUR: I disagree with you, Stephen; absolutely, entirely disagree.
'MORE: I can't help it.
'EDWARD MENDIP: . . . You can't afford –
'MORE: To follow my conscience? That's new, Mendip.
'MENDIP: Idealism can be out of place, my friend.
'THE DEAN: The Government is dealing here with a wild lawless race, on whom I must say I think sentiment is rather wasted.
'MORE: God made them, Dean.
'MENDIP: I have my doubts . . . My dear friend, are you to become that hapless kind of outcast, a champion of lost causes?
'MORE: The cause is not lost.
'MENDIP: Right or wrong, as lost as ever was cause in all this world. There was never a time when the word "patriotism" stirred mob sentiment as it does now. 'Ware "Mob", Stephen – 'ware "Mob"!'

(John Galsworthy, *The Mob*. This play was produced early in 1914, at Manchester. It is concerned with a war of conquest against an unspecified coloured people, but evokes the jingo atmosphere of the Boer War. The hero More, an idealistic M.P., is deserted by his friends, supporters and wife, and finally a mob of rowdies and students breaks into his house and he is murdered.)

Shining Armour and Mailed Fist

'One of the great dangers, as I recollect Sir Charles Dilke remarking to me . . . was the warlike tone of our constituencies, and the fact that the greater the progress of democracy in England, the less the people would be disposed to accept a "peace at any price" policy.'

(Sir Horace Rumbold, *Further Recollections of a Diplomatist*, 1903. Advocates of democracy had always expected it to bring peace and international fraternity.)

'On a dark morning in February 1854, I went to see my friends in the Scots Fusilier Guards ... parade in the barracks preparatory to their departure for Malta. I think it was the most impressive moment that I had experienced in my life. War we had read of; now we knew it was near in all its grim reality ... War was declared on February 21, 1854. All the spring and summer were spent in anxiety, and we thought and dreamed of nothing but of our army in the East; for fighting, say what you will, is dear to the hearts of all Englishmen in whatever cause their country may be embarked.'

(Sir Algernon West, *Recollections, 1832 to 1886* (1889). The Crimean War was Britain's first European conflict since Waterloo. West was later private secretary to Gladstone.)

'It is terrible to see our middle-class journals and speakers calling for the destruction of Delhi, and the indiscriminate massacre of prisoners ...

'To read the letters of our officers at the commencement of the outbreak, it seemed as if every subaltern had the power to hang or shoot as many natives as he pleased, and they spoke of the work of blood with as much levity as if they were hunting wild animals ...

'It will be a happy day when England has not an acre of territory in Continental Asia. But ... where do we find even an individual who is not imbued with the notion that England would sink to ruin if she were deprived of her Indian Empire? Leave me, then, to my pigs and sheep, which are not labouring under any such delusions ...'

(Letter from Cobden to John Bright, 22 September 1857, in John Morley, *The Life of Richard Cobden*, 1881. Delhi was the headquarters of the revolted sepoys.)

'We are met to do honour to a soldier who volunteered to serve on the staff of General Wolseley in the recent war . . . Lieutenant Wauchope, on his arrival at the Gold Coast, was appointed one of the officers of the Haussas . . . The War Office, finding that the Ashantis were more formidable than was at first expected . . . resolved to send out British troops. This meeting must feel proud, as an assemblage of Scotsmen, that the 42nd Royal Highlanders was one of the chosen regiments . . . Our gallant guest was wounded . . . but continued to push forward, and . . . entered the now famous city of Kumasi.'

(Provost Wood of Portobello (near Edinburgh) proposing the toast to Lt. A. G. Wauchope, guest of honour at a town hall banquet after the second Ashanti War in 1873–4; cited by W. Baird, *General Wauchope*, 1900. Wauchope finally lost his life in the Boer War.)

'I am at Swinford on a visit to Austin . . .

'In the afternoon we all sat talking on the lawn . . . and it was suggested that each of us should give his ideas of Heaven . . . Austin's idea was to sit . . . in a garden, and while he sat to receive constant telegrams announcing alternately a British victory by sea, and a British victory by land.'

(Wilfrid Scawen Blunt, 27 June 1897, in *My Diaries*, 1919–20. Alfred Austin was Tennyson's successor as poet laureate. Blunt was a determined anti-imperialist, but of the most aristocratic and therefore isolated and ineffective wing.)

'There are things worse than war . . . The cankers of a long peace are worse than the sufferings of a war. In a long peace men come to think more of wealth than of honour. The moral fabric of the community is slackened . . . When war prevails, the higher qualities of our race come to the surface . . . [This is] the highest form of Christianity.'

(Editorial in *The Scotsman*, 13 December 1899, attacking the anti-war Liberal M.P. Sir Wilfrid Lawson.)

'We had our little service of Intercession this morning . . . with special hymns and a tactful little sermon from Mr

Clement Smith . . . but I can't enter into the Old Testament spirit shown in the prayers for victory and boasting of our cause as righteous . . . war is so eminently unchristian, so full of evil that I cannot bring myself to pray that we may slaughter our enemies . . . I am quite out of place in these war-like circles where the only cry is "Let us slay the Amalekites!" '

(Letter from a lady-in-waiting at Osborne, 11 February 1900, in *Life with Queen Victoria: Marie Mallet's Letters from Court 1887–1901*, ed. V. Mallet, 1968.)

'We swore to be revenged. And so well did we avenge them that Lord Roberts himself wondered why the 72nd never took any prisoners. He said to our General, Sir James Baker, "How in the world, sir, is it that all the other regiments in the division take so many prisoners, and the 72nd never take any?" Sir James Baker knew the reason, but he simply said, "No, the 72nd never take any prisoners." The Captain, with the story-teller's art, left his hearers to infer the rest.'

(Speech by Capt. Lauder, Seaforth Highlanders, sympathetically reported by the *Daily News*, 17 May 1900: cited in F. W. Hirst, etc., *Liberalism and the Empire*, 1900.)

' "We tore up the hill and into the intrenchments, and the Boers saw we had them; so they dropped their guns and went down on their knees and put up their hands clasped, and begged for mercy. And we gave it them – *with the long spoon.*"

'The long spoon is the bayonet. See *Lloyd's Weekly*, London, of those days.'

(Mark Twain, *To the Person Sitting in Darkness*, in *North American Review*, February 1901, quoting from *Lloyd's Weekly* a letter written by a British soldier. Mark Twain was a strong critic of imperialism, which America had lately embarked on by conquering the Philippine Islands.)

'The law of the stronger is the law of nature . . . Life is war . . .'

(J. Ellis Barker, *The Rise and Decline of the Netherlands*, 1906. The verdict of history as delivered by a contemporary historian.)

The Civilizing Mission and Its Other Side

'We are all anxiously waiting for Lord Raglan to storm Sebastopol . . . What should be done is to go at it at once, without more dilly-dallying!

'I have not seen a clergyman or a missionary yet. How I should enjoy meeting one who would talk to the men simply about the Cross of Christ! The Holy Ghost always blesses such preaching. We have meetings in my tent for Scripture-reading as often as we can get together, and delightful seasons they are.'

(Letter from Capt. Vicars in the Crimea to his sister, 29 November 1854; Anon., *Memorials of Captain Hedley Vicars, Ninety-Seventh Regiment*, 1856. This young officer, who had previously served in the West Indies, was killed in action soon after. The book (by Miss C. M. Marsh) sold over 100,000 copies.)

Epitaph on General Gordon

'Warrior of God, man's friend, and tyrant's foe,
Now somewhere dead in the far waste Soudan,
Thou livest in all hearts, for all men know
This earth has never borne a nobler man.'

(Tennyson; written for a Boys' Home near Woking.)

'This Empire has been raised up by the same Providence that called the Roman Empire into existence, and as God used the one towards the attainment of His Own Divine purpose of mercy, so does He seem to be using the other.'

(Circular letter from Cardinal Vaughan to his clergy, 20 December 1899; cited in W. S. Adams, op. cit.)

'During the last few years political feeling [in India] has become much embittered, extremists have openly revealed themselves, and diabolical crimes have been committed in the name of patriotism. It is needless to say that every form of influence possessed by missionaries has been exerted against evil deeds . . . Missionaries in India, as elsewhere, are sympathetic with all that is best in the national life of the people among whom they live ... At the same time they recognize the present need of the strong arm and impartial policy of the British Government.'

> (Report of Commission VII, on *Missions and Governments*, of the World Missionary Conference, Edinburgh, 1910.)

'No impartial observer can fail to see that on the whole the empire of England is a factor in the world which makes for righteousness. Wherever our flag is planted there follow the arts of peace. And there follows also the spirit of fair play and of just dealings with native races ...'

> (W. A. McArthur, M.P., 'The Imperial Aspect', in *The Destitute Alien in Great Britain*, ed. A. White, 1892. McArthur adds that John Bull will have to learn to play 'the wise elder brother of the English family', instead of 'the all-powerful father'.)

'The prosperity visible in the country [Ladakh] compared with the picture given of its former state might be a lesson to those people at home who accept their own peace and security as a mere matter of course, but utter cries of protest against a Government which proceeds to extend these benefits to others who are under its protection. Can there be a nobler mission for a great nation than to rescue the oppressed, to prevent slavery, and to give the peaceably disposed liberty to go about their daily work unmolested? ... I myself, when I was in Syria a few years ago, heard the natives say how they wished their country could be as Egypt is. But nothing will convince some stay-at-home Britons, who always know so much better than those who go abroad and see things for themselves.'

> (Jane Ellen Duncan, *A Summer Ride through Western Tibet*, 1906.)

'My father belonged to the old conservative school in politics, which regarded the British Empire established abroad as almost divine in its foundation, and as likely to lead, through righteous administration, to the relief of the miseries and evils of the world. The unity of the British

Empire was a sovereign thought with him: he would have died for it. British rule in India was regarded by him as a sacred trust given to England by God Himself. He used to tell me with glowing enthusiasm how nobly England had fulfilled that trust, and what benefits had been conferred thereby on India itself.'

(C. F. Andrews, *The Indian Problem*, 1923. The author went to India as a missionary, grew disillusioned with British rule, and became an admirer of Gandhi.)

'Let us have the courage to repudiate the pretence which foreigners laugh at and which hardly deceives ourselves that we keep India only for the benefit of their country and in order to train them for self-government. We keep it for the sake of the interests and the honour of England . . . (*Asiatic Quarterly*, 1889).

'Englishmen won India by the sword, and we hold it today as our forefathers did before us, and our children will hold it after us (*Morning Post*, 29 December 1893).'

(Prem Narain, *Press and Politics in India 1885–1905* (1970).)

'It is in general sadly true that Englishmen in India live totally estranged from the people among whom they are sojourning. This estrangement . . . might in great part be removed if Englishmen would make up their minds (but how can they be ordered to do so?) to assume a less contemptuous attitude . . . The English contempt proceeds in the main from English ignorance, and English ignorance is accompanied, as so often happens, by English bluster . . . The army of the "damned nigger" Philistines is strong.'

(Letter from an Englishman in India, published in H. M. Hyndman, *The Awakening of Asia*, 1919.)

'One always rather likes the Nigger; evidently a poor blockhead with good dispositions, with affections, attachments, – with a turn for Nigger Melodies, and the like: – he is the only Savage of all the coloured races that doesn't die out on sight of the White Man; but can actually live beside him, and work and increase and be merry. The Almighty Maker has appointed him to be a Servant. Under penalty of Heaven's curse, neither party to this pre-appointment shall neglect or misdo his duties therein . . .'

(Thomas Carlyle, *Shooting Niagara: and After?*, 1867. About this time Carlyle, along with Kingsley, Ruskin, Tennyson and others, was active in defending Governor Eyre of Jamaica, charged with excessively brutal repression there in 1865.)

' "Never could see any good in any d—d foreigner, Dutch, Dago, Nigger, or Chink," said the "Old Man" sturdily.
' "Good old John Bull!" I murmured to myself.
' "Don't you think so too, Doc?" he said, turning to me.
' "Thinking so is the secret of England's greatness," I answered diplomatically.'

(J. J. Abraham, *The Surgeon's Log*, 1911, a narrative of a voyage round eastern Asia.)

The Jingoism of Common Man and Common Soldier

'Have faith in dear Old England!
    Her lion-hearts lie dead;
But tens of thousands ready wait
    To battle in their stead.
They know from history's reddest page,
    That nations, when opprest,
Must point their swords for arguments
    Against the tyrant's breast . . .'

(Edward Capern, 'The Lion-Flag of England', in *Poems*, 2nd edition, 1856. Capern was a Devonshire postman. There is an unconscious irony in these lines, written during the Crimean War, in view of the approaching Indian Mutiny.)

'Ye sons of Mars, come, join with me,
And sing in praise of Sir Herbert Stewart's little army
That made ten thousand Arabs flee
At the charge of the bayonet at Abu Klea.

General Stewart's force was about fifteen hundred all told,
A brave little band but like lions bold.
They fought under their brave and heroic commander,
As gallant and as skilful as the great Alexander.

And the nation has every reason to be proud,
And in praise of his little band we cannot speak too loud,
Because that gallant fifteen hundred soon put to flight
Ten thousand Arabs, which was a most beautiful sight . . .'

> (William McGonagall, poet and tragedian, 'The Battle of Abu
> Klea'. This battle was fought in the Soudan in 1885. McGonagall
> recited for pennies in public houses when hard up.)

'Bank Holiday at the Crystal Palace. Among the Ethno-
logical Models.

'WIFE OF BRITISH WORKMAN (*spelling out placard under
Hottentot Group*): "It is extremely probable that this inter-
esting race will be completely exterminated at no very
distant period." Pore things!

'BRITISH WORKMAN (*with philosophy*). Well, *I* sha'n't go
into mournin' for 'em, Sairer!

'LAMBETH LARRIKIN (*in a pasteboard "pickelhaube", and a
false nose, thoughtfully, to* BATTERSEA BILL, *who is wearing an old grey chimney-pot hat, with the brim uppermost, and
a tow wig, as they contemplate a party of Botocudo natives*).
Rum the sights these 'ere savidges make of theirselves,
ain't it, Bill?

'BATT. BILL (*more thoughtfully*). Yer right – but I dessay if
you and me 'ad been born among that lot, *we* shouldn't
care 'ow we looked!'

> ('F. Anstey', *Voces Populi*, 2nd series, 1892, a collection of
> sketches from *Punch*. The great humourist – author of *Vice Versa* –
> was no doubt caricaturing these Cockneys, but with some sub-
> stratum of realism.)

'I was full corporal in the 93rd Southern Highlanders, and
I can get the best of characters from my commanding
officers . . .

'I've served in India, and I was at the battles of Punjaub, 1848, and Moultan, 1849 . . .

'Although I had served ten years and been in two battles, yet I was not entitled to a pension. You must serve twenty-one years to be entitled to 1s. 0½d. I left the 93rd in 1852, and since that time I've been wandering about the different parts of England and Scotland, playing on the bagpipes . . .

'I'd rather than twenty thousand pounds I'd been in my health to have gone to the Crimea, for I'd have had more glory after that war than ever any England was in . . .'

(A Highland veteran, reported by Henry Mayhew in *London Labour and the London Poor*, 1861.)

'About 8 o'clock we received the word "forward", and with a true British cheer, we advanced . . . till we came to a nullah some eight or nine feet deep. We soon crossed this but several of our men got winged . . . We dashed on to a large . . . building . . . entrenched and enclosed on all sides by loopholed walls some 10 or 12 feet high. From this place the enemy peppered us in grand style when advancing. We were not long in bursting open the doors of this refuge place, and the massacre which took place in it was frightful; our Grenadiers soon had the place covered with the dead and dying . . .

'In India the men of the Army generally is looked upon as so many pieces of one great machine that is passive in the hands of the engineer; and as to sense or feeling, that is not thought of. The private soldier is looked upon as the lowest class of animals, and only fit to be ruled with the cat o' nine tails and the provost-sergeant. Such a course is not likely either to improve or to correct their morals, and I am sorry to say that it is very bad.'

(*The Memoirs of Private Waterfield*, ed. A. Swinton and D. Scott, 1968. The first extract relates to an action near Multan in 1848; the second to a soldier's execution at Meerut for striking an officer.)

'British private soldiers called all Indians "Moors", and

wanted to kill them indiscriminately. "They had been brought all the way from England to kill Moors, and why should they not begin at once?" . . . The hero of the affair was an honest fellow, who had disembarked with his head full of the Nana and the fatal well. His story was simple: – "I seed two Moors talking in a cart. Presently I heard one of 'em say 'Cawnpore'. I knowed what that meant; so I fetched Tom Walker, and he heard 'em say 'Cawnpore', and he knowed what that meant. So we polished 'em both off.'"

(G. O. Trevelyan, *The Competition Wallah*, 1864. These soldiers had been hearing stories of the rebel leader Nana Sahib, and of Englishwomen at Cawnpore being massacred and thrown into a well.)

'[Execution of a Mutiny suspect at Cawnpore, 1857] The condemned man was timid, but not without self-possession . . . When all was over, one of the sailors got up on a wall to address the public . . . "First of all, understand," he said, "that you are all rascals! And now you have seen a rascal die. But what is one rascal? My opinion is that not only one black rascal should be hung, but every black rascal in the country! And then you black rascals would learn how to behave yourselves." '

(J. W. Sherer, an eye-witness, *Havelock's March on Cawnpore 1857* (1910), a re-hash of an account written at the time.)

'He had visited stranger spots than any seaside cave; encountered men more terrible than any spirit; done and dared and suffered in that incredible, unsung epic of the Mutiny War; played his part with the field force of Delhi . . . when . . . the fate of the flag of England staggered. And of all this he had no more to say than "hot work, sir", or "the army suffered a great deal, sir", or "I believe General Wilson, sir, was not very highly thought of in the papers". His life was naught to him, the vivid pages of experience quite blank . . .'

(An old tramp in the Scottish hills whom R. L. Stevenson got to know, described in the essay on 'Beggars' in *Across the Plains*, *with other Memories and Essays*, 1892. Probably few of the soldiers who helped to conquer the empire comprehended or remembered more than this man of what they had seen and done.)

The Labour Movement and Imperialism

[Joseph Arch, farm labourers' leader, questioned by Royal Commission on Agriculture, 1881]

'How do you set about ensuring the labourers getting higher wages? – We have reduced the number of labourers in the market very considerably . . . We have emigrated about 700,000 souls, men, women and children within the last eight or nine years.

'How have those 700,000 souls been emigrated; out of what funds? – I went over to Canada, and I made arrangements with the Canadian Government to give them so much, and we found them so much from the funds of our trade.'

(Cited in J. B. Jefferys, *Labour's Formative Years* (*1849–1879*), 1948.)

'Chamberlain had turned his coat and was riding on the rising tide of Imperialist enthusiasm. The people of Birmingham were as clay in his hands. On one occasion Andrews stood in the tense, close-packed mass which invariably filled the City Hall for the Empire-builder's meetings. Chamberlain walked stiffly on to the platform and was given a tremendous ovation lasting five minutes. He stood motionless, staring straight before him, with no sign of emotion on his sharp, tight-drawn face. It would have been a brave man to utter a whisper of opposition in such a crowd under his influence.'

(R. K. Pope, *The Life and Times of W. H. Andrews, Workers' Leader*, n.d. This meeting took place in 1891. Andrews emigrated to South Africa, where he became a left-wing Socialist.)

'You ask me what the English workers think about colonial policy. Well, exactly the same as they think about politics in general: the same as what the bourgeois think. There is no workers' party here, there are only Conservatives and Liberal-Radicals, and the workers gaily share the feast of England's monopoly of the world market and the colonies.'

(Engels to Kautsky, 12 September 1882, in *Karl Marx and Friedrich Engels, Correspondence 1846–1895*, ed. Dona Torr, 1934.)

'Great efforts are now being made in England to convince the trade unionists that the colonial policy is in their interests ... But the English trade unionists are not to be caught with those fine words ... And if the jingoes rejoice in the fact that England has become a great country on which the sun never sets, then I say that in England there are thousands of homes on which the sun has never risen.'

(Pete Curran, of the I.L.P., at the 1900 Congress of the Second International; cited in J. Lenz, *Rise and Fall of the Second International*, 1932.)

'What Imperial extension, what the blessings of our beneficent rule, what the opening up of new territories *are supposed* to mean we all know. What these high-sounding terms *really* mean, few of us distinctly realise. The working-class at home see that they are not materially benefited by the expansion of Greater Britain, as it is called. But they are assured by their pastors and masters that it is a necessary and glorious thing, and as this thought affords them some amusement now and then at the music halls, in the shape of refrains and cheers, they are content to let the matter slide.'

(Belfort Bax, *Essays in Socialism New and Old*, 1906.)

7

Poverty and Progress, 1870–1914

THEO BARKER

In the half century or so before the First World War, and particularly from about 1890 onwards, increasing attention began to be paid to the yawning gap between rich and poor. The bright lights and ostentatious luxury of the West End, for instance, struck more and more people from all walks of life, including the rich themselves, as being immoral as well as wasteful when so many others were living in want. Out of this growing concern, given greater political strength by the extension of the franchise in the mid 1880s, emerged the new climate of public opinion which led to an acceptance of greater state activity in social matters during the Edwardian period. This growing concern about poverty, however, did not mean that poverty itself was becoming worse or more extensive. Indeed, the reverse was the case, for the dramatic fall in the cost of living, and particularly in the cost of basic foodstuffs, in the later nineteenth century benefited the poor most of all. Although world prices moved up a little in Edwardian times, this loss was small compared to previous gains; and there were by then certain compensations such as increased public, and especially local government, expenditure.

No, poverty begins to attract much more attention in this period primarily because men of social conscience, notably the shipowner Charles Booth and the chocolate manufacturer Seebohm Rowntree, began to investigate it, to quantify it and to reveal its reality and extent in irrefutable detail for the first time. Thirty per cent of London's population at the beginning of the 1890s fell on or below Booth's poverty line (which meant, of course, that the percentages in certain parts of London were far higher, 68 per cent in Southwark, for instance, and 65 per cent in Greenwich), and Rowntree's figure for York in 1899 was not much lower. Cases of real want could no longer be dismissed as unrepresentative. Nor, in many cases, could they be attributed to an unwillingness to work. So low or inter-

mittent were earnings that many families had incomes below the level needed for the maintenance of physical health and strength even if superb housekeepers had been available to devote every farthing to the essentials of life, to the exclusion of all else. Just what this physical efficiency minimum meant was carefully spelt out by Rowntree in language clearly intended for middle-class readers:

'A family living upon the scale allowed for in this estimate must never spend a penny on a railway fare or omnibus. They must never go into the country unless they walk. They must never purchase a half-penny newspaper or spend a penny to buy a ticket for a popular concert. They must write no letters to absent children, for they cannot afford to pay the postage. They must never contribute anything to their church or chapel, or give any help to a neighbour which costs them money. They cannot save, nor can they join a sick club or Trade Union, because they cannot pay the necessary subscriptions. The children must have no pocket money for dolls, marbles or sweets. The father must smoke no tobacco and must drink no beer. The mother must never buy any pretty clothes for herself or her children . . . Should a child fall ill, it must be attended by the parish doctor; should it die, it must be buried by the parish. Finally, the wage earner must never be absent from his work for a single day.'

In the York of 1899, 9.91 per cent of the total population (15.46 per cent of all wage earners) lived in primary poverty below even this spartan minimum; and this figure was believed to be not untypical of other provincial towns. Small wonder that just over a third of the men who volunteered for military service between 1893 and 1902 were rejected on medical grounds, and fears of national physical deterioration began to alarm the more conservative elements in the country and allied them with those whose consciences had been stirred by the social investigators' 'arithmetic of woe'.

The plight of the poor was made worse to some extent by the fact that many more of them now lived in towns. The urbanization theme, frequently encountered in earlier chapters, now reaches its climax. In

*1871, 62 per cent of the population of England and Wales was
classed by the census as urban: by 1911 it reached 80 per cent of a
much larger total. In these extracts, for reasons of space, we shall,
therefore, concentrate upon urban, rather than rural, examples. They
emphasize not only the extreme hardship endured by many town
dwellers but also the spirit of these people which enabled them to
sustain the struggle to survive.*

Poverty and Hardship amidst Plenty

'Look at the people who swarm the streets to see the Lord
Mayor's Show, and where will you see a more pitiable sight?
These beef-eating, port-drinking fellows in Piccadilly,
exercised, scrubbed, groomed, they are well enough to be
sure; but this other side of the shield is distressing to look at.
Poor, stunted, bad complexioned, shabbily dressed, ill-
featured are these pork-eating, gin-drinking denizens of the
East End. Crowds I have seen in America, in Mexico, and in
most of the great cities of Europe . . . Nowhere is there such
squalor, such pinching poverty, so many undersized, so many
plainly and revoltingly diseased, so much human rottenness
as here . . .'

(Price Collier, *England and the English From An American Point of
View*, 1909. The author was a visiting American.)

'[There are] whole rows of houses in little out-of-the-way
streets where a rude sort of family life obtains. In the evenings the men can be seen at their doors, pipes in their mouths
and children on their knees, wives gossiping and laughter
and fun going on. The content of these people is manifestly
great, for, relatively to the wretchedness that encompasses
them, they are well off. But at the best it is a dull, animal
happiness, the content of the full belly . . .'

(Jack London, *The People of the Abyss*, 1903. Jack London,
already author of a two-volume work about life in the Klondyke,
came to London in the summer of 1902 at the age of twenty-six.
He bought some old clothes and went to live down by the docks
for two months.)

'24 December 1901. I walked along the Embankment this morning at two o'clock . . . Every bench from Blackfriars to Westminster Bridge was filled with shivering people, all huddled up – men, women and children. The Salvation Army people were out giving away hot broth, but even this was merely a temporary palliative against the bitter night. At Charing Cross we encountered a man with his wife and two tiny children. They had come to town from Reading to look for work. The man had lost his few shillings and they were stranded . . .'

(*R.D.B.'s Diary*, 1930. R. D. Blumenfeld, born in Wisconsin in 1864, came to England in the 1880s. Later, as editor of the *Daily Express*, he played a notable part in the shaping of popular journalism.)

'The first act of welcome Canon Barnett met with from one of his future parishioners on entering Commercial Street to take possession of St Jude's vicarage was to be knocked down and have his watch stolen. Later, a like greeting met the late J. M. Dent, the well-known publisher and founder of the Everyman's Library, who was tripped up and suffered a similar loss.'

(Thomas Okey, *A Basketful of Memories*, 1930.)

'There were no drink restrictions, hours were very long, and there was an immense amount of drunkenness, and at any time you walked through these slum areas [of London] you would see tens, if not scores, of people drunk, women and men lying about, perhaps dancing to a barrel organ . . . [My step-father] was in Glasgow one Sunday, and he wanted very much to find the time of day, and he couldn't see a sober man at all to ask the time, and at last he saw a very, very tall, respectable man in a top hat standing at the side of the pavement, and he went up to him and said, "My dear sir, can you possibly tell me the time?" And the man looked stonily at him, and fell perfectly flat on his face on the ground. I don't think London was so bad as that, but it was very, very bad.'

(Sir Charles Tennyson, BBC Archive Disc.)

'Many an artist was ruined by drink – my father was one of them. He died of alcoholic excess at the age of thirty-seven . . .

'Mother had now sold most of her belongings. The last thing to go was her trunk of theatrical costumes . . . Like sand in an hour-glass our finances ran out, and hard times again pursued us. Mother sought other employment, but there was little to be found. Problems began mounting. Instalment payments were behind; consequently Mother's sewing machine was taken away. And Father's payments of ten shillings a week had completely stopped . . . There was no alternative: she was burdened with two children, and in poor health; and so she decided that the three of us should enter the Lambeth workhouse . . . there we were made to separate. Mother going in one direction to the women's ward and we in another to the children's. How well I remember the poignant sadness of that first visiting day: the shock of seeing Mother enter the visiting-room garbed in workhouse clothes. How forlorn and embarrassed she looked! In one week she had aged and grown thin, but her face lit up when she saw us . . . She smiled at our cropped heads and stroked them consolingly, telling us that we would soon all be together again. From her apron she produced a bag of coconut candy which she had bought at the workhouse store with her earnings from crocheting lace cuffs for one of the nurses . . .'

(Charles Chaplin, *My Autobiography*, Penguin edition, 1966. Charlie Chaplin was born in 1889 at Walworth and grew up in Lambeth and elsewhere south of the river.)

'Every crossing in London had an old crossing-sweeper who had no payment at all and relied on the kindness of people giving him an occasional penny. And possibly the saddest sight, and one I shall not forget, is the fact that whenever you took a horse cab, in the horse cab days, from any of the big stations, two runners followed you wherever you went, to take the luggage off at the other end, and I have actually seen men leave to follow our cab from Victoria to Holborn, a distance of possibly 2½ to 3 miles, pelting along, and they were there to take the luggage off at the other end. And what was their reward? Well in those days, the reward was 4d, a ghastly state of affairs. But when you gave them 4d, they could get a cup of tea and two slices of bread and butter, and put 2d in their pocket.'

(Claude Hamilton Fletcher, BBC Archive Disc.)

'Mothers used to make all the clothes for the girls, like the underclothes and all those . . . In fact, the mothers in those days used to do all the work, all the work that could be done, like after cleaning the house, and all that sort of thing, she used to set to and make the clothes . . . Even me, she'd make my short trousers . . . They were very good, the mothers in those days.'

(Sergeant B. Jones, BBC Archive Disc.)

'Most people kept what they possessed clean in spite of squalor and ever-invading dirt. Few who were young then will forget the great Friday night scouring ritual in which all the females of a house took part. (Dance halls closed on Friday evenings for lack of girls.) Women wore their lives away washing clothes in heavy, iron-hooped tubs, scrubbing wood and stone, polishing furniture and fire-irons . . . Only too well known was the Saturday morning custom common then and for a long time after of cleaning and colour-stoning the doorstep and then the pavement across the width that took in one's frontage. This chore helped to project the image of a spotless household into the world at large.'

(Robert Roberts, *The Classic Slum*, 1971. The author grew up at a corner shop in one of the poorest parts of Salford in the years before 1914.)

'I went to a big old rectory in Staffordshire. I went there as a between maid, and that was really a very hard place. There was no gas or anything in the rectory. The place was lit with oil lamps; and I had to clean the big range and get the fire going before I could boil a kettle. And then I used to scrub the big kitchen which had a floor like gravestones, and scrub the tables, and then take the cook a cup of tea before seven. Then I had to clean the servants' hall, and there were always a lot of people staying in the house, because they were very rich people ... They used to have huge dinners at nine o'clock at night, which used to go on till ten or ten thirty, before dinner was over, and me being the in-between maid, had all the washing up to do, and all the vegetables to clean – I had all the rough work. We had one day a month off, and I lived in Staffordshire, and I went home one day a month.'

(Alice Cairns, BBC Archive Disc.)

'Another difficulty which dogs the path of the Lambeth housekeeper is, either that there is no oven or only a gas oven which requires a good deal of gas, or that the stove oven needs much fuel to heat it. Once a week, for the Sunday dinner, the plunge is taken. Homes where there is no oven send out to the bakehouse on that occasion. The rest of the week is managed on cold food, or the hard-worked saucepan and frying-pan are brought into play. The certainty of an economical stove or fireplace is out of the reach of the poor. They are often obliged to use old-fashioned and broken ranges and grates which devour coal with as little use to the user as possible ...'

(Mrs Pember Reeves, *Round About a Pound a Week*, 1914.)

'The Edwardian slum child, like his forebears, felt an attachment to family life that a later age may find hard to understand. Home, however poor, was the focus of his love and interests, a sure fortress against a hostile world. Songs about its beauties were ever on people's lips. "Home, sweet home", first heard in the 1870s, had become "almost a second national anthem". Few walls in lower working-class houses lacked "mottoes" – coloured strips of paper, about nine inches wide and eighteen inches in length, attesting to domestic joys: EAST, WEST, HOME'S BEST; BLESS OUR HOME; GOD IS MASTER OF THIS

HOUSE; ... HOME IS THE NEST WHERE ALL IS BEST. To hear of a teenager leaving or being turned out of it struck dark fear in a child's mind. He could hardly imagine a fate more awful.'

(Robert Roberts, op. cit.)

'Inside they were singing Sankey's hymn, "Safe in the arms of Jesus"; outside, as I stood on the lighted porch, I heard childish voices shouting from the darkness, "Let's come in, Guv'nor, we won't make no noise; we'll behive ourselves". Going towards them, I made out several small, rough-looking children peering through the railings from an adjoining field. I suggested they would be better at home and in bed at this time of night; to which a girl of about eight (and little at that) replied in saucily precocious style, speaking for herself and a companion, "Garn, we're ahrt wiv ahr blokes; that's my bloke". "Yus", said the other girl, "and that's mine" (they pointed to two boys about their own size). At this there was a general shout of laughter; and then came a plaintive plea from the first child, "Give us a penny, will you, Guv'nor?" Regular cockney arabs these.'

(Charles Booth, *Life and Labour in London*, 3rd edition, 1902–3.)

'There is one beautiful sight in the East End, and only one, and it is the children dancing in the street when the organ-grinder goes his round.'

(Jack London, op. cit.)

'A street of working-class houses ran the length of our garden and we were not allowed to speak, much less play, with the children in this street. On the other side of the house the son of ... a wealthy Manchester merchant ... lived with his family. They had a nurse-maid in cap and apron to look after the three children. *They* were not allowed to play with *us*. We used to stand on the flat top of our summer house and look at both lots of children and say how daft it was that we could not all make up a game of rounders.'

(C. Stella Davies, *North Country Bred*, 1963. The writer was born in 1895, the fourteenth of fifteen children, five of whom died in infancy. Her father, a commercial traveller, died when she was eight. The family lived at Higher Crumpsall, near Manchester.)

'It is pathetic, especially on cold, wintry mornings, to note the rivet boys and others of the poorest class as they approach the entrance by the coffee stalls. Their eyes are fixed longingly on the steaming urns and piled-up plates of buns . . . But such luxuries are not for them. They have not a halfpenny in the world, so they content themselves with a covetous look and pass on to the labour . . . All the money is needed elsewhere – for clothes, boots, and household requirements.'

(Alfred Williams, *Life in a Railway Factory*, 1915. The passage refers to the G.W.R. works at Swindon where the author worked for twenty-three years.)

'Well, we had to start work more or less when we were 14 years of age, sometimes earlier than that, and we were more or less kept working all day long and felt much too tired to do anything as they do now, like they do now, at night time. I just say we had to work, and if you didn't work, you didn't eat. As far as living was concerned, well, I mean, for the poorer class of people, it really was bad. It was a very common sight to see, even in my own home town, Edinburgh, children going about in the snow with no boots on. And a great big patch on either knee, and a patch behind. That was a very common sight . . . I used to work a fair amount when I went to school, you know, after school hours and things like that, sometimes till 11 at night, the shops never shut till 11 at night, in those days. It was very hard work, messenger boy, really, we had no bicycles to ride on, we used to carry the stuff on our head . . . I think for the whole week's job I got about five shillings, working about 60 hours.'

(Sergeant-Major Anderson, BBC Archive Disc.)

'One afternoon all the scholars were allowed to climb on the desks and look out through the window to see a boy of our school being carried home with his head cut off. He was a notorious "mitcher". That day he had been playing in a canal boat at the bottom of a quarry incline about a mile down the valley. A tram, half-way up the mountain side and loaded with quarry stones, had run wild down the incline, dashed over the bank across the boat in which Alec was playing, caught his neck against the top of the boat side, and severed his head from his body as evenly as a sword could have done it. We were advised not to be "mitchers" like Alec and then we should not have our heads cut off.'

(Joseph Keating, *My Struggle for Life*, 1916. The writer was born of Irish parents at Mountain Ash in 1871 and started school at the age of three and a half.)

'We hardly got settled here [in 1905] when my poor sister Florrie was brought home from the telephone exchange in dreadful agony. She had the newly diagnosed appendicitis ... The operation was considered to be extremely dangerous and our doctor would not advise it. Florrie died a week later of, I suppose, peritonitis and her screams ring in my ears as I record this.'

(C. Stella Davies, op. cit.)

'Want of food, irregularity and unsuitability of food, taken together are the determining cause of degeneracy in children. The breakfasts that these children get are nominally bread and tea, if they get it at all. There is bread and margarine for lunch, and the dinner is normally nothing but what a copper can purchase at the local fried fish shops, where the most inferior kinds of fish such as skate are fried in unwholesome, reeking cottonseed oil. They frequently supplement this with rotten fruit, which they collect beneath barrows ... One of the most important points to which I would draw your attention is the absence of fresh milk. In these districts the only milk which any of the children know is tinned milk which does not possess the nutritive power of fresh milk ... As regards meat, if they get it at all, it is for the most part once a week on Sundays and then very little and of the poor sort . . .'

(Evidence of Dr Alfred Eichholz, H.M.I., to the Interdepartmental Committee on Physical Deterioration, 18 December 1903. Eichholz had been Medical Inspector of Schools for Lambeth since 1898. He was later Chief Medical Officer at the Board of Education.)

'Those meals! Those endless, extravagant meals, in which they all indulged all the year round! Sebastian wondered how their constitutions and their figures could stand it; then he remembered that in the summer they went as a matter of course to Homburg or Marienbad, to get rid of the accumulated excess, and then returned to start another year's course of rich living. Really, there was very little difference essentially between Marienbad and the vomitorium of the Romans.'

(V. Sackville-West, *The Edwardians*, 1930, a novel prefaced by the note that 'no character in this book is wholly fictitious'.)

'22 June 1887 . . . I think it a strange habit for business men of all ranks to knock off at eleven o'clock in the morning and go out to a public-house for a drink. I noticed this particularly in the City in the neighbourhood of the Bank. Champagne at sixpence a glass appears to be the favourite tipple.

'24 December 1901 . . . This being the day before Christmas has brought out everybody for final shopping. I went in a hansom along Regent Street and down Tottenham Court Road, where most of the shoppers congregate. Maple's and Shoolbred's great establishments were packed with people and the furniture shops in Tottenham Court Road were thronged . . . Bond Street, on the way back, was less crowded. Luxury-buying is less apparent this year. Everybody is buying gramophones and ping-pong sets.'

(*R.D.B.'s Diary.*)

'So most of the women were idle in the sense that there was very little real work which they had to set their hands or minds to do whether they liked it or not. They all "filled in time". One method was paying calls; they all paid calls, not because they liked doing it or because they really thought that social good accrued from it, but because it was an accepted social duty and the only way open to them of getting to know a new neighbour. An introduction on neutral ground could never be followed directly by an invitation to tea or dinner. An invitation issued in so casual a way would have been social heresy . . .'

(Katharine Chorley, *Manchester Made Them*, 1950. The writer grew up in a large house at Alderley Edge before the First World War.)

'Women's clothing was extremely decorous. Dresses were long enough to hide ankles, and so highly boned to the chin that practically no neck was visible. No respectable girl went hatless or gloveless. Evening dresses were also ankle length . . .'

(May Hankey, BBC Archive Disc.)

'14 October 1900. [Paquin] says that the skirt two inches off the ground is all right for dry weather, as it leaves both hands free, but not so in muddy weather . . . The short skirt, to be safely left alone in muddy weather, says the fashion dictator, needs to be at least six inches off the ground; and who dares to wear it!'

(*R.D.B.'s Diary.*)

'2 Sept. 1902. Over 70 miles in the [motor] car without a mishap – lovely travelling.

'23 Sept. 1902. The motor behaved splendidly; lit my acetylene lamp for the first time – first rate.

'Returning home [to Essex from Devon], sometimes at 60 miles an hour, never under forty. The pace very fast, the bumping occasionally disagreeable, and the dust (chalk) awful. I could see our track behind us for miles, and people meeting us had to hide their heads. I was ashamed of it. The A.A. Scouts [*sic*] always saved us from a police trap.'

(J. O. Thompson (compiler), *Diary and Reminiscences of Dr. Salter*, 1933.)

'One of the leading house painters and decorators in Birmingham tells the writer that people are spending their money on automobiles and their upkeep instead of on the redecoration and painting of their houses ... People ... were living more in hotels and on the roads ... People were spending less time at home, caring less for the attractiveness of the home and devoting their surplus money, and even more than their surplus, to the purchase of automobiles and their upkeep; many, it being stated, purchasing motor cars without any idea as to their cost of maintenance and the loss through depreciation.'

(Report by the U.S. Consul in Birmingham, Albert Halstead, 1911.)

'There was, I suppose, a great deal of poverty. Naturally, I didn't know much about that as a child. My own dear nurse and the two faithful maids who served us – they never complained of poverty, and when they retired, they were comfortable and had nice places to live, and were always nicely dressed, and could go off for little holidays. It's difficult to know what poverty is.'

(Mrs E. Sillar, BBC Archive Disc.)

Progress

The growing urbanization of the country which, many people thought, aggravated the problems of the poor also made it easier to deal with the worst social injustices. Towns provided an increasing range of free services. Indeed, local government expenditure almost doubled between 1900 and 1913. It was in towns that free school meals and school medical inspection began. Better medical attention was becoming available, too, in hospitals, which catered mainly for working-

class patients rather than for the rest of the community who at that time still preferred to be treated (much less satisfactorily) in their own houses or in primitive private nursing homes. Workmen's trains and, from the 1890s onwards, electric tramcars – and cheap, second-hand bicycles – enabled many a wage earner to escape from the congested central areas of towns into the suburbs, leaving more room for those who still had to remain. And the spread of multiple shops, such as Sainsburys and Liptons, from the 1860s onwards, was also essentially an urban phenomenon, as were the sporting events on Saturday afternoons, trips by excursion train, the music halls, and, later on, silent films. Another innovation was the new and more attractive public house with its bright lights and large expanse of plate glass and mirror; and even here there was considerable progress, for there was a definite decline in high alcohol consumption (particularly spirits) and drunkenness from 1900 onwards. This marked a clear break with the past. But so, too, did the increase in cigarette smoking.

Women were perhaps the main beneficiaries of change before 1914. The preference for smaller families, which became more marked in the middle classes in the later nineteenth century, and began to spread to certain sections of the working classes, was making the life of many married women considerably easier; and the coming of the typewriter and the telephone were among the developments which provided more employment opportunities for girls. More scholarships, often to the new schools and technical colleges, gave bright young people of both sexes a better start in life than their parents had had.

All these changes, however, were coming about slowly. There may have been more women teachers and nurses, shop assistants and telephonists, typists and machine operators; but there was still a vast army in domestic service. Old age pensions began to be paid by the state only at the beginning of 1909 and health and unemployment benefit not until the beginning of 1913. Poverty was still alarmingly extensive in 1914.

'[When I first went to live at Camberwell in 1900] our sole communication with London . . . was a few erratic horse omnibuses and lines of slow-moving, two-horse trams . . . [Now] we have fast lines of electric trams, brilliantly lighted, in which reading is a pleasure, hurrying us down from over the bridges at half the time expended under the old conditions. Each workman today in the district has had an hour added to his life – half an hour actually saved from the transit and half an hour given back to him in the transit. And you can see the young of both sexes – especially the young working girls – eagerly using that half hour . . . Family after family are evacuating the blocks and crowded tenements for little four-roomed cottages, with little gardens, at Hither Green or Tooting.'

(C. F. G. Masterman, writing *c.* 1906, quoted in Lucy Masterman, *C. F. G. Masterman*, 1939.)

'Travel by train or motor anywhere in England and you see games being played – particularly if it be a Saturday – from one end of the country to the other. The open spaces of England seem to be given over to men and some women batting, kicking or hitting a ball. The attendance at games on a Saturday is very large . . . Even at the beginning of the foot-ball season the gate receipts show an attendance of more than 200,000 people. When the big and final games take place, I have calculated that out of the male adult population in England and Wales on a great foot-ball Saturday, one in every twenty-seven is in attendance at a Game of some sort, and this leans to the error of being too few rather than too many.'

(Price Collier, op. cit.)

'There has been a great development and improvement upon the usual public-house sing-song, as to the low character and bad influence of which there are not two opinions. The story of progress in this respect may be traced in many of the existing places which, from a bar parlour and a piano, to an accompaniment on which friends "obliged with a song", have passed through every stage to that of music hall . . . The audiences are youthful. They seek amusement and are easily pleased . . . The increase in the number as well as size of halls has been rapid . . . The

taste becomes a habit and new halls are opened every
year . . .'

(Charles Booth, op. cit.)

'Once a year, during Wakes Week, when the mills closed
down . . . the [Rossendale] valley was all but deserted . . .
Wakes Weeks are staggered, each town in the industrial area
taking different weeks throughout the summer for their
holiday . . . The overwhelming majority of people went to
Blackpool though some, eccentrically, went to Morecambe
or even Rhyl. Blackpool, therefore, was full at any one time,
with neighbours from the same town and no one need feel
isolated or lonely. Groups of relatives and friends would
share lodgings or take them in the same street and young
and old, children, courting couples and sober married folk
alike, would spend a year's savings in one glorious spree.'

(C. Stella Davies, op. cit.)

'When the men come back to work after the Whitsuntide
holidays, they usually find the official notice boards covered
with posters containing the preliminary announcements of
the annual Trip, and, very soon, on the plates of the forges
and walls, and even outside in the town, the words "Roll on
Trip" or "Five weeks to Trip" may be seen scrawled in big
letters . . . "Trip Day" is the most important day in the
calendar at the railway town. For several months preceding
it, fathers and mothers of families, young unmarried men,
and juveniles have been saving up for the outing. Whatever
new clothes are bought for the summer are usually worn for
the first time at "Trip"; the trade of the town is at its zenith
during the week before the holiday . . . A general exodus
from the town takes place that day and quite twenty-five
thousand people will have hurried off to all parts of the
kingdom . . . About half the total number return the same
night; the others stop away till the expiration of the holiday,
which is of eight days duration [but unpaid].'

(Alfred Williams, op. cit., writing about the railway works at
Swindon.)

'Sheffield has 17 cinematograph theatres, whose total intake is about $7,300 [£1,500] per week.

'More than 60 per cent of the films used in this city are American ... The reason given for the popularity of the American-made film is not that the photography is any better, but rather that the subject matter at present suits the popular taste. The American film generally portrays the so-called western drama, with stirring, forceful action, put on in the open ... Five years ago the popular film was the home drama, where the action was built on a purely fictitious plot. Roughly speaking, two years ago the American cowboy came on the stage and rapidly became the popular hero of the moving-picture palaces ... In many picture houses films entitled "The Happenings of the Week" are now shown. These features were at first rather under-valued, but their popularity has so grown that now no manager can afford to omit them.'

(Report by the U.S. Vice-Consul in Sheffield, Rice K. Evans, 1912.)

'At the club-house, after a ride through the lanes of Cheshire or over the Derbyshire hills, we ate an enormous tea of ham, pickles, jam and cake of such solidity that we called it a "tram-stopper" ... Washing-up followed, after which we cleared the tables away for either a meeting, a play or a concert, finishing the evening by dancing ... By ten o'clock we were shooting down Schools Hill, bunches of wild flowers tied to our handle-bars, apples in our pockets, the wind lifting our hair ...'

(C. Stella Davies's memories of the Clarion Cycle Club, op. cit.)

'Taking the wear of both sexes, but especially that of women, the greatest feature of the period was the immense develop-ment of ready-made clothes. These were so much improved in quality, that they no longer differed obtrusively from the bespoke garments worn by richer people; while their cheapness enabled all the poorer classes to raise their standards of clothing. Although it remained for the war to level up the dress of people in all classes . . . a distinct start was observable some years before 1914. Its importance will not be underestimated by anyone who remembers what a cruel and unescapable badge of inferiority clothes had till then constituted.'

(R. C. K. Ensor, *England 1870–1914* (1936). The writer lived in Poplar, which he represented on the L.C.C. from 1910–13.)

'Clogs and shawls were, of course, standard wear for all. The girl who first defied this tradition in one of Lancashire's largest mills remembered the "stares, skits and sneers" of fellow workers sixty years afterwards. Her parents, urgently in need of money, had put her to weaving, where earnings for girls were comparatively good. They lived, however, in one of the newer suburbs with its parloured houses and small back gardens. To be seen in such a district returning from a mill in clogs and shawl would have meant instant social demotion for the whole family. She was sent to the weaving shed wearing coat and shoes and thereby shocked a whole establishment . . . Nevertheless, before 1914 even, continued good wages in weaving and the consequent urge to bolster status, had persuaded not a few to follow the lone teenager's example.'

(Robert Roberts, op. cit.)

'5 October 1900. Lord Iveagh, the great Irish brewer, is authority for the statement that women clerks in offices are a great success. He recently tried the experiment of employing lady clerks on the staff of the Guinness Brewery, mostly daughters of employees, and there has not been a single failure.'

'6 November 1900. Mrs Rendell and Miss Tattershall write from Baker Street that they have opened a new tea room in which there are to be found lady proprietors, lady waitresses in pretty frocks, and ladies to bake cakes, pastries and scones, and where the walls are decorated with attractive pictures and hangings, and so on. The new woman progresses.'

(*R.D.B.'s Diary.*)

'Now London and other large towns teem with restaurants, tea shops, fruit shops and sweet shops ... The coming of girls into business and their consequent possession of personal incomes accounts to some extent for the kind of food offered and for the premises in which it is served, and possibly the fact that the young women drink but little alcohol, allied to the fact that they have more pocket money, explains the growing demand for sweets ...'

(Mrs C. S. Peel, *A Hundred Wonderful Years*, 1926.)

'Many mothers nowadays to all intents and purposes are as young as their daughters. In fact, the disappearance of the middle-aged woman is a marked sign of the period ...'

(*The Queen*, 1910.)

'They [women] read more, they think more, they do more, and this shows in their conversation. Subjects are discussed which would not have been whispered about a generation or two ago.'

(*The Lady*, 1910.)

'I have visited schools in London and ... I have made special visits to West Ham, Manchester, Salford and Leeds ... In the better districts of the towns there exist public elementary schools frequented by children not merely equal but often superior in physique and attainments to rural children. And these schools seem to be at least as numerous as schools of the lowest type ... All evidence points to active improvement, bodily and mental, in the worst districts, so soon as they are exposed to better circumstances, even the weaker children recovering at a later age from the evil effects of infant life. Compulsory school attendance, the more rigorous scheduling of children of school age and the abolition of school fees in elementary schools have swept into the schools an annually increasing proportion of children during the last thirty years.'

(Dr Alfred Eichholz, H.M.I., reporting to the Interdepartmental Committee on Physical Deterioration, 1904.)

'The importation of American breakfast cereals into the country continues on a great scale . . . During the past year approximately 200,000 cases were imported direct to Manchester. Present indications point to an increasing demand in Great Britain for cereal breakfast food.'

(Report by the U.S. Consul in Manchester, Church Howe, 1912.)

'I think that everyone who knows the effect which smoking has upon children will be shocked to see how this habit is growing . . . I asked where did they get the tobacco from, and it seems there is a regular trade now in cheap cigarettes . . . I am informed that they can get cigarettes in packets of five for a penny. But I was told that some of the girls were following suit, and there was a school mentioned to me . . . in which one or two girls had actually been caught in the passage of the school smoking.'

(Dr J. Cunningham, Professor of Anatomy at Edinburgh, to the Interdepartmental Committee on Physical Deterioration, 1904.)

Postscript. A 1970s problem in 1904:
lack of educational opportunities in deprived areas

'Elementary education has contributed to the stratification of the large urban population into a distinct series of social levels. There is an upper class, well-to-do and well cared for, to whom our methods afford every chance of mental and physical improvement . . . At the other end of the scale we find the aggregations of the slum population ill nourished, poor, ignorant, badly housed, to a small extent only benefited by our methods of training . . .'

(Dr Alfred Eichholz, H.M.I., op. cit.)

8

The Inferno: 1914–18

JOHN A. TERRAINE

It is doubtful whether British society has ever been so beset with contradictions as it was in 1914. A Liberal Government was in power – but only just; it depended on the support of Labour and the Irish in the House of Commons. A vast programme of social reform lay behind it, but a vast agenda of social unrest awaited it every day. There was working-class unrest; beginning in 1910, a wave of strikes, conducted with extreme bitterness on all sides, swept through the country, with every prospect of a final confrontation in the autumn of 1914. Ben Tillett, the Dockers' leader, looking back on these years, called them:

'A strange, hectic period of our economic history! It was a great upsurge of elemental forces. It seemed as if the dispossessed and disinherited class in various parts of the country were all simultaneously moved to assert their claims upon society.'

(Ben Tillett, *Memories and Reflections*, 1931.)

Parallel with the upsurge of the working class was the revolt of women: the militant Suffragette movement. In the first seven months of 1914 the Suffragettes set fire to no fewer than 107 buildings; their leader, Mrs Emmeline Pankhurst, went to prison four times during the same period. Parallel with the Suffragette agitation were the Irish Home Rule issue, the Ulster crisis, and the Tory revolt. In March, fifty-seven officers of the 3rd Cavalry Brigade, stationed at the Curragh Camp outside Dublin, declared that they would resign their commissions rather than coerce Protestant Ulster into accepting Home Rule. The Army was split by divided loyalties, reflecting a nation equally divided. Professor Gilbert Murray recalled the mood of the occasion:

'Some time in March 1914, in the midst of the Curragh crisis, I happened to be in the gallery of the House of Commons. The sight of the House rather shocked me. The opposition seemed wild with delight. There was a mutiny: There was to be a rebellion: The Government would fall and the Conservatives get office: All the questions, all the speeches had a ring of triumph. A powerful counter note was struck by a Labour Member, Colonel Ward, but it was a note almost equally dangerous. In ringing tones he warned the Tories that, if they wanted a Civil War they could have it. If there was to be a mutiny in the Army, it would not be a Tory mutiny but a mutiny of the working class. The debate was exciting, but deplorable. It seemed as if nobody cared for the community as a whole; it was all party or class.'

(J. A. Spender and C. Asquith, *Life of Herbert Henry Asquith*, 1932.)

It was to a country in this condition of disruption and self-contradiction that war came in August. At once another contradiction was exposed. The ruling Liberal Party was strongly tinged with pacifism – yet it was the Party which had carried through, under Lord Haldane, the most effective military reforms in British history. The nation was largely unaware of them; indeed, it was largely unaware of its Army altogether, except when war was actually in progress, or when disagreeable occurrences like the Curragh Mutiny reached the headlines. Britain was a naval power, the greatest in the world. The Royal Navy was the shield of British democracy, much admired. The Army was something else. Rudyard Kipling's poem, ' Tommy', expresses a widespread national attitude:

'I went into a public-'ouse to get a pint o' beer,
The publican 'e up an' sez, "We serve no redcoats here."
The girls be'ind the bar they laughed an' giggled fit to die,
I outs into the street again an' to myself sez I:
O it's Tommy this, an' Tommy that, an' "Tommy go
    away";
But it's "Thank you, Mister Atkins", when the band begins
    to play –

The band begins to play, my boys, the band begins to play,
O it's "Thank you, Mister Atkins", when the band begins
   to play.'
   (Definitive edition of Rudyard Kipling's Verse, 1940.)

*It was particularly in the lower middle class, and the 'respectable
working class', with special emphasis in certain regions (e.g.
'chapel-going' areas, like much of Wales), that this hostility to the
Army was most pronounced. Brigadier Stanley Clarke recalls a by no
means untypical case which he encountered:*

'My R.S.M. was a Drill-Sergeant from the Grenadier
Guards and I remember him telling me that his father was a
small farmer in Gloucestershire. When he told his parents
he wished to join the Army he was abused for wanting to
join "that scum" and told that if he did they never wished
to have anything more to do with him. I asked him what he
had answered. He said he was joining, and as far as their
ultimatum went it was a game two could play. He added:
"I never did have anything more to do with them."'

   (Quoted in John Baynes, *Morale*, 1967.)

*But the most remarkable example of this frame of mind is to be
found in the letter of a Mrs Robertson to her son, on hearing that he
had enlisted:*

'My very Dear Boy
   'you never could Mean what you put in your Letter on
Sunday . . . and what cause have you for such a Low Life . . .
you have as Good Home as any one else in our Station . . .
you have kind and Loving Sisters . . . you know you are
the Great Hope of the Family . . . if you do not like Service
you can do somethink else . . . there are plenty of things
Steady Young Men can do when they can write and read
as you can . . . [the Army] is a refuge for all Idle people . . .
I shall name it to no one for I am ashamed to think of it . . .
I would rather Bury you than see you in a red coat . . .'

   (Quoted in Victor Bonham-Carter, *Soldier True*, 1963.)

Mrs Robertson's son, William, was the only man to make the long march from private to field-marshal, taking in on the way the highest post that the Army can offer, Chief of the Imperial General Staff (1916–18): Field-Marshal Sir William Robertson, Bart, G.C.B., G.C.M.G., K.C.V.O., D.S.O.

And so it was a nation which relished its military glories, but had little regard for or understanding of the men who won them, which now found itself engaged in a war which would affect every part of it as no other had ever done. The prevailing mood, in the early August days of 1914, was one of euphoria. The weather had a lot to do with it; Charles Carrington remembers the approach of war while he was staying at a country vicarage at the age of seventeen:

'I lay in a hammock and ate plums – too many plums – in a garden full of delphiniums which seemed to go on flowering week after week in that splendid summer of 1914. We started a grand offensive (there was a family) against wasps' nests, and were not very brave. One of the girls was frightened of the dark even more than of wasps, and when I walked down the lane with her to a late party I shamefully showed that a very dark lane made me feel creepy too. I might have gone to school for another year, but one day there was a crisis in Serbia reported in the morning paper, and I wilfully said that I would enlist as a soldier to fight for the Serbians . . .'

(C. E. Carrington ['Charles Edmonds'], *A Subaltern's War*, 1929.)

When war actually came, only those with unusual insight echoed in their thoughts the words of the Foreign Secretary, Sir Edward Grey: 'The lamps are going out all over Europe; we shall not see them lit again in our lifetime.' Most people envisaged a somewhat dangerous but predominantly glorious spree; Michael MacDonagh of The Times *wrote in his diary on 4 August:*

'It was in the streets after the House of Commons had adjourned that I found myself in an atmosphere of real passion. Parliament Street and Whitehall were thronged with people highly excited and rather boisterous. A brilliant sun shone in a cloudless sky. Young men in straw hats were in the majority. Girls in light calico dresses were numerous. All were already touched with the war fever. They regarded their country as a crusader – redressing all wrongs and bringing freedom to oppressed nations. Cries of "Down with Germany!" were raised. Germany was the aggressor. She must be made humbly to ask for peace. The singing of patriotic songs, such as "Rule Britannia", "The Red, White and Blue", and also "The Marseillaise", brought the crowds still closer in national companionship. They saw England radiant through the centuries, valiant and invincible, and felt assured that so she shall appear for ever.'

(Michael MacDonagh, *In London During the Great War*, 1935.)

National unity was suddenly reborn; the new mood was caught and heightened in the Press; men of letters made their contribution. Rudyard Kipling was only exercising once again his reporting talents when he wrote:

> 'For all we have and are,
> For all our children's fate,
> Stand up and take the war.
> The Hun is at the gate! ...
> No easy hope or lies
> Shall bring us to our goal,
> But iron sacrifice
> Of body, will and soul.
> There is but one task for all –
> One life for each to give.
> What stands if Freedom fall?
> Who dies if England live?'

(Definitive edition, op. cit.)

On 9 September The Times *published Thomas Hardy's poem,* 'Men Who March Away'; *this also caught a nation-wide sentiment:*

> 'In our heart of hearts believing
>   Victory crowns the just,
>   And that braggarts must
>   Surely bite the dust,

Press we to the field ungrieving,
In our heart of hearts believing
Victory crowns the just.'

(Quoted in John H. Johnston, *English Poetry of the First World War*, 1964.)

But of all the War poets, none captured the naïve enthusiasm of the first days as Rupert Brooke did in his sonnet sequence, '1914':

'Now, God be thanked Who has matched us with His hour,
And caught our youth, and wakened us from sleeping,
With hand made sure, clear eye, and sharpened power,
To turn, as swimmers into cleanness leaping,
Glad from a world grown old and cold and weary,
Leave the sick hearts that honour could not move,
And half-men, and their dirty songs and dreary,
And all the little emptiness of love!'

(ibid.)

It must have come as rather a shock, in the midst of so much lofty feeling, for the readers of The Times *to be informed that the latest marching song from Aldershot went (more or less) as follows:*

'Send out the Army and the Navy,
Send out the rank and file.
(Have a banana!)
Send out the brave Territorials,
They'll face the danger with a smile.
(I don't think!)
Send out the boys of the girls' brigade,
They will keep old England free;
Send out my mother, my sister and my brother,
But for Gawd's sake don't send me!'

(Anon; Regular Army.)

This was the voice of the Army – the Regular Army; this was the sardonic, unemotional, matter-of-fact voice of once-despised 'Tommy', who as usual was being expected to do the dirty work, and was quite prepared to do it, but not to sentimentalize about it. The Army – that old British Regular Army of 1914 which the Kaiser called 'a perfect thing apart' – had few illusions; its attitudes, had they been aware of them, would have shocked its fellow-countrymen. Major Tom Bridges, of the 4th Dragoon Guards, wrote:

'Certainly the 2nd Cavalry Brigade to which I belonged was in a high state of efficiency and was quite ready to fight anybody. There was no hatred of Germany but in the true mercenary spirit we would equally readily have fought the French. Our motto was, "We'll do it. What is it?"'

(Lieut.-Gen. Sir Tom Bridges, *Alarms and Excursions*, 1938.)

Sixty per cent of the men in the ranks of the 1914 British Expeditionary Force were reservists, called back to the colours. For many of them, this return to Army life was a distressing uprooting from their homes and occupations; but for many others there was an odd satisfaction in obeying the call. Private Frank Richards of the 2/Royal Welch Fusiliers tells how it came to him:

'On the fourth of August, 1914, I was at Blaina, Monmouthshire, having a drink in the Castle Hotel with a few of my cronies, all old soldiers and the majority of them reservists. One had took us around South Africa; there wasn't a Boer left in South Africa by the time he had finished his yarn. Next I took them around India and Burmah, and there wasn't a Pathan or Dacoit left in the world by the time I had finished mine. Now another was taking us through North China in the Boxer Rising of 1900; and he had already got hundreds of Chinks hanging on the gas brackets when someone happened to come in with a piece of news. He said that war had broken out with Germany and that the Sergeant of Police was hanging a notice up by the post office, calling all reservists to the Colours. This caused a bit of excitement and language, but it was too late in the evening for any of us to proceed to our depots so we kept on drinking and yarning until stop-tap. By that time we were getting a little top-heavy . . .'

(Frank Richards, *Old Soldiers Never Die*, 1933.)

Until a shocked public awoke to their plight, the wives of some reservists found themselves in appalling circumstances: they were the first British victims of the war.

'Hundreds of reservists had been called to the colours, and their families were left entirely without support. Women were starving, for many of the factories where they had worked were closed, in panic of the unknown. A man earning fourteen to eighteen shillings a week before the war, sole support of wife and half a dozen or more children, had not been able to save. Prices had risen sharply in the shops on the day after war was declared; and they went on rising daily ... As the hot August days went on, some families were threatened with eviction unless the weekly rent, which had taken up to a third of the former weekly wage, was paid. There was a small unemployment benefit available to a few trades, under the National Insurance; but this affected only about one family in six. Again, Poor Law relief applied only to the crippled, not to the able-bodied; so this could not help the wives whose men had gone. Breasts of nursing mothers shrunk bag-like from lack of food.'

(Henry Williamson, *How Dear Is Life*, 1954.)

In 1914, the Territorial Army was considered as basically a force for Home Defence, though many men in it were willing to serve overseas. The Regular Army, even with its reservists, was simply not large enough for the needs of continental war. There would need to be something else – and this need was quickly perceived by Lord Kitchener, the new Secretary of State for War. Out of his perception came the 'Kitchener Armies', or 'New Army', an extraordinary manifestation of patriotism which brought over 2¼ million volunteers to the colours in the first fourteen months of the war. Michael MacDonagh describes how the first appeal was made:

'August 6th: The first appeal for recruits appears on the walls of London today. It is printed in the national colours. Within a deep red border, in vivid blue letters on a white ground, are the words, "Your King and Country need You" – "YOU" being heavily underscored. "In this crisis," the poster says, "our country calls on all her young unmarried men to rally round the Flag and enlist in the ranks of the Army" – ages 18–30 years. Another poster is headed "A Call to Arms", and says: "An addition of 100,000 men to His Majesty's Regular Army is immediately necessary in the present grave national emergency." Lord Kitchener, who has been appointed Secretary of State for War, is confident "that this appeal will be at once responded to by all those who have the safety of our Empire at heart". Thus the young men in straw hats who were clamouring for war in Whitehall early in the week are now afforded the opportunity of demonstrating their patriotism in a more practical form. Their response has been immediate.'

(Michael MacDonagh, op. cit.)

Arthur Behrend was a railway trainee, on a salary of £40 a year at Lime Street Station. He was one of the hundreds of thousands of young men who felt the impulse to join up – though in his case not in the 'Kitchener Army':

'Mobilization was on the point of starting, and since my duty was mainly by night my memories are of special troop trains and of noisily drunken Army and Navy reservists being seen off by tearful and equally drunken wives, and if this seems unkind I would mention that those were the days when drink was strong and cheap. Anyhow I still remember the phenomenal number of empty bottles which had to be swept up and removed from the platforms after the departure of every train . . . The desire to be in some kind of uniform had already got under my skin, and since I had now received permission from Euston to join the Territorials I sent off a telegram on the morning of August 6th to an army friend of the family, a regular who . . . had just been seconded by his Regiment, the Lilywhites or East Lancashires, to become the Adjutant of their 4th Battalion at Blackburn. His reply arrived the following day and read: COME TO-MORROW PREPARED TO STAY BRING ALL NECESSARY KIT . . . I told my mother not to worry because the fighting would be over long before I was trained to fight, spread a dust-sheet over my new Douglas motor-cycle, and departed for Blackburn. I was not yet nineteen, I was in love only with the railway, and the war was my oyster.'

(Arthur Behrend, *Make Me a Soldier*, 1961.)

So now the nation was at war – the unimaginable war which would totally transform its way of life. Shocks and sensations were abundantly in store for it, and they began at once. It was no surprise that the first service to be active was the Royal Navy; 'instant readiness' was part of the Navy's tradition, and in 1914 this meant that the Fleet went straight from its annual exercises to its war stations six days before hostilities began.

The surprise lay in what followed: instead of the expected 'Trafalgar' against the German High Seas Fleet, the Grand Fleet found its enemies locked in their harbours, where (except for occasional sorties) they would remain for nearly two years. This meant that the Grand Fleet itself was very much tied to its base, Scapa Flow, a bleak, uninviting anchorage almost devoid of shore amenities. One sailor said:

'Scapa left its mark on all who served there. To go to Scapa was to join a club whose membership you could never quite disown . . . There were times when men spat the name out like a four-letter word . . .'

(Brown and Meehan, *Scapa Flow*, 1968.)

Cheated of its expected naval triumph, the British public soon had to adjust itself to strange news of the Army. On Monday, 24 August, it learned from a cryptic Press Bureau release that: 'The British forces were engaged all day on Sunday and after dark with the enemy in the neighbourhood of Mons, and held their ground . . .' The Battle of Mons was, in fact, little more than a skirmish, in which the B.E.F. did, indeed, hold its ground all day, but at the end of the day was compelled to retire to avoid encirclement. So began the long Retreat from Mons, presented in alarming terms to readers of the British Press. Private Frank Richards tells how it all began:

'We were issued out with an extra fifty rounds of ammunition, making in all two hundred rounds to carry. We marched all night again and all next day, halting a few times to fire at German scouting aeroplanes but not hitting one . . . We reservists fetched straight out of civil life were suffering the worst on this non-stop march, which would have been exhausting enough if we had not been carrying fifty pounds weight or so of stuff on our backs. And yet these two days and nights were only the start of our troubles . . . I don't believe any one of us at this time realized that we were retiring, though it was clear that we were not going in the direction of Germany. Of course the officers knew, but they were telling us that we were drawing the enemy into a trap.'

(Frank Richards, op. cit.)

On 26 August the II Corps of the B.E.F. fought the Battle of Le Cateau, another admirable, but this time more costly, rearguard action. Already what was to become an outstanding characteristic of the war was becoming apparent. Private John Stiles of the 1/Gloucestershire Regiment wrote in a letter:

'People who say that the German artillery fire is no good simply don't know what they are talking about. I can only figure it out as being something worse than the mouth of hell.'

(Letter quoted in the Press.)

The retreat continued; many units were broken up, contacts were lost, wild ideas circulated among the exhausted soldiers. A staff officer wrote:

' "Who are you?" I would call out, as a dozen tired and footsore men approached.

' "We're the sole survivors of the Blankshire Regiment, sir," an old soldier would reply. "All the rest got done in yesterday. Not a soul except us is left alive."

' "All right. Keep straight on for a couple of miles or more and you will find three or four hundred other sole survivors of your regiment bivouacking in a field."

'This happened not once, but twenty times.'

(Brig.-Gen. C. D. Baker-Carr, *From Chauffeur to Brigadier*, 1930.)

Wild ideas . . . wild hallucinations . . .

'. . . there is the story of the "Angel of Mons" going strong through the 2nd Corps of how the angel of the Lord on the traditional white horse, and clad all in white with flaming sword, faced the advancing Germans at Mons and forbade their further progress. Men's nerves and imagination play weird pranks in these strenuous times . . .'

(Brig.-Gen. J. Charteris, *At G.H.Q.*, 1931.)

'We retired all night with fixed bayonets, many sleeping as they were marching along. If any angels were seen on the Retirement, as the newspaper accounts said they were, they were seen that night. March, march, for hour after hour, without no halt: we were now breaking into the fifth day of continuous marching with practically no sleep in between . . . Stevens said: "There's a fine castle there, see?" pointing to one side of the road. But there was nothing there. Very nearly everyone were seeing things, we were all so dead-beat.'

(Frank Richards, op. cit.)

While the army continued its retreat from Mons to the Marne, the Home Front was waging battles of its own:

'Sir,

'Yesterday morning came the news of a serious setback to our armies. Yesterday afternoon, while Lord Kitchener was telling of the bravery of our wounded and dead, while he was asking for men to take their places, every lawn tennis court in the space near me was crowded by strapping young Englishmen and girls. Is there no way of shaming these laggards? The English girl who will not know the man – lover, brother, friend – that cannot show an overwhelming reason for not taking up arms – that girl will do her duty and will give good help to her country.

> Your obedient servant,
>   Henry Arthur Jones
> Reform Club, Pall Mall, S.W., Aug. 26th.'

(Letter to *The Times*, published 1 September 1914.)

'. . . never have the public houses been so full of women as they have been since the war began, and this, too, in the morning. Many of these women have more money in their hands than they know what to do with. Why not close the public houses entirely to women during the war?'

(Extract from letter to *The Times*, published 9 October 1914.)

Two thousand similar letters on the same pressing topic were received; they reflected only one of the nation's obsessions at the time. On 19 October a Times *leader stated: 'Public dissatisfaction with the Home Office in regard to the question of enemy aliens is rising to a flood . . .'*

Michael MacDonagh wrote in his diary:

'A large section of the public continue to suffer from the first bewildering shock of being at war. Their nerves are still jangling, and they are subject to hallucinations. They seem to be enveloped in a mysterious darkness, haunted by goblins in the form of desperate German spies, and they can find no light or comfort afforded them by Press or Government . . . The wildest stories are being circulated by these people of outrages committed by Germans in our midst. Attempts have been made to destroy the permanent ways of railways and wreck trains! Signalmen in their boxes, armed sentries at bridges, have been overpowered by bands of Germans who arrived speedily on the scene and, their foul work done, as speedily vanished! Germans have been caught red-handed on the East Coast, signalling with lights to German submarines! More damnable still, bombs have been discovered in the trunks of German governesses in English county families!'

(Michael MacDonagh, op. cit.)

An officer at the War Office wrote:

'You never know what ferocity means until you have been approached by a titled lady who has persuaded herself that she is on the track of a German spy.'

(Sir C. E. Callwell, *Experiences of a Dug-Out, 1914–1918* (1920).)

The B.E.F. at last reached the area of the River Marne, where the Allies turned and struck back at the advancing Germans. There followed the Battle of the Aisne, ending in stalemate, and then the B.E.F. moved to a new sector which was to become one of the greatest and bloodiest British battlegrounds in history: Ypres. Here, as the Regulars were slowly ground down in the fiercest fighting so far, their first support arrived from the Citizen Army. The first Territorial battalion to go into action was the London Scottish, at Messines; now it was their turn to experience twentieth-century war.

'The blows of the gunfire seemed to arise through the bones of his heels upon the hard cobbles.

'Then his mouth filled with water as a coarse downward buzzing grew louder and louder and in the field three hundred yards away on the right four massive black eruptions arose and instantly seemed to break the very day with four stupendous crashes.

' "Halt!"

'The rear companies waited, white-faced, while the leading company marched on, to allow an interval between them.

' "Them's Jack Johnsons,* " said a cavalry soldier, one of a score guarding horses tied to a picket line on the grass near the road. Leaning against branches were clusters of lances with bright points, and pennons below the blades.

' "What's it like up there?" asked Elliott.

' "Bloody terrible, mate." '

(Henry Williamson, op. cit.)

---

* 'Coal-Box'; German 5·9-inch howitzer shell, or larger.

By the end of the battle, the old Regular Army had practically ceased to exist. This was not yet the real era of the barbed-wire war, but a song from that era expresses the truth of 'First Ypres':

> 'If you want the old battalion,
> I know where they are, I know where they are,
> If you want the old battalion,
> I know where they are,
> They're hanging on the old barbed wire.
> I've seen 'em, I've seen 'em,
> Hanging on the old barbed wire,
> I've seen 'em,
> Hanging on the old barbed wire.'

(Anon.)

Christmas came, the first Christmas of the war which was to be 'over by Christmas'. On some sectors of the British front a strange phenomenon, never repeated, was now seen: the truce between the lines:

'We mucked in all day with one another. They were Saxons and some of them could speak English. By the look of them their trenches were in as bad a state as our own. One of their men, speaking in English, mentioned that he had worked in Brighton for some years and that he was fed up to the neck with this damned war and would be glad when it was all over. We told him that he wasn't the only one that was fed up with it.'

(Frank Richards, op. cit.)

Even in the front line, there was some attempt to make Christmas Day a special occasion. Frank Richards tells us:

'We had a decent Christmas dinner. Each man had a tin of Maconochie's and a decent portion of plum pudding.'

(ibid.)

Maconochie's — regarded by some as one of the minor, but effective, horrors of war — was tinned meat and vegetables ('M and V'); it, too, was awarded its place in song:

'Oh, a little bit of everything got in a tin one day,
And they packed it up and sealed it in a most mysterious way;
And some Brass Hat came and tasted it,
And "Pon my Sam," says he,
"We shall feed it to the soldiers,
And we'll call it M. and V." '

(Anon.)

The Home Front, except for the poor, fared rather better:

'There have been the customary crowds of shoppers in the
West End. The Strand, Piccadilly, Regent Street and Oxford
Street were as thronged as I have ever seen them at Christ-
mas-time ... In the suburbs the butchers' shops were
bulging with beef and mutton; the poulterers' with geese
and turkeys; the grocers' with wine, spirits and beer; the
fruiterers' with apples and oranges. Yes, supplies were
abundant; prices were only a little in advance of those of
last year; and money seemed to be plentiful. As for the
"Compliments of the Season", friends were moved, because
of the War, to shake hands with heartier vigour, and wish
each other a Merry Christmas in sincerer and more glad-
some voices ... Moreover, there are no widespread mis-
givings as to the future. The belief as well as the hope
prevails that long before next Christmas we shall have
celebrated the restoration of peace to Europe by the
victories of the Allies.'

(Michael MacDonagh, op. cit.)

*But 1915 was a year of disappointment on all sides. For Britain,
the sadness of the year was epitomized in the Dardanelles Campaign,
whose failure spelt also a failure of British sea-power. The attempt
to force the Dardanelles Straits was a direct application of sea-
power to the seemingly insuperable stalemate of the war on land. It
was also, for many (until they actually arrived at Gallipoli), a
wonderful adventure in the glamorous East.*

'I had not imagined Fate could be so kind ... Will Hero's
Tower crumble under the 15-inch guns? Will the sea be

polyphloisbic and wine-dark and unvintageable? Shall I loot mosaics from St Sophia, and Turkish Delight and carpets? Should we be a Turning Point in History? Oh God! I've never been quite so happy in my life I think. Never quite so pervasively happy; like a stream flowing entirely to one end. I suddenly realize that the ambition of my life has been – since I was two – to go on a military expedition against Constantinople.'

(Rupert Brooke, letter quoted in *Collected Poems*, 1915.)

But Rupert Brooke died of blood-poisoning without ever setting foot on Gallipoli, and those who did arrive encountered a stalemate as deadly as that of the Western Front. Arthur Behrend, in the 42nd East Lancashire Division (T.A.), was one of the second wave to land at Cape Helles:

'There, below the pontoon we had to cross from RIVER CLYDE, the water was six feet deep and so crystal clear that on the bottom we could see, lying in perfect preservation, the uniformed bodies of the soldiers who had been hit or who had fallen in while scrambling ashore ten days earlier.'

(Arthur Behrend, op. cit.)

This was not an auspicious beginning; but neither was the campaign itself in any way auspicious. Typhus and dysentery added their horrors to heat, flies, dust, stench – and the resistance of a stubborn enemy. Corporal Alec Riley wrote:

'Day after day we watched the P.B.I.* going up and down the nullah to and from the trenches. Some of them looked like old, tottering men, bowed stooping, and most of their faces were colourless, except that they were grey or dirty . . . Most of us had sick minds in sick bodies. We were becoming mentally dulled, living for the day and the hour, for food and sleep, and for very little else. It seemed impossible that a day would come when we should leave this place of torment.'

(Diary, in the Imperial War Museum; quoted by R. Rhodes James, *Gallipoli*, 1965.)

* Poor Bloody Infantry.

Every attack broke down; every ruse failed. Gallipoli became more and more a place of martyrdom. Douglas Jerrold, describing an experience of the Royal Naval Division, wrote:

'. . . many hundreds of men lay dead and dying, where a burning sun had turned the bodies of the slain to a premature corruption, where there was no resting-place free from physical contamination, where the air, the surface of the ground, and the soil beneath the surface were alike poisonous, fetid, corrupt.'

(Douglas Jerrold, *The Royal Naval Division*, 1923.)

At the end of the year the Gallipoli Peninsula was evacuated; by then the British casualties numbered 213,980 – and it had all been for nothing. This was the last attempt to use sea-power in this fashion, the end of a traditional mode of British warfare, a turning-point in history indeed, but not as Rupert Brooke had hoped.

And so, in 1916, the centre of gravity of the war lodged itself irrevocably on the Western Front, and Western Front characteristics have dominated all memories and imaginations of it ever since. Chief of these characteristics was that it was an artillery war; artillery was the great killer, and also the great destroyer of the human spirit and personality. By the numbers of men killed, by the horrible manner of many of their deaths, by the continuous attrition of the nerves, the guns made themselves the masters of the war.

'We are the guns, and your masters! Saw ye our flashes?
Heard ye the scream of our shells in the night, and the shuddering crashes?
Saw ye our work by the roadside, the shrouded things lying,
Moaning to God that He made them – the maimed and the dying?
    Husbands or sons,
Fathers or lovers, we break them. We are the guns!'

(Gilbert Frankau, 'The Voice of the Guns', from *The City of Fear*, 1917.)

In all the great battles of the war which now followed in terrible succession, the weight of artillery mounted and its effects became more deadly. The Battle of the Somme (1916) cost the British Army 415,000 casualties; the Battle of Arras (early 1917), 158,000; the Third Battle of Ypres ('Passchendaele', late 1917), 244,000. As personal experiences, there was not much to choose between them. The storm of gunfire merely mounted to higher crescendos.

'At 9.30 they started with Jack Johnsons. By Jove they are HELL. You hear them coming for about ten seconds and then the shell explodes. The concussion of the air is so great, if they are anywhere near, that you feel as if your hands and face were chapped ... One big one hit the parapet about thirty yards from me and blew three men to pieces. One fellow we carried away and buried in five oilsheets ... The real enemy during a shelling is time. With these big ones coming about every one-and-a-half minutes, you feel as if a quarter of an hour would never end, much less a morning or a day ... Am in superb spirits ...'

(Lord Chandos, letter in *From Peace to War*, 1968.)

'We wander on and our luck remains out, for, at the junction of Elgin Avenue and the fire trench we meet a man with a human arm in his hand. "Whose is that?" I ask. "Rifleman Broderick's, Sir," is the reply. "Where's Broderick?" is my next question. "Up there, Sir," says my informant, pointing to a tree top above our heads. There sure enough is the torn trunk of a man fixed securely in the branches of a shell-stripped oak. A high-explosive shell has recently shot him up to the sky and landed him in mid-air above and out of the reach of his comrades.'

(Brig.-Gen. F. P. Crozier, *A Brass Hat in No Man's Land*, 1930.)

'It was only a matter of luck whether we would make a rapid exit into the next world or not. Some men were perfect philosophers under heavy shellfire, whilst others used to go through severe torture and would cower down, holding their heads in their hands, moaning and trembling. For myself I wasn't worrying so much if a shell pitched clean amongst us: we would never know anything about it. It was the large flying pieces of a shell bursting a few yards off that I didn't like: they could take arms and legs off or, worst still, rip our bellies open and leave us still living. We would know something about *them* all right.'

(Frank Richards, op. cit.)

'Never before, despite my capacity for fear, had I felt myself for so long in the grip of a terror so absolute. All around us was the continuing threat of instant death. Yet I saw no one fall. I saw men crying, and would have cried myself, had I the tears. The company that night was in the grip of a sort of communal terror, a hundred men running like rabbits. I prayed that I would never see its like again.'

(E. N. Gladden, *Ypres 1917* (1967).)

'You're quiet and peaceful, summering safe at home;
You'd never think there was a bloody war on! . . .
O yes, you would . . . why, you can hear the guns.
Hark! Thud, thud, thud – quite soft . . . they never cease –
Those whispering guns – O Christ, I want to go out
And screech at them to stop – I'm going crazy;
I'm going stark, staring mad because of the guns.'

(Siegfried Sassoon, *Repression of War Experience*, 1925.)

It was in 1916 that the unimaginable became reality. This was war on a scale never envisaged, least of all by the sheltered British. The much-maligned General Headquarters, now under Sir Douglas Haig as Commander-in-Chief, was the instrument through which control had to be exercised over the largest army ever put into the field, with all its undreamt-of paraphernalia. One of Haig's staff officers wrote:

'Here at G.H.Q. . . . nearly every one of the ramifications of civil law and life has its counterpart in the administration departments. Food supply, road and rail transport, law and order, engineering, medical work, the Church, education, postal service, even agriculture, and for a population bigger than any single unit of control (except London) in England. Can you imagine what it is to feed, administer, move about, look after the medical and spiritual requirements of a million men, even when they are not engaged in fighting, and not in a foreign country? . . . The work goes on continuously; office hours are far longer than of any civilian office in peacetime. There are few, if any, officers who do not do a fourteen-hour day, and who are not to be found at work far into the night.'

(Brig.-Gen. J. Charteris, op. cit.)

To cope with these complexities, skilled civilian specialists were brought in as staff officers. Sir Eric Geddes, Managing Director of the North-Eastern Railway, was made Director-General of Transport with the rank of Major-General. Haig wrote in his diary:

'There is a good deal of criticism apparently being made at the appointment of a civilian like Geddes to an important post on the Headquarters of an Army in the field. These critics seem to fail to realize the size of this Army, and the amount of work which the Army requires of a civilian nature . . . To put soldiers who have no practical experience of these matters into such positions, merely because they are generals and colonels, must result in utter failure.'

(*The Private Papers of Douglas Haig*, ed. Robert Blake, 1952.)

The statistics of the War are baffling, fantastic, barely comprehensible; here are just a few of them:

Army ration strength, August 1914: 164,000 men, 27,500 animals

Army ration strength, November 1918: 5,363,352 men, 895,770 animals

Maximum strength of the B.E.F. in France: 2,046,901 officers and men

Petrol consumption by B.E.F., 1914: 250,000 gallons per month

Petrol consumption by B.E.F., 1918: 10,500,000 gallons per month

3,092 locomotives and tractors sent to France by December 1918

Total gun ammunition expenditure in France: 170,385,295 rounds

Preliminary bombardment for Third Battle of Ypres (17–31 July 1917): 4,283,550 rounds, costing £22,211,389 14s. 4d.

Maximum ammunition expenditure in 24 hours (Noon, 28–9 September 1918): 943,847 rounds, costing £3,871,000

1910: Royal Aero Club issues 22 flying certificates

1918: Strength of Royal Air Force: 30,122 officers, 263,410 other ranks, 22,000 aircraft

Contributions of Voluntary Organizations:
1,742,947 mufflers
1,574,155 mittens (pairs)
3,607,059 socks (pairs)
6,145,673 hospital bags
12,258,536 bandages
45,503,001 dressings
16,000,000 books
232,599,191 cigarettes
256,487 lbs. of tobacco

Life at the front settled into its beastly patterns; when the dangers of battle were absent, there remained squalor, discomfort and everlasting fatigue. Stretcher Bearer Frank Dunham of the 1/7th London Regiment describes a typical introduction to the front line: through the Lille Gate at Ypres:

'So far things had seemed strangely quiet, the only sound being that of our transport taking rations and ammunition up to the line dumps, but passing through the Gate, we found ourselves on the open roadway, and Very lights could be seen bursting in the distance. This road was ankle deep in mud and slush, and in a very bad state owing to continual shelling, and was crowded with all kinds of transport, guns and troops – naturally the infantry came off the worst, as the horses splashed us all over with mud. Of course, the remnants of the old Battalion had seen this sort of thing before, but to our draft it was all new, and it didn't leave a good impression.'

(War diary of Frank Dunham, *The Long Carry*, 1970.)

'The other night I fell into a ditch when on rounds ... There is so little cover from the enemy that we can seldom use our electric torches to pick the way, with the result that I again stumble into a ditch and am sorry to confess that my curses must have been heard afar. A little later, as if in reproof for them, I sink, *speechless* with anger, through what appears to be a firm surface, up to the waist in a cess-pool. At 2 a.m. I reach my trench shelter. It is too cold to sleep and the coke embers have almost died out.'

(*General Jack's Diary*, ed. John Terraine, 1964.)

'On the night of the 26th all the good gas cylinders were carried to the left flank and if the man who invented them had all the good wishes of the men that were carrying them he would have been in untold agony both before and after his death. The Old Soldier was in magnificent form and going round the trench during the night I met him and the young soldier carrying one of the cylinders. They had a rest and he swore for some minutes, hardly using the same word twice.'

(Frank Richards, op. cit.)

'Long waders were issued to the men going in the front line, which reached to the top of the thigh. They were all right for walking through water but were a nuisance when the trenches were very muddy; often when walking down a communication trench a man would sink in mud above the knees and in trying to get one leg free the other would be sinking deeper. He generally released himself by pulling one leg out of the wader and putting one of his boots on, which we carried with us tied around our necks, and then doing the same with the other leg; and against he had pulled and tugged to release his waders, and fell on his backside in the mud, his curses would be loud and deep enough to blow up every wader factory in the world.'

(ibid.)

Meanwhile the War was making its novel impact on the home population. The inhabitants of coastal towns could expect to be bombarded by sea-raiders, but now the new dimension of air warfare opened up inland towns and the capital itself to attack. As early as September 1914, Sir George Arthur, an eminent Civil Servant, wrote in a letter:

'. . . the King is concerned with nothing except winning the war; even when Winston Churchill casually remarked that if Buckingham Palace were bombed by a Zeppelin it would have a very stimulating effect upon the people, the King only mildly suggested it might have a very depressing effect on him.'

(*Further Letters of a Man of No Importance*, 1932.)

In all, the German Zeppelin airships made some forty raids on Britain, dropped 220 tons of bombs, killed 537 people and injured 1,358. This was not a very impressive record in itself, but it had a considerable shock effect. Michael MacDonagh wrote after the raid of 9 September 1915, in which thirty-eight were killed and 124 injured:

'I had another novel War experience last night. I was writing in my study about twenty minutes to eleven o'clock when the roar of bombs and guns broke upon my meditations, and, stepping out upon a little balcony of the room at the back of the house, commanding a wide sweep of the sky north-east, I saw an amazing spectacle. High in the sky was a Zeppelin picked out of the darkness by searchlights, a long narrow object of a silvery hue! I felt like what a watcher of the skies must feel when a new planet swims into his ken. For it was my first sight of an enemy airship!'

(Michael MacDonagh, op. cit.)

More dangerous, and above all more ominous for the future, were the raids by Gotha aeroplanes which began in 1917. These killed

*836 people and injured 1,982. On 7 July, Michael MacDonagh
witnessed the raid on London carried out by twenty-two Gothas,
which killed fifty-seven people and injured 193:*

'I heard the weird swish of a bomb as it plunged downwards
through the air and the roaring, rending explosion of its
fall. Instantly the scene in the streets was wholly transformed.
The policeman standing near the monument of Queen
Victoria worked himself into a state of excitement, shouting
"Take cover! Take cover!" and wildly waving his arms.
Everybody ran hither and thither for shelter. I joined the
rush for the Blackfriars station of the Underground. We
tumbled down the stairs to the platform of the trains going
west, and ran along it to its end, some distance under the
roadway. A second terrific explosion had given added
swiftness to our feet. The girls of the Lyon's and ABC tea-
shops at the station were in our wake, some of them being
helped down, screaming hysterically. For my part, I felt that
I had been plunged suddenly into a confused phantasmal
state of being encompassed with dangers as in a nightmare.
"The raiders have London at their mercy," I kept saying
to myself; "there are no defences against them."'

(ibid.)

*The feeling of helplessness against attack from the air bred
hysteria out of all proportion to the damage done. Sir William
Robertson (C.I.G.S.) wrote to Sir Douglas Haig on 9 July:*

'The result of the air-raid on Saturday was the calling of a
special Cabinet meeting in the afternoon at which much
excitement was shown. One would have thought that the
world was coming to an end.'

(John Terraine, *Douglas Haig: The Educated Soldier, 1963.*)

*Home Front panics ... Home Front victories ... one pre-War
struggle at least was now decided without further ado. Mr J. L.
Garvin, editor of the* Observer, *wrote in a leader on 13 August
1916:*

'Time was when I thought that men alone maintained the State. Now I know that men alone never could have maintained it, and that henceforth the modern State must be dependent on men and women alike for the progressive strength and vitality of its whole organization.'

Michael MacDonagh reported on 29 March 1917:

'The House of Commons yesterday recognised the services of women to the State by approving, by 341 votes to 62, woman suffrage, which is included in a scheme of electoral reform to come into operation at the end of the War. The motion was moved by Asquith, who in a fine speech recanted the stout opposition which he gave to votes for women before the War. Women, he said, had worked out their own salvation in the War. The War could not have been carried on without them: and he felt it impossible to withhold from them the right of making their voice heard on the problems of the country's reconstruction when the War was over.'

(Michael MacDonagh, op. cit.)

It was the mass participation of women in the War effort – in industry, in the Civil Service, and in the Forces – which produced this result so deeply desired by the pre-War Suffragette Movement. It was not greeted with universal enthusiasm; nor were the means by which it was obtained always admired. One soldier at the Front wrote to his wife in May 1918:

'Well, I am afraid there will be trouble if they try to take married women into the W.A.A.C. We men can stand a lot, but they are nearing the danger zone when they wish to force our wives into service. Goodness, the damned infernal impudence of wanting our wives! Why, if anyone came for you whilst I was at home, I'd slit his throat open. I'm not bragging I'm saying what I mean. How little they understand us, they are running up against trouble with a vengeance, they will find they have signed their death warrant.'

(Censor's extract from letter, quoted in John Terraine, *Impacts of War, 1914 and 1918,* 1970.)

The Front-line war continued, the endless casualty lists recorded the toll of human life; the physical destruction mounted day by day. It was not surprising that nerves frayed, and revulsion mounted among those who had to endure these sufferings.

'Evil and the incarnate fiend alone can be master of this war, and no glimmer of God's hand is seen anywhere. Sunset and sunrise are blasphemous, they are mockeries to man, only the black rain out of the bruised and swollen clouds all through the bitter black of night is fit atmosphere in such a land. The rain drives on, the stinking mud becomes more evilly yellow, the shell-holes fill up with green-white water, the roads and tracks are covered in inches of slime, the black dying trees ooze and sweat and the shells never cease . . .'

(Paul Nash, war artist, quoted in A. Marwick, *The Deluge*, 1965.)

'. . . this country stinks of corruption. As far as the eye can reach is that brown and torn sea of desolation and every yard there is a grave, some marked with rifles, others with crosses, some with white skulls, some with beckoning hands. But everything is dead: the trees, the fields, the corn, the church, even the prayers of those that went there in their Sunday clothes with their sweaty pennies for the plate: it is all dead and God has utterly forsaken it.

' "O prosper thou the work of our hands upon us", forsooth. But the pipes and the saffron kilts brought us back to life and the warm red blood of youth and laughter, and we walked among the dead and thought only of the spring and its awakening.'

(Lord Chandos, op. cit.)

To make all this endurable, the soldiers invented a vocabulary, a style of humour (closely modelled upon that of the old Regulars) all of their own. They cheered and braced themselves with sardonic sayings:

'Dear Mother, this war's a bugger. Sell the pig and buy me out. John. Dear John, pig's gone. Soldier on.'
'Dear Aunty, hoping this finds you as it leaves me. We are

wading up to our necks in blood. Send fags and a life-belt.'
'Some fell by the wayside, and the Sergeant-Majors sprang
up and choked them.'
'Are we downhearted?
No!
Then you bloody soon will be!'
'Oh, to be shot at dawn!'
'Roll on, Duration!'
'What did you do in the Great War, daddy?
Shut up you little bastard! Get the Bluebell and go and clean
my medals.'

(All Anon.)

*And steadily, year by year, the Home Front learned the meaning of
total war – conscription, bombardment, shortages, rationing. F. S.
Oliver wrote in a letter to Canada in September 1917:*

'I never knew till last summer what a delicious thing a
potato was, that is, when I couldn't buy any; nor did I ever
realise the transcendant luxury of white bread. The stuff
you get from the baker really automatically rations the
consumer because it is so abominable now as to destroy any
greediness which may still lurk in our natures.'

(F. S. Oliver, *The Anvil of War*, 1936.)

In March 1918 he wrote:

'We are not exactly starving; but we are pretty pinched. I
daresay it is quite good for some of us. I have lost a stone
since June. We practically never have butcher's meat. Two
very small pats of butter a day is my own allowance, and the
equivalent of one good slice of bread per diem divided
unequally between breakfast, lunch and dinner. The people,
bless them, bear it very well. But there is no use pretending
that the food problem is not serious; for it is damnably so.'

(ibid.)

'After the experience which tens of thousands of people
must have undergone during the past week-end it is idle to

mince words. The whole country is confronted with a meat famine.'

(*The Times*, 7 January 1918.)

'There is reason to fear that the persistence of the unequal distribution of food and of its offspring, the queue system, is beginning to tell on the tempers of numbers of people. Here and there the discontent engendered by the scramble for margarine and meat which has been the cause of the insistent and universal demand for rationing, is finding an outlet in demonstrations and disorderliness . . .'

(*The Times*, 18 January 1918.)

'We are all on an equality under this system of rationing. The papers announce that the King and Queen have received their cards from the Westminster food committee, and that everyone in Buckingham Palace is on rations.'

(Michael MacDonagh, op. cit.)

March and April 1918 were the period of the great German offensives against the British Army in France. This was probably the period of the most savage fighting of the War – in six weeks British casualties practically equalled those sustained in the fourteen weeks of 'Passchendaele'. It was certainly a period when the danger of outright defeat loomed very large. Then followed an interval of recuperation, as the Germans turned their attention to the French. G.H.Q. decided that this was the time to test the mood of the Army; the Censorship department undertook a close scrutiny of soldiers' letters. Some, as might be expected, reflected the hard times so recently endured:

'You will probably have seen a few bits about us in the newspapers (Glorious Deeds!). If you ever hear anybody say that the troops are in excellent spirits just refer them to this battery. The sooner one side wins the better and we know who will win (*not us*).'

'I am sure we are on the wrong side, what do you think about it? I think we get worse off every day for food, and it's a misery to be under the officers that are coming out now.'

'Any one reading the papers can see that our Government is full of corruption, that is what has made a chap sick of the whole business out here, there are a good many out here my dear like myself fed up and don't care a damn which side wins. After four years and now we are being pushed back and no end in sight.'

'We are expecting Fritz over any time now. I think the quicker he drives us out of France the better, it is quite time to end it somehow or other . . . everybody is fed up with the war out here and don't care who wins so long as we can get it over.'

(Censor's extracts, *Impacts of War*, op. cit.)

The pessimists were only a minority. Despite the gruelling battles which had just taken place, and despite the fact that the ranks were now being filled with young conscripts of a very different type from Lord Kitchener's 1914 volunteers, the bulk of the letters inspected by the Censor reflected only that wonderful devotion which had sustained the Army for nearly four years. This was the true mood of the Expeditionary Force in France in 1918:

'The night previous to our departure from the billet for the trenches we were all singing and a chap just remarked "You would think we were going home instead of going into the arena", but this is where we beat Fritz; in dark days or bright, we don't lose heart, "Jerry" may give us a smack today, but he will get a harder one tomorrow. Really I am so proud to be a British soldier and to be able to fight to the bitter end for British interest and it is the same with us all here.'

'They may attack any day, but we shall obey our chief's command and have our backs to the wall, and not one inch will we retire. No one knows it better than the Huns.'

'I can bear testimony to the splendid qualities of our troops, they are perhaps the biggest lot of growsers under the sun, but they have their growse and finish with it and always fight well. No task is too great for them to undertake, but they must have their growse with it, it is part of their lives. I really believe as you say that Jerry will not digest the lump he has bitten, on the contrary I think he will receive a severe attack of indigestion from us before long.'

'It is no use being pessimistic Clara for I tell you we are bound to win with the men we have got. I have just seen a battalion of them going into the trenches. They look into the gates of Hell and laugh, this every day and night, and I tell you the boys of Britain cannot be beat.'

'For God's sake don't talk about us being beat. Fancy if a letter like that fall into German hands they would think we were really beaten and we are far from that yet. You must not think about being beat. Never mind what you hear we will win yet. I would rather see you all in the grave as see the Bosche win.'

(Censor's extracts.)

This was the spirit which made possible the magnificent revival of the Army in the summer of 1918, and the series of great victorious battles which brought the war to an end. The British role in those final victories has rarely been appreciated; it is best summarized in the following striking statistics for the period 8 August (opening of the Battle of Amiens) to 11 November:

	Prisoners	Guns
Captures by British Army	188,700	2,840
All other Allies (France, America, Belgium)	196,700	3,775

Here at last was the fruit of the great battles of attrition which had taken such a terrible toll during the middle years. A Times *Special Correspondent wrote on 26 August:*

'These are great days. It surely must be that they will even loom greatly in history, but they are certainly great to live in . . . The sweep of our advance is so rapid that no man can say where our advanced line as a whole may stand at any given moment, for every half-hour brings news that this or that village is in our hands, or that an airman has seen the khaki figures somewhere where we never dreamed that they had reached . . . When one remembers what the names of Thiepval, and Fricourt, and Mametz and Contal-maison meant in the old days of 1916, and Le Sars and Warlencourt, it is difficult to realize that we have again swept over all that ground between Friday night and Sunday morning . . .'

(*The Times*, 26 August 1918.)

The transformation of the war which had taken place is summed up in an order of Field-Marshal Sir Douglas Haig to his Army Commanders:

'Risks which a month ago would have been criminal to incur ought now to be incurred as a duty.'

(Order of the Day, 22 August 1918.)

But Haig now had his eye firmly fixed on the greatest prize of all. The Minister of Munitions, Mr Winston Churchill, visited him at G.H.Q. to discuss production programmes, and Haig noted in his diary:

'His schemes are all timed for completion next June. I told him we ought to do our utmost to get a decision this autumn.'

(*The Private Papers of Douglas Haig*, op. cit.)

Thanks to sound leadership and the wonderful spirit of the soldiers, the decision was reached that autumn – on 11 November at 11 a.m. the Armistice came into force. Stretcher Bearer Frank Dunham wrote:

'This morning news of the Armistice reached us, but there was little excitement in our vicinity and discipline seemed to relax at once. My pal Percy, now on leave in London, took the opportunity to send me a postcard on this day and it proves what a friend he was.'

(Dunham, op. cit.)

So, on a note as characteristically matter-of-fact as that with which the old Regulars had gone to war, the new Regulars greeted the coming of peace. Arthur Behrend wrote:

'November 11 found the majority of us still at Salesches – ten or more miles behind our infantry and at least twenty from the nearest Germans – and a small group of officers assembled outside the Adjutant's office and greeted eleven o'clock with a half-hearted cheer. We had no beer, no gin, no cigarettes.'

(Arthur Behrend, *As From Kemmel Hill*, 1963.)

General J. L. Jack, now commanding the 28th Brigade in the 9th (Scottish) Division, wrote:

'At last I lie down tired and very happy, but sleep is elusive ... Incidents flash through the memory: the battles of the first four months; the awful winters in waterlogged trenches, cold and miserable; the terrible trench-war assaults and shell-fire of the next three years; loss of friends, exhaustion and wounds; the stupendous victories of the last few months; all our enemies beaten to their knees. Thank God! The end of a frightful four years ...'

(*General Jack's Diary*, op. cit.)

Robert Graves, on leave in Wales on Armistice day, recalled in later years:

'The news sent me out walking alone along the dyke above the marshes of Rhuddlan, cursing and sobbing and thinking of the dead.

'Siegfried's* famous poem celebrating the Armistice began:

"Everybody suddenly burst out singing,
      And I was filled with such delight
      As prisoned birds must find in freedom ..."

'But "everybody" did not include me.'

(Robert Graves, *Goodbye to All That*, 1929.)

*Siegfried Sassoon.

9

The Hungry Years, 1918–40

DONALD NICHOLL

Every future historian of modern England should be compelled to take a good long slow walk round Gateshead. After that he can at his leisure fit it into his interpretation of our national growth and development.

(J. B. Priestley, *English Journey*, 1934.)

For historians of England 'the hungry years' began in 1929 with the Depression, but for many of the workers they never had a beginning, since depression, unemployment and hunger were a permanent condition of their lives and one from which they received only occasional relief. Already in 1922, for instance, 43 per cent of Jarrow's employable persons were out of work, whilst 47 per cent in Brynmawr and 60 per cent in Hartlepool were in the same condition.

Similarly, even before the end of the First World War the divisions of England, later to be signalized by the General Strike of 1926, were already being widened. There were mutinies in the armed forces which reminded the upper classes uncomfortably of the Russian Revolution; they were followed by a series of strikes which led The Times *to proclaim that 'this war, like the war with Germany, must be a fight to a finish' (27 September 1919).*

This civil strife arose principally amongst the miners, ship builders, railwaymen and farm workers, that is, in the declining sections of the economy. Consequently, when the showdown came in 1926 it was not really a 'fight to the finish', because the power had shifted to other sections of the economy; and after ten days of General Strike all the workers gave in, except the miners – and even they were forced to surrender five months later.

In comparison with the unforgiving bitterness of class war abroad, however, the social divisions within England, at least, were almost always mitigated by a number of factors: a common memory of what it means to be an Englishman; reverence for the monarchy; a residual common religion; the instinctive communion of sport; and a saving humour.

Not all these factors were present to the same degree in the three cultures that were becoming so clearly delineated after 1926, but they were present in each of them to some degree or another. The first, and oldest, of these cultures was the rural one in which archaic relationships still persisted between labourers, farmers and landowners. The second, itself already beginning to seem archaic, was the industrial culture that had scarred Northern England, the Black Country, South Wales and Clydeside. The third of these cultures was only now beginning to emerge, along the arterial roads connecting South-east England with the Midlands; it was centred not around agriculture or heavy industry, the church or the chapel, the cricket and football pitch and the Co-op, but around the light industries, electronics and plastics, the service and entertainment trades, the semi-detached house and the private car. In many respects this third England was America.

But it was upon the second of these cultures, the industrial one, that the burden of 'the hungry years' fell heaviest. Bare statistics do, in this case, give some impression of the burden. Unemployment, for instance, devastated Jarrow, Merthyr Tydfil and Maryport in 1934 to the extent that 68 per cent, 62 per cent, and 57 per cent respectively of the insured workers of these towns were out of work whereas in High Wycombe it was 3·3 per cent, Coventry and Oxford 5 per cent and not much more in most of the South-east. Unemployment meant that people did not have enough money for food, houses, clothing or medicine. Already at the beginning of the century it had been found that twelve-year-old boys at private schools were on average five inches taller and correspondingly heavier than their working-class counterparts, and in 1935 it was still true that 62 per cent of the volunteers for the Army – almost entirely working-class – were found to be below the comparatively low standard of physique required.

Inadequate food inevitably resulted in bad health, a high death rate among expectant mothers and many deaths among newly born children. The connection was vividly demonstrated in 1936 when as a result of the food distribution in the Rhondda Valley, at the instigation of Lady Williams, maternal mortality fell by 75 per cent. Once again comparisons are relevant: in 1935, when the infant death rate was only 42 per thousand live births in the Home Counties, it was 63 in Glamorgan, 76 in Durham, 77 in Scotland, 92 in Sunderland and 114 in Jarrow.

But in addition to these burdens so vividly recorded in statistics the people had to bear the further burden of knowing that they and their culture were under oppression from the wealthier, better-fed, better-housed, educated, powerful élite who ran the country. Their consciousness of oppression was now sharpened by the fact of having to listen to slights from the rich on the radio, in the newspapers and in the compulsory school system. Some of them, under the sting of poverty and arrogance, abandoned their traditional cultures. Over a million people between the ages of fifteen and forty-five emigrated into the South-east between 1923 and 1938.

Those who remained tried to defend themselves in a variety of ways: they organized strikes and gave their support to left-wing political parties. But their most dramatic gesture, calling attention to their plight, was the Hunger March upon London, whether from Glasgow or Jarrow or South Wales. In November 1936, for instance, almost a quarter of a million of these Hunger Marchers gathered in Hyde Park, and the English élite responded, as was their habit, by invoking the spectre of Communism.

Yet what enabled the people to survive the hungry years was the strength of their traditional way of life, sustained by the comradeship of the workshop or the mine, relaxation in the public house, worship in the church or chapel and – for more and more – the hope of quick wealth through gambling. Also in these years a new factor was emerging: they became aware of other working classes, either the Irish emigrants whom they still saw as a threat, or the Spanish ones whose cause they passionately supported in the Civil War.

Victory

'Ahr soldiers goin' to war
Ahr soldiers feightin'
Ahr soldiers stickin bayonets
Up the Germans' ahrsole

Djers goin' to war
Ahr soldiers feightin'
Ahr soldiers stickin bayonets
Up the Germans' . . .'

(Street song of West Riding children, in 'Memories of a York-shire Boyhood', an unpublished manuscript by Donald Nicholl.)

'Many a time I were in t' trenches an' it were a bit quiet I used to daydream about what it'd be like when it were all over an' we went 'ome.

'I could see all t' battalion gettin' off t' train at t' station an' marchin' up 'Orton Street, wearin' us medals, an' all t' lasses cheerin' us and t' band playin'. An' t' Mayor comin' to welcome us back.

'But when I did get back it were at night, on t' last train from Bradford. An' I were t' only one 'at gott off at t' station. An' as I walked up 'Orton Street it were that quiet, just sound o' mi boots on t' pavement.

'I were forced to smile to miself remembering how I used to dream about what it would be like.

'Th' only person I saw were a bobby, as I passed t' Town 'All. An' he said, "Good night, lad", an' I allus remember 'earin t' Town 'All clock strikin' twelve.

'Then I walked up t' lane, an' there were no band playin'. But I didn't mind 'cos I were 'ome again.'

(George Harrison of Halifax, ibid.)

'But the old world was restored and we returned
To the dreary field and workshop, and the immemorial
feud
Of rich and poor. Our victory was our defeat . . .'

(Herbert Read, 'To a Conscript of 1940', *Collected Poems*, 1946.)

'We all know that in the industrial world the capitalists would give us peace tomorrow if we would surrender. But I am not going to surrender. I am not going to be a pacifist in the industrial movement. I believe that even in our own country there will have to be the shedding of blood to attain the freedom we require . . .'

(Ernest Bevin, labour leader, speaking in the Leeds Coliseum on 3 June 1917, quoted in Alan Bullock, *The Life and Times of Ernest Bevin*, Vol. I, 1960.)

'I was a sergeant and I marched the troops off the dock in spite of all the colonels and majors and lesser fry . . . and the guard of marines opened the gates to let us out. When I got them about half a mile from the huts, I halted them, and addressed them from the top of a bank and told them to stand firm, as the authorities would be giving them some soft soap as well as threats, which afterwards proved to be the case.

'The next day the General came down from the Admiralty (we being under the discipline of the marines) and formed us up in three sides of a square, drove his motor car into the centre, read the Army Act out, and then invited any man to step out and go to work who liked; I was made to fall out on the right by myself.

'You can imagine my feelings, as being an old soldier of over twenty years service, of course, I knew the consequences of my act.

'But I never saw such loyal men in my life, not one man moved. I could hear the sergeants in the rear of the men telling them to stand by me, and it was well they did or I should have got ten years or so.

'The following Monday one thousand of us were demobbed, my name at the head of the list.'

(G.P. from North Shields, in Tom Wintringham, *Mutiny*, 1936.)

The Older World

'Myself, my family, my generation, were born in a world of silence; a world of hard work and necessary patience, of backs bent to the ground, hands massaging the crops, of waiting on weather and growth; of villages like ships in the empty landscapes and the long walking distances between them: of white narrow roads, rutted by hooves and cart-wheels, innocent of oil or petrol, down which people passed rarely, and almost never for pleasure, and the horse was the fastest thing moving. Man and horse were all the power we had – abetted by levers and pulleys. But the horse was king, and almost everything grew around him: fodder, smithies, stables, paddocks, distances and the rhythm of our days. His eight miles an hour was the limit of our movements, as it had been since the days of the Romans. That eight miles an hour was life and death, the size of our world, our prison.

'This was what we were born to, and all we knew at first. Then, to the scream of the horse, the change began. The brass-lamped motor-car came coughing up the road. Soon the village would break, dissolve and scatter, become no more than a place for pensioners.'

(Laurie Lee, a Gloucestershire man, *Cider With Rosie*, 1959.)

'The hirings reminded me of slave markets. I left school at the age of thirteen and a half in 1917 and was hired to a farmer for £12 for one year, being classed as a "lad" on the farm. On Martinmas Day a year later I received my £12 and was free for further employment. This was when we used to say:

> Good morning, Mister Martinmas,
> You've come to set me free.
> I don't give a toss for my master
> And he don't give one for me.'

(An East Riding man of about thirty, in Leslie Baily and Charles H. Brewer, *Scrapbook*, 1937.)

Fight to a Finish

'1922 March, the *Daily News* reported that an ex-soldier of the Royal Field Artillery was living with his wife and four children in London under a patchwork shack of tarpaulins, old army groundsheets and bits of tin and canvas. "If they'd told me in France that I should come back to this I wouldn't have believed it. Sometimes I wished to God the Germans had knocked me out."'

(John Montgomery, *The Twenties*, 1970.)

'In the interests of economy they condemned hundreds of children to death, and I call it murder ... It is a fearful thing for any man to have on his soul – a cold callous, deliberate crime in order to save money. We are prepared to destroy children in the great interest of dividends. We put children out in the front of the firing line.'

(Jimmy Maxton, of the Independent Labour Party, in the House of Commons, June 1923. C. McAllister, *James Maxton*, 1935.)

'Look, Dad, if any trouble's being caused it can't be blamed on us. The war's been over for years and where's the homes fit for heroes? They say we won the war – and where are the winnings? In the pockets of the big boys and it's mugs like us being asked to take the can back as per usual. Ten per cent off wages and a longer working day, that's what the coal owners are shouting for.'

(Jim Moleyns, of Salford, in Walter Greenwood, *There Was a Time*, 1967.)

'We lived in a colliery house, and me mother, she was such a conscientious woman she would never go to bed except on a Saturday, because you had me father in one shift, our Jimmy in another shift, me in another shift and Tommy in another.

'And it sometimes meant the clock round, one coming in and one going out, and she was so conscientious that if there was an hour or two hours to spare between one and the other, she would just sit in the rocking chair in front of the fire, and I've known for months on end the only time me mother got to bed was a Saturday night when there was no work at the pit.'

(Monty Lowther, of Durham, BBC Archive Disc.)

'Our case is simple. We ask for safety and economic security. Today up and down our coalfields the miner and his family are faced with sheer starvation. He is desperate. He will not, he cannot stand present conditions much longer. He would be a traitor to his wife and children if he did. Until he is given safety in mines, adequate compensation, hours of labour that do not make him a mere coal-getting medium, and decent living conditions, there can be no peace in the British coalfields.'

(A. J. Cook, miners' leader, in Leslie Baily and Charles H. Brewer, op. cit.)

'Sir John Simon says the General Strike is illegal under an Act passed by William the Conqueror in 1066. All strikers are liable to be interned in Wormwood Scrubs. The three million strikers are advised to keep in hiding, preferably in the park behind Bangor Street, where they will not be discovered.'

(Kensington strike bulletin, issued after Sir John Simon's pronouncement that the General Strike was illegal. Allen Hutt, *The Post-War History of the British Working Class*, 1937.)

'Keep smiling. Refuse to be provoked. Get into your garden. Look after the wife and kiddies. If you have not got a garden, get into the country, the parks and the playgrounds.'

(Cardiff Strike Committee, in T. A. Critchley, *The Conquest of Violence*, 1970.)

'"Bastards," Jack Lashwood said bitterly, to the congregation of strikers on our street corner. He was an elderly collier, a tall, scrawny man with a thin neck and blue marks on his skull which showed through his close-cropped hair, relics, they were, of roof falls, "I know what I'd like to do with 'em."

'"It's a game for them, Jack," James Moleyns said.

'"Game?" he retorted with pop-eyed indignation, "Six loaves of bread a week, that's what two shillin's wage cut means to me. Game? Kids goin' short o' grub? It's a fine bloody game.'''

(Jack Lashwood, of Salford, in Walter Greenwood, op. cit.)

'The old crystal set was the vogue then and there was an eagerness to receive the news and like the old story-teller, anybody who had a crystal set, even in 1926, was continuously being asked: "What's the news?"'

(BBC Archive Disc.)

'We heard Jimmy Thomas almost crying as he announced the terms of what we thought were surrender, and we went back with our tails between our legs to see what the bosses were going to do with us. I was told within a couple of days that I had been dismissed the service – a very unusual thing, and I think that very few station masters in the Kingdom can say that they had had the sack, but that was the case with me, and I know at least two more who had the same experience.'

(Railwayman, BBC Archive Disc.)

'There is no moral justification for a General Strike of this character. It is therefore a sin against the obedience which we owe to God ... All are bound to uphold and assist the Government, which is the lawfully-constituted authority of the country and represents therefore, in its own appointed sphere, the authority of God himself.'

(Cardinal Bourne, Roman Catholic Archbishop of Westminster, in Westminster Cathedral, 9 May 1926, quoted in Julian Symonds, *The General Strike*, 1957.)

LOVING MEMORY
'Some time we know we'll meet them,
  Sometime, we know not when,
  In a beautiful land of sunshine,
  Never to part again.'

(In Memoriam from local English newspapers.)

'One Whose life I revere and Who, I believe, is the greatest Figure in history, has put it on record: "Those who take the sword shall perish by the sword" . . . If mine was the only voice in this Conference, I would say in the name of the faith I hold, the belief I have that God intended us to live peaceably and quietly with one another, if some people do not allow us to do so, I am ready to stand as the early Christians did, and say, "This is our faith, this is where we stand, and, if necessary, this is where we will die."'

(George Lansbury, Labour M.P., in R. Postgate, *Life of George Lansbury*, 1957.)

'The government has gained immense prestige in the world and the British Labour movement has made itself ridiculous. A strike which opens with a football match between police and strikers and ends nine days later with densely-packed reconciliation services will make the continental Socialists blaspheme. We are all of us just good-natured stupid folk.'

(Beatrice Webb, a Fabian Socialist, in Kitty Muggeridge, *Beatrice Webb*, 1967.)

The Divisions of Society

'I happened to be standing beside Lady Astor, M.P., and she said, "McGovern, this is a wonderful scene. This is what makes Old England such a great nation." I replied, "But there are two Englands . . ." [As the King finished his Speech] I called out, "What about the restoration of the cuts in the unemployed allowances and the end of the Means Test" . . .

'Two Conservative M.P.s caught hold of my arms. I said in a loud and angry voice, "Let me go, you gang of lazy, idle parasites, living on the wealth produced by the workers. You ought to think shame on yourselves with all this splendour, pomp and ceremony while millions are starving outside." '

(John McGovern, of the Independent Labour Party, *Neither Fear Nor Favour*, 1960.)

'[A Socialist speaker had won my admiration until he said] "What is this England you are supposed to love? It is only a tiny portion of the earth's surface. Why should you be expected to love it, or be prepared to die for it any more than you would for Russia, or China, or Greenland."

'I was thunderstruck. "Because it's England!" I yelled out in fury.

'Didn't he know that most of the happiness that ever I had came from this love of England that he spoke so contemptuously about? Didn't they know that in the early winter mornings when the frost glittered on the half frozen fields and the air was so clear and sharp that it hurt one's nostrils, or in the hot summer afternoons when the forest of Sherwood was quiet under the heavy heat except for the popping of the bursting broom-pods – that England spoke to you? How she told you the wonderful stories of famous men who fought and ruled and died because of their love for her. Of the simple men who toiled, ploughed, reaped, loved every handful of her brown soil and died still loving her.'

(G. A. W. Tomlinson, a Nottinghamshire coal miner, *Coal Miner*, 1937.)

[On the conveyor belt car industry]

'The whole business, in my opinion, was one of human degradation. Any man of spirit preferred the dole rather than the comparatively high pay that might be earned . . . The type of man who was ready to submit to such regimentation was not the type with whom I, for one, had been accustomed to mix. I found them a craven lot, spineless, money-grabbing, selfish, without a sense of fraternity or loyalty to their fellow-workers . . . Even to this day, such is my revulsion that I cannot see one of their cars on the road without a feeling of disgust.'

(Walter Greenwood, of Salford, *How the Other Man Lives*, 1939.)

'We are happy in our own little world, and we know how to get along. Ma over her fish and chips is happier than many a rich lady at her banquet. And we know how to work things out in our own little world so that we get along some way. But you take us into another world – we're not fit for it. What an ass So and So has made of himself up there in Parliament! What does he know about ruling the country? No, there are them as are made to manage the country's affairs, lad, and they've got the brains to do it.'

(A Cockney worker in E. Wight Bakke, *The Unemployed Man*, 1933.)

'We had seen the changing of the guard, and the crowd had melted. We had stepped across into the Park to rest a while, for Laura was just a little tired. She sat facing the Palace; I sat with my back to it. "Jack look," she cried. I turned to find her on her knees, pointing at a car in which the King was sitting.

' "Don't point, girl." The King noticed, smiled, raised his hat, all in less time than it takes to tell, and he was gone. Laura knelt watching the motor-car until it was out of sight.'

(Jack Jones, from Merthyr Tydfil, *Unfinished Journey*, 1937.)

'As we stood waiting for His Majesty, amid the gold and crimson of the Palace, I could not help marvelling at the strange turn of Fortune's wheel, which had brought MacDonald, the starveling clerk, Thomas the engine-driver, Henderson the foundry labourer and Clynes, the mill-hand to this pinnacle.'

(J. R. Clynes, ex-mill-hand, Minister in the Labour Government, quoted in C. L. Mowat, *Britain Between the Wars*, 1955.)

Unemployed

'Everybody does some work in this world. You can go back as far as Adam, and you'll find that they all work some way, with their brains if not with their hands. That's one thing that makes us human; we don't wait for things to happen to us, we work for them. And if you can't find any work to do, you have the feeling that you're not human. You're out of place. You're so different from all the rest of the people around that you think something is wrong with you.'

(A Midlands worker in E. Wight Bakke, op. cit.)

'Just watch those children sitting on the dockyard wall
Watching their father do nothing at all
Some day or other they'll be dockyardees too
Just like their father with nothing to do.'

(Anonymous poem from Liverpool, BBC Archive Disc.)

'Two years last July the mill closed down. It was a struggle on the full employment allowance, but we made ends meet somehow. Didn't get into debt. Then seven months ago we were put on the Means Test. They gave us 31s. It was no good. God knows we watched every halfpenny, cut out everything we didn't need. But it couldn't be done. You can't feed six on 31s. when you have to pay 8s. rent.

'"We've got crooked for the first time in our married life," says the woman. "We're £12 in debt in six months." '

(Husband and wife from Great Harwood, Lancashire, in A. Fenner Brockway, *Hungry England*, 1932.)

'Another woman, asked, "Ever get a bit of pleasure?" "Yes: once a week we go to the pictures. The three children at 2d. each; I have to pay 5d. That's 11d. in all. It's a big slice in the week's money, but for me it's pictures or going mad. It's the only time I forget my troubles. I wish Hugh – my husband – would come. It would do him good, even if it meant going short of a little more food. But he won't. Says he hasn't any troubles to forget! He goes to the Weavers' Club and waits for us, though what he does there I don't know. Just talks, I suppose. He doesn't drink. He hasn't drunk for seven years." '

(A Lancashire woman, in ibid.)

'I remember walking through the streets – they lived near Merthyr – and being amazed simply by the number of people there were in it. The street was simply crowded and you could hardly move. The extraordinary thing about it was that the people were not doing anything – they were not moving, they were leaning against lamp posts, smoking cigarettes – those who had some – almost immobile, as if they were turned to stone, and I suddenly realised that this was what went on every day of the week in Merthyr. The entire population was unemployed and that is almost literally true, apart from the shopkeepers and they were giving credit to people who couldn't afford it, and this was really like seeing a world turned to stone, absolutely dead. And as far as one could see, without any hope whatever of ever reviving again.'

(G. Rees, a Welshman, BBC Archive Disc.)

'What we cannot buy we cannot have. It means having chilled meat once a week, half a pint of milk a day instead of a pint, no eggs, no jam and three-quarters of a pound of butter. We miss the eggs and milk most for we are not big meat-eaters at the best of times. I have a small garden and I grow potatoes to last half the winter and some summer vegetables too. That makes a big difference to us. My wife bakes a small cake once a week, and that is the extent of our diet – no meat after Sunday, no fish, bacon, eggs or jam. And I must say we miss these things more as time goes on and we grow more tired of bread and butter and cheese.'

(Unemployed millwright from Derby, quoted in H. L. Beales and R. S. Lambert, *Memoirs of the Unemployed*, 1934.)

'Nobody was well off. For instance, it was common when we left the yard at dinner time to find outside the yard hoards of children with no shoes on their feet, begging, "Any left, please, any left?" and that would be any left from our snacks, which we used to take out and give to them.'

(Hubert Medland, of Liverpool, BBC Archive Disc.)

'In one of the older streets containing a large proportion of back-to-back houses with very small, airless rooms, little access to sun, and leaking roof and walls oozing with damp as many as 17 cases [of consumption] were notified from the 29 houses in the street . . . In one such case one of the two small bedrooms was given up to a dying girl, while the father and mother and six children crowded into the second bedroom and living room (used also as a bedroom). It is not to be wondered at that two other children contracted the disease, and that two out of the three infected children died within two years.'

(Hilda Jennings, in *Brynmawr*, 1934.)

'Every day I walked down a little grey street and I had to pass a window which had no curtains; on a bed just inside a man was dying of a disease contracted in the mine, and they'd gradually sold everything in the house to pay for his illness and they'd finally had to sell the curtains, so he was dying in full view of the street.'

(Beverley Nichols, journalist.)

'Our observations did not disclose any widespread manifestation of impaired health which could be attributed to insufficiency of nourishment. In this view we are confirmed by the opinions of the medical practitioners who have the best opportunities of watching the physical condition of families.'

(Report of Ministry of Health Investigation in the Coalfield of South Wales and Monmouth, 1929.)

'I have been coming to the view since I began these investigations that as regards social conditions and business practice affecting the common people of this land of ours, no one knows anything about anything that really matters.'

(John Hilton, a Bolton worker who became a professor, *Rich Man, Poor Man*, 1944.)

Resistance

'I am one of those men who come from a town that has been
fighting for seven weeks . . . I am one of those men who have
been knocked and kicked about by the police for the last
few weeks . . . I was running six looms for a matter of 35s.
a week, and I had five bellies to fill out of that wage. Now
the employer has come along and says he wants 3s. 4d. out
of that. Isn't that enough to get a man's back up? We have
got eight thousand people in Burnley fighting on 12s. 4d.
a week and they are as firm as a rock . . .'

(Burnley working man, in Branson and Heinemann, *Britain in the
Nineteen Thirties*, 1971.)

'I lowered the newspaper I was glancing through as the
wireless filled our living-room with music, dance music.
When the "number" being played ended, a most irritating
voice topped the background of chatter and laughter
against which the band had been playing to inform us that
we were listening to so-and-so's band from the Savoy Hotel,
London – "turn that off, son," I shouted. "Why?" said
David. I got up and turned it off myself . . . "Dance music
from the Savoy Hotel, London, and the men of the mining
valleys rotting in heaps." '

(Jack Jones, op. cit.)

'There are hundreds and thousands of young men who do
not show any disposition to bestir themselves to get out of
unemployment into employment. They are content with a
life of laziness . . . there is a slackness of moral fibre and of
will as a muscle . . . Salutary action is necessary beyond
dispute . . . the breakdown of morale can only be made
good by applying compulsion.'

(*The Times*, 22 February 1938.)

'I have suffered hardships for many years. Rain and cold
and wind on the way will mean nothing to me after that. I
have suffered all that a man may suffer. Nothing that can

happen on the road between here and London can be worse.'

(A Jarrow man, aged sixty, dead within a month. Ellen Wilkinson, *The Town That Was Murdered*, 1939.)

'Some of them were young, some of them in their teens and some between 20 and 30, had never had any kindness, and had nothing but poverty and destitution, and to meet the people on the way down as we had met them, and the meals that they'd getten on the visits to the various places, well it just gave them an eye opener. And I think it was one of the finest things that ever happened to our townspeople going down to the South was to recognise that there were some decent people left in the country.'

(Paddy Scullion, from Jarrow, BBC Television Schools Programme, 29 December 1970.)

'Saturday was a day of exploded myths for many in Chiswick. The marching miners arrived during the afternoon, not the footsore, disorderly band of rebels that certain reports had led one to believe they were, but a vigorous body of orderly men with the soft and pleasant accent of the Welsh valleys. They spoke of the kindness they had met with everywhere on the road, and were very indignant about the reports of the march that had appeared in some of the papers. They spoke with affection of their leaders and mentioned that A. J. Cook had met them several times on the road and spent three nights sleeping on the bare boards with them.'

(*Brentford and Chiswick Times*, November 1927.)

'Good afternoon. A terrible mine disaster in North Wales. There was an explosion followed by fire in Gresford Colliery near Wrexham early this morning. Of the men working in the mine at the time, more than two hundred safely reached the surface, but for the rest, we regret to say, the position is extremely serious. Good progress is being made in subduing the fire and the rescue work is being vigorously continued in the hopes of getting to the area

where the men are cut off. But the work is tragically difficult, and already three members of the rescue party have
lost their lives. We would like to express on behalf of our
listeners our profound sympathy with the relatives of those
involved in this terrible disaster.'

(BBC announcer, 22 September 1934. 247 miners died.)

'You've heard of the Gresford disaster,
 The terrible price that was paid;
 Two hundred and sixty-two colliers were lost,
 And three men of a rescue brigade.

'It occurred in the month of September,
 At three in the morning, the pit
 Was racked by a violent explosion,
 In the Dennis where gas lay so thick.

'The gas in the Dennis deep section
 Was packed there like snow in a drift,
 And many a man had to leave the coal-face
 Before he had worked out his shift.

'A fortnight before the explosion
 To the shotfirer, Tomlinson cried:
 "If you fire that shot we'll all be blown to hell",
 And no one can say that he lied.

'The fireman's reports they are missing,
 The records of forty-two days;
 The colliery manager had them destroyed
 To cover his criminal ways.

'Down there in the dark they are lying,
 They died for nine shillings a day,
 They have worked out their shift and now they must lie
 In the darkness until Judgement Day.

'The Lord Mayor of London's collecting,
 To help both our children and wives;
 The owners have sent some white lilies
 To pay for the poor colliers' lives.

'Farewell, our dear wives and our children,
Farewell, our old comrades as well;
Don't send your sons down the dark dreary pit;
They'll be damned like the sinners in hell.'

(A young miner named Ford, in A. L. Lloyd, *Come All Ye Bold Miners*, 1952.)

'I was very unhappy when I was fourteen or fifteen – it was miserable at home – and one day I said to our French master that I didn't think life was worth living. He was a poor Jew from Manchester and he said, "Well just you think of the smell of fish-and-chips *with vinegar on*" – and I was won for the living-on just as surely as Goethe's Faust was by the sound of Easter hymns.'

(West Riding scholarship boy, in Richard Hoggart, *The Uses of Literacy*, 1957.)

'We march up the village playing "Hail Smiling Morn", and some time after eight we form up there at the bottom of Bill o' Jacks Road, with everybody spruced up and the trees all out. Often as not I can't play for a lump in the throat – why, when we play Silver Hill, anybody who's not moved must have a heart of stone.'

(George Gibson, from Saddleworth, in Graham Turner, *The North Country*, 1967.)

'He bought a 22-room mansion in South London and I saw the laughter slowly go out of his eyes. To begin with, he lost his little friends, the ha'penny cornet buyers. He also lost his mother who suffered a heart attack on hearing of his win. Then he became the centre of litigation over claims to shares in his winnings . . . Sudden wealth made him the unhappiest man alive.'

(Journalist describing the fate of Emilio Scala, the cornet-vendor from Battersea who won £354,544 on the Grand National, in Leslie Baily and Charles H. Brewer, op. cit.)

Wider Horizons?

'Why the hell's he got the right to go over there and do a dirty trick like that! It'll have the whole world against us now. Who'll trust us? It's like throwing your own kid to the wolves. We helped make it a country and then Chamberlain comes along and wants to buy that swine off. There'll be a war sooner or later, then there'll be nobody to help us.'

(London bus conductor, after the 1938 Munich agreement, in Branson and Heinemann, op. cit.)

'These Irish come over here. My God, they're half wild when they get here. Strong? You never saw anything like the strength these men have. I'm not passing this around, but I've got it from one who knows, the Government wants them over here to marry with the Englishwomen and have bigger children for the army. They're big enough, all right. But no brains.'

(A Cockney worker, in E. Wight Bakke, op. cit.)

'Just then I came across George Bright. George was a carpenter, over sixty years old. He had come to Spain to do carpentry, being too old to fight. George had been well known to me during the unemployed struggles in London. I asked him what the hell he was doing here, and just as he opened his mouth to answer there was a very quiet plop and a small red hole appeared in his forehead. He died instantly. His Union card fluttered out as he fell.'

(Fred Copeman, one of the leaders of the Invergordon mutiny, an International Brigadier, *Reason in Revolt*, 1948.)

War

'Now we know where we are. No more bloody allies.'

(Tug skipper on the Thames, after the fall of France, in A. Calder, *The People's War*, 1969.)

'I saw 'Arry 'Artley gettin' off t' bus this morning. 'E's just back from Dunkirk. An 'e does look well, all sunburnt, an 'is cheeks 've right filled out since 'e went in t' army. Must be all that good food they get. An 'e's not wounded, or owt.'

(West Riding housewife, in Donald Nicholl, op. cit.)

'Wat's ta think o' Churchill for Prime Minister, Willie? In't e one o't pig-stickin lot? Shootin' t' Indians, turnin' troops ont' miners, an all that?'

'Aye, that's reight. 'E's allus been seekin' a feight. Well 'e's got wun now, and no mistake. We'll 'ave 'im to 'elp us feight 'Itler an' as soon as it's all ovver we'll get rid o't' owld bugger.'

(Conversation in Working Man's Club, in ibid.)

10

Semi-Detached

ASA BRIGGS

*At the end of the First World War many people in Britain hoped
that peace had been secured for all time. They had been encouraged to
believe also that a 'new order' was likely to begin in the domestic
affairs of the country. The slogans were catchy – among them 'a land
fit for heroes to live in' – yet even the White Papers and Blue Books
identified a new mood:*

'Few can fail to feel the force of inspiration and experience
which is being born of the war, or to recognise the strength
of the new hope with which the people are looking forward
to the future. The nation ardently desires to order its life
in accordance with those principles of freedom and justice,
which led so many of its best sons to the field of battle . . . No
one can doubt that we are at a turning point in our national
history. A new era has come upon us. We cannot stand still.
We cannot return to the old ways, the old abuses, the old
stupidities. As with our international relations so with the
relations of classes and individuals inside our own nation,
if they do not henceforth get better they must needs get
worse, and that means moving towards an abyss. It is in
our power to make the new era one of such progress as to
repay us even for the immeasurable cost, the price in lives
lost, in manhood crippled and in homes desolated . . . We
stand at the bar of history for judgement, and we shall be
judged by the use we make of this unique opportunity.'

(*Interim Report of the Adult Education Committee,* 1918.)

*Already by the end of the 1920s, half-way between two World
Wars – although no one, of course, then knew it – it was clear that
the 'unique opportunity', if there really had been one, had been lost,*

and that the 'new era' carried with it its own 'stupidities' and 'abuses'. Certainly there was little 'inspiration'. The old pre-1914 bearings had disappeared, and there was no sense of common direction.

Different individuals and different groups reacted in different ways to the facts of the post-1918 world. Some were better off than others, materially and psychologically, since social distinctions, while less taken for granted than before 1914, were still real. Different generations had their own responses, too, in an age when much was made of the clash between the values of the old and the young and of the ominous gap left by the 'missing generation' lost during the First World War. Writers and artists usually expressed the underlying 'anxiety' which never completely disappeared even at moments of political optimism: during the 1930s many of them were to pass from anxiety to concern and commitment. Because they often came from relatively well-off families they were often in revolt against their families and against their schools.

The well-to-do could still enjoy a rising standard of living – and of comfort – during the 1920s and 1930s, and it was possible either to evade the problems of society or (despite the declining number of domestic servants) to escape from them. Even the less well-to-do, provided that they were employed, could react in these ways, since for the first time in history the benefits of industrialization began to be applied on a large scale to the home as well as to the factory. New industries, geared to consumer demand, prospered while old basic industries languished. Meanwhile 'mass entertainment', becoming an industry and sustained by new technical media, often encouraged the flight from the uneasy present, and the holiday resorts boomed.

The experience of the 1930s remained fragmented and divided, yet as the decade went by it proved increasingly difficult completely to ignore the international 'crises'. There was no domestic crisis comparable to the General Strike of 1926, but the economic recovery after 1934 which raised the country out of the trough of unemployment and hunger was limited and precarious. It was recognized, indeed, that in part the recovery depended on a rearmament programme which might ultimately involve Britain in another World War. There was great fear of such an outcome, and the widespread, *if not universal, reaction to the news of the Munich agreement signed by Chamberlain and Hitler in 1938 at the expense of Czechoslovakia was one of relief.*

Chamberlain appealed to the semi-detached mind when he told his fellow-countrymen just before Munich, when the sandbags were already being piled up outside public buildings and the gas masks distributed, that it was wrong to be drawn into 'a quarrel in a faraway country between people of whom we know nothing'. This approach to 'foreign affairs' was shared by many people without power. The critics were always in a minority. They included politically conscious, ideological enemies of 'Fascism' (including some who fought in the Spanish Civil War) and hard-headed realists who knew that however much individuals or groups might evade or escape from the facts of their time, the country as a whole could not indefinitely do so. 'People seem unable to differentiate between physical relief and moral satisfaction,' Harold Nicolson complained just after Munich. 'Naturally we were all over-joyed to have removed from us the actual physical fear which was hanging over us. My moral anxiety remains.' The poet Louis MacNeice put it differently:

'But once again
    The crisis is put off and things look better
And we feel negotiation is not in vain –
    Save my skin and damn my conscience.
And negotiation wins,
    If you can call it winning,
And here we are – just as before – safe in our skins;
    Glory to God for Munich.'

The 'crisis' could not always be put off, and the relief of Munich was very short-lived. Yet even after the Second World War had begun in September 1939, there was still no sense of common direction. The government, still the 'National' government which had been returned to power with a huge majority during the economic crisis of 1931 and ratified in office in 1935, was not fully representative of the nation. The war itself was fought so fitfully – mainly by propaganda – that it was called at the time 'the phoney war'. It was not until the blitzkrieg *of the summer of 1940, when Hitler's armies over-ran Holland, Belgium and France, and the formidable air attack on Britain in the September of that year (also called the blitz), after France had fallen, that a new government, led by Churchill, was able to mobilize the full support of the vast majority of the people. The support was given not just for reasons of high policy but because there was a strong popular feeling that the world could not remain safe or happy so long as Hitler was ruling Germany and dominating Europe.*

1940 was the year when the 'semi-detached' period of history came to an end. In retrospect, the years between 1919 and 1940 were to look like 'the years that the locusts had eaten', years of wasted hopes and of wasted resources and people. Yet this was not what they seemed to be like at the time to the growing numbers of people who felt themselves to be 'middle-class'. There was much to enjoy and much to be thankful for. The very contrasts of society – in health, education, housing, food and leisure – were a measure of how fortunate they were.

The housing figures (both of municipal and private housing estates*) speak for themselves and were a sign of how much England, a country of smaller families, was changing. So, too, were the figures of car ownership. There was surprisingly little vox pop *on radio programmes, but there was a great vogue for cinema documentary particularly among the politically conscious minority in the late 1930s, and in 1937 Mass Observation was founded to note directly (without intermediate comment or theory) what people were saying about anything and everything in streets and public houses.*

J. B. Priestley portrayed the setting of all this in his English Journey *(1934) which should be compared with* Cobbett's *Rural Rides. In it we read of an*

'England of . . . filling stations and factories that look like exhibition buildings, of giant cinemas and dance halls and cafés, bungalows with tiny garages, cocktail bars, Wool-

---

* 1,807,682 houses were built between January 1935 and the outbreak of war, more than three quarters of them by unsubsidized private enterprise.

worths, motor-coaches, wireless, hiking, factory girls looking like actresses, greyhound racing and dirt tracks, swimming pools, and everything given away for cigarette coupons.'

Settings

'Men drawing comfortable salaries were soon tempted to acquire not only their jerry-built villas, but cheap cars, wireless sets, furniture and other amenities, on the 'never-never' system. With each new obligation they became more and more the slaves of their employers. "Very well, Mr Smith, I'm sorry. But if you are not satisfied, you know your remedy." This familiar phrase, translated into plain English, meant "another word from you and you'll find yourself on your backside in the street". Mr Smith may have been a hero at Mons, but he became a terrified rabbit when he thought of his "little palace" at Colindale, his Kozy Kot at Wembley, or his overdue instalment on his Austin Seven.'

(D. Goldring, *Nineteen Twenties*, 1945.)

'In the land of lobelias and tennis flannels
The rabbit shall burrow and the thorn revisit
The nettle shall flourish on the gravel court,
And the wind shall say: Here were decent godless people:
Their only monument the asphalt road
And a thousand lost golf balls.'

(T. S. Eliot, *The Rock*.)

'Get there if you can and see the land you once were proud to own,
Though the roads have almost vanished and the expresses never run:

'Smokeless chimneys, damaged bridges, rotting wharves and choked canals
Tramlines buckled, smashed trucks lying on their side across the rails;

225

'Power stations locked, deserted since they drew the boiler
    fires;
Pylons fallen or subsiding, trailing dead high-tension wires;

'Head-gears gaunt on grass grown pit-banks, seams aban-
    doned years ago
Drop a stone and listen for its splash in flooded dark below.'

(W. H. Auden.)

'Among the upper and middle classes the word "garden
city" stands more for a working class housing estate, with
perhaps just a touch of philanthropy. It has, therefore,
been something to approve of but on no account to live in.
Welwyn has done much to kill this prejudice but not all that
is necessary.'

(Sir Frederick Osborn.)

Class

'On one point I should imagine every one will agree, that
class distinctions have been positively toppled over since
the Great War, or rather social barriers have been removed,
not entirely by the upper classes becoming less exclusive,
but much more by a general uplifting in the standard of
living ... Luxuries once enjoyed by the few are now
regarded as ordinary expenditure by young people whose
immediate antecedents were unaccustomed to such amenities, and in the case of the same people their standard has
gradually altered in the same way. Take for example the
telephone, wireless, electric light, motor-cars, pictures. It
might be said that these are all recent inventions brought
into common use by the developments of science; but unless
the standard of living had been considerably raised, these
would still have been considered great luxuries to be used
only by the wealthier classes ... [Yet] the landed aristocracy have been almost taxed out of existence, and are
mostly living in a much less luxurious way than before the
War; and the middle classes are undoubtedly labouring

under a burden of taxation such as they have never before
been called upon to bear . . .'

(Yorkshirewoman, quoted in F. W. Hirst, *The Consequences of the
War to Great Britain*, 1934.)

'As children, we lived on the lower-class fringe of an upper-
class suburb . . . We were constantly being pulled up for
some real or fancied coarseness of enunciation or vulgar
phrase. I soon found that speech, which distinguished man
sharply from animals, distinguished Briton from Briton
almost as sharply . . . I saw that learning to speak English
with a genteel accent was more important to getting on
than learning to speak French or German.'

(Man from Pinner, quoted in T. H. Pear, *English Social Differences*,
1955.)

'Both the new rich and the new poor have learnt that the
old social orders were not immutable, that the roles of
Lazarus and his patron were interchangeable. It is significant that you seldom hear nowadays the phrase which was
once so common, "know my station" . . . '

(Woman Oxford Graduate, quoted in F. W. Hirst, op. cit.)

'The classification of our schools has been on the lines of
social rather than educational distinction; a youth's school
badge has been his social label. The interests of social unity
demand the removal of this source of class prejudice and
the drastic remodelling of the national structure to form a
coherent whole.'

(Letter from Stanley Baldwin to the teaching profession, 1929.)

'Whatever the political changes in this country during the
next few years one thing surely is almost certain: the class
distinctions will not remain unaltered and the public school,
as it exists today, will disappear.'

(Graham Greene, *The Old School*, 1934.)

'I signed on at Chelsea as a member of the London Auxi-
liary Fire Service. The assembled recruits were already in

their shirt sleeves, revelling in the lovely weather, the healthy occupation, the novelty of digging up municipal territory to fill sandbags, and the opportunity to meet strangers without introduction. Among them I found an attitude of almost incredible optimism. That it should take a war to produce this holiday mood was a reflection of the dullness of people's lives and the prison of class distinction in English society. There were bearded artists who talked of keeping their hands in by joining the camouflage corps. There were university graduates "marking time" till their chance came to join one of the Services. There were middle-aged ladies whose lonely lives had been brightened by the announcement "Your Country Needs You". I felt happy for them. They had little to lose and great energy to give . . .'

(J. Byrom, *The Unfinished Man*, 1957.)

'I noted at once that the "working class", if franker about their motives for joining National Service, were less public spirited. Nor were they carried away by the community spirit the hour fostered. Many of them were there because they were out of a job, because they were lonely or because business was bad . . .'

(ibid.)

'For several days I've reported, or repeated to you, calls for ambulance drivers, stretcher bearers, and personnel of the civilian defence. It might be useful to request the services of a good sociologist because if this business of repeated air alarms goes on, the sociological results will be considerable. This is a class-conscious country. People live in the same small street or apartment building for years, and never talk to each other. The man with a fine car, good clothes and perhaps an unearned income doesn't generally fraternise with the tradesmen, day labourers and truck drivers. His fences are always up. He doesn't meet them as equals. He's surrounded with certain evidences of worldly wealth calculated to keep others at a distance, but if he's caught in

Piccadilly Circus when the sirens sound, he may have a waitress stepping on his heels and see before him the broad back of a day labourer as he goes underground. If the alarm sounds about four in the morning, his dignity, reserve and authority may suffer when he arrives half-dressed and sleepy, minus his usual defences and possessed of no more courage than those others who have arrived in similar state.'

(Ed Murrow, broadcast of 4 September 1939, printed in *In Search of Light*, 1968.)

'We once bought two dozen granadillas, and gave instructions to our cook to scoop them out and serve them with the sweets at a rather ambitious little dinner of our own. She had never seen anything like them before, and, with a stupidity which had, perhaps, entered into league with her strong resentment of innovations, she threw away the inside of the fruit and served only a dishful of empty, shrivelled husks. This was nothing to the anguish felt by a friend of ours who ordered no less than a pound of caviare for a dinner party and having no ice box placed it in a basin in her stone pantry sink so that it would keep cool overnight. The next morning the kitchen-maid informed her that she had thrown away a lot of nasty black grease which the master must have brought in from his motor car.'

(June and Doris Langley Moore's textbook of hospitality, *The Pleasure of Your Company*, 1936 edn.)

'Breakfast, Wednesday: Bread and dripping, tea. Dinner: Liver and onions, bread and butter and tea. Tea: bread and butter, beetroot, tea. Supper: Cocoa. Breakfast, Thursday: Bread and dripping, tea. Dinner: Sausages and potatoes, tea. Tea: Bread and butter, jam, tea. Supper: cocoa. Breakfast, Friday: Bread and dripping, tea. Dinner: Cod and chips, bread and butter and tea. Tea: Bread and butter, tomatoes, jam, tea. Supper: None. Breakfast, Saturday: Bread and dripping, tea . . .'

(B. S. Rowntree, *Poverty and Progress*, 1941.)

'Coming now to weights, which, as stated, reflect physical fitness more reliably than do heights, we note that taking the average figure for children of all ages there is a difference of $5\frac{3}{4}$ pounds between the average weight of girls in Classes A and B and D and E, while the girls in Class X are on the average $12\frac{1}{4}$ pounds heavier than those in Classes A and B. The boys in Classes D and E are $4\frac{3}{4}$ pounds heavier and those in Class X are $8\frac{1}{4}$ pounds heavier than those in Classes A and B.'

(ibid.)

'It is customary to present the finger bowl and the dessert plate together, with a silk or lace mat which the guest arranges to the left of his plate. The hostess here takes almost her last opportunity of showing with what taste and skill she presides over her dining table and each bowl contains one or two flowers and leaves, while the water is faintly redolent of perfume. Rose water or verbena are the best scents for the purpose.'

(June and Doris Langley Moore, op. cit.)

'Mother was glad to see Dick, and Catherine was glad to see him too. Visitors were rare. No one goes to see poor people. Even relatives stay away ... [Dick] belonged to that aristocracy of Labour who have hot dinners with vegetables every day, eat real butter on Sundays, and have fresh cows' milk with their tea. Mother made him a cup of tea and cut him a slice of bread and margarine, a sincere gesture of hospitality. She wanted him to feel at home.'

(William Cameron, *Common People*, 1938.)

'I am so sorry we cannot spare a bed for your maid whom I know you would like to have with you. But there are several comfortable rooms, not at all dear, to be had in the village, and I will gladly engage one on your behalf if this plan suits you.'

(June and Doris Langley Moore, op. cit.)

The Generations

'The post-war generation suffers from a sort of inward instability, a lack of character, due, probably, to the somewhat hysterical atmosphere of their childhood. There seems nowadays to be no desire to provide for the future or look beyond tomorrow. The War shattered that sense of security which brooded over Victorian homes, and made men buy estates and lay down cellars against their old age and for the benefit of their sons . . . Before the War children (in better class families at least) were kept apart from their elders, had their own good plain food in the nursery and found their own simple amusements. Now they mix more freely with their elders, sit down to table with them, play the same games, and expect and get much more attention and amusement . . . But it is a great reflection on the common sense of parents of today that the indulgence and lack of discipline which were pardonable in wartime should be allowed to remain, and the fact that for four years Age *had* to stand aside and admire the feats of Youth is a poor defence for the absence of respect from the younger generation to the older in 1933.'

(Woman Oxford Graduate, quoted in F. W. Hirst, op. cit.)

' I am a young man. At least I am just thirty, and that seems to me young. But more and more for some while now I have been aware of a younger generation than my own growing into manhood and into achievement, and quite lately it has been brought home to me in more than one connection that I really know very little – *very* little – of what these younger men and women think and feel about things. One tends to believe that others of one's age, and younger, agree with one by nature and necessity. But do they?'

(Geoffrey West, in *The Twentieth Century*, March 1931.)

'Knock knock
Who's there?
It's the younger generation.

What's your ambition?
To change the world.
Youth is painfully fighting for an outlet which will offer escape from obscurity into the public eye. The *Mirror* is offering that outlet.'

(Passage from the *Daily Mirror*, quoted in H. Cudlipp, *Publish and be Damned*, 1953.)

'Never, within the memory of anyone now living, has Britain produced a finer generation of boys and girls than those begotten between 1915 and 1925. The young men who fought the Battle of Britain and, when at last they were provided with adequate arms and reasonably competent leadership, won victory after victory, were conceived by parents who had fought for Freedom and were inspired by Hope.'

(D. Goldring, op. cit.)

The Sexes

'One great change is the increased employment of women ... About forty years ago we were employing no women other than those in two departments, which are recognised as women's work. Outside these departments, all clerical and administrative, warehouse and general work was done by men. The introduction of women to do men's operations was a temporary measure during the War, and has practically ceased. We do, however, employ a large number of women and girls as typists, clerks and on warehouse work and many other occupations about the factory, where they are most useful ...'

(A boot and shoe manufacturer, quoted in F. W. Hirst, op. cit.)

'But whether you behold her in her box
Diaphanously clad, with purple locks,
Or jazzing with contortions that outdo
The gestures of a boxing kangaroo,

Tarantulated by the fearsome tunes
Played by a band of epileptic coons –
Glorinda holds the centre of the stage,
The most conspicuous monster of our age.'

(*Punch*, 1922.)

'As women, even in these levelling times, are at leisure much oftener than men, we give a separate list of pastimes essentially feminine:

'Sewing, embroidering, crochet work, and knitting in all their branches.

'Macramé (string work useful for bags, belts, coarse laces, etc.)

'Fancy cooking (toffee, sweets, etc.)

'The making of artificial flowers and floral ornaments

or

'Perfumes, pot pourri, and scented sachets

or

'Cold cream and cosmetics

or

'Babies' toys in felt, plush and velvet.'

(June and Doris Langley Moore, op. cit.)

Mobility and Settlement

'Owing to the increased speed and ease of travel contacts between guest and host are in almost every possible respect more quickly severed than they ever have been before. Where a visit to a country house would have once lasted a week, it now lasts a weekend. Where a dance would have begun at ten at night and gone on till five or six in the morning it now starts at twelve and is completely over by three. The sherry and the cocktail party exhibit the best of this tendency to get things over quickly. The guests have come and gone before one has had time to appreciate their presence.'

(ibid.)

'I deliver milk all over the estate, so I think I know practically everybody on the estate. And I can tell you that when they move down here – I suppose it's just that they've got a new house – they just think they're a cut above everybody else.'

(Milkman, quoted in M. Young and P. Willmott, *Family and Kinship in East London*, 1957.)

'In fact, these houses of suburbia, built to tempt one of the keenest buyers' markets of all time, and soon to be rocked on their footings by Hitler's bombs, had to be built rather well. The developers threw everything into the fight. Free removal costs, free legal charges – even a free bus service for residents. Building societies cut back their mortgage rates down to $4\frac{1}{2}$ per cent. "In 1937," the estate agent remembers, "you could buy a semi-detached house on one estate – with a garage and a big garden – for £479. You put down a deposit of £49, and your repayments were 11s. 1d a week."

'Many of these homes were built on the very land of the displaced squires, as the builders were pleased to point out. Each one of the new houses was built to satisfy the very same dream that the squire enjoyed there ... Each of the little castles on the ground was designed on the assumption that all the other houses in suburbia are invisible. They started life, these houses, in the picture books and models at the Ideal Home exhibitions of the twenties. When they chose their home, the man and his wife were wrapt in a private dream of owning their *own* home, for their own children. No word of neighbours, community, no pictures of people complicate the brochures of the estates. One house alone is shown, and it is all yours. On the maps the estate is coloured green, as if it is your parkland. Beyond the estate, where there will in fact be other estates, the builders drew Noddyland trees and toytown railways. "When you buy a house you buy security for the days when your earning capacity shall have ceased; you buy peace of mind for yourself and your wife."'

(Peter Way, 'Once it was All Fields', in *The Sunday Times Magazine*, 11 February 1968.)

The Motor Car

'In 1933 . . . there were just over 1,200,000 private cars in use . . . The motor car by this time had become a utility vehicle and had long left behind its prime characteristic of a "pleasure" conveyance. There were also in use more than half a million motor cycles. There were also 46,000 omnibuses and motor coaches. . . The average rate of increase of numbers in use was, taking all classes of vehicles, in the terms of about 20 per cent annually. So we find that the motor vehicle from being merely one which ministered to the pleasures of the "idle rich" – a term much beloved by the opponents of motoring in the early days of the automobile movement – has become a vital link in the life of the nation. It has enabled new areas of the country to be opened up to trade and residence. It alone has made slum clearance and the removal of slum dwellers to the open countryside possible. It has vastly facilitated the exchange of commodities and the development of internal trade. By its aid rural communities have been brought into closer touch with those living around them than could have been possible through any other medium. In a word, it has so altered our whole conception of communal life that I would go so far as to say that if we had to choose between dispensing with one of our two principal forms of transport, road or rail, the nation would suffer less by the loss of the latter, because the motor vehicle can do most things the railways do, while the railways could in no possible way assume the important services that are every day rendered to the people by road transport.'

(Sir Malcolm Campbell, *The Roads and the Problem of their Safety*, 1937.)

Holidays

'Brighton and Hove are going gayer than ever this Coronation Summer. What fun you can have there – what endless entertainments. What glorious air and sunshine, what superb coast and downland scenery . . .'

(Newspaper advertisement, 1937.)

'We must always keep in mind that Blackpool . . . is not just a place of bricks and mortar. There are dream-builders as well as brickbuilders, and the dream-builders really lay the foundations for the brickbuilders.'

(A. Clarke, *The Story of Blackpool*, 1923.)

'Morecambe and Heysham provides a wide variety of first class entertainments for all tastes. There are four modern ballrooms, each equipped with its own resident orchestra; four theatres, one of them the largest and best equipped Variety theatre in the country; seven cinemas screening the latest films, and four resident concert parties. During the Autumn a special feature is made of decorative and artistic illuminations which transform the resort into a glowing fairyland of light and colour.'

(*Lancashire; the Official County Handbook.*)

The Cinema

'At the age of twenty-five, I have literally gone to the cinema all my life. I first entered a cinema (in my mother's arms) at the age of one month. I have therefore been going to the cinema for exactly a quarter of a century. Apart from that my life so far has been commonplace and dull enough. My parents are working-class (my father is a works electrician). I am a clerk in a printing office . . . My nationality is English, with, possibly, a touch of Irish and Welsh. Last, but not least, I am a bachelor and have never experienced anything in the nature of romance or sexual love . . . I have vivid recollections of such events of the early 'twenties as *Metropolis* . . . Clara Bow in *It* and Rudolf Valentino . . . In those days all films came alike to me. Of course, I liked Westerns and exciting sword-and-cloak pictures; but at the same time I could sit through sentimentalities and love scenes without becoming bored . . .'

(Clerk, quoted in J. P. Mayer, *British Cinemas and Their Audiences*, 1948.)

'Now I go to the pictures every week. Every week I find something to like in the pictures I see. Without films I am miserable. Sometimes I think they have become a habit, almost a drug; but I can still criticize films and while I can I am in no danger of becoming a film drug addict. Meanwhile films continue to give me more pleasure than anything else in life . . .'

(Regular filmgoer, quoted in ibid.)

'Films have influenced me. I've imagined myself in the roles of Cowboys, Indians and Bad men, and as a hero. I've been a little frightened of terror films, but later on I've realised they were only celluloid characters . . . I often get a lump in my throat during a sad scene.'

(Shop assistant, quoted in ibid.)

'The amount of pleasure we got for fourpence was amazing.'

(Typist, quoted in ibid.)

'It is all very well seeing marvellous houses and apartments on the screen, but how do you think we feel when we see our own home? I personally look at my home, in a semi-detached flat, with disgust, and I don't invite my friends home because I don't want them to see the place where I live.'

(Bank clerk, quoted in ibid.)

'When I see what beautiful houses the flim [sic] stars live in, then my ambition is to live in one of those houses and have a private swimming pool in my garden. I cannot say that flims have ever made me dissatisfied with life but I can safely say flims do make me dissatisfied with my neighbourhood and towns. From what I have seen they are not modern; for instance, there are no drug stores on the corner of the street where you can take your girl friend and have some ice-cream or a milk-shake. In our town there are no skyscrapers or really high buildings and there are not half as many buildings which are really lit up as those on flims such as Broadway . . .'

(Schoolboy's comments, quoted in ibid.)

The Wireless

'Our thoughts also turn to the poor, that vast majority whose children look on the streets as their playground and attend when they can the performances of the nearest Picture House. The possibilities of "the pictures" were enormous, and at the outset it was firmly believed that here was to be found the means of educating the masses. The ethical and educational value of the cinematograph was allowed to be superseded by sensationalism . . .'

(J. C. W. Reith, *Broadcast over Britain*, 1924.)

'The policy of the BBC being to bring the best of everything into the greatest number of homes, it follows that if this policy be carried out many educative influences must have been stirred . . . Entertainment, pure and simple, quickly grows tame; dissatisfaction and boredom result.'

(ibid.)

'Till the advent of this universal and extraordinarily cheap medium of communication, a very large proportion of people were shut off from first-hand knowledge of the events which make history. They did not share in the interests and diversions of those with Fortune's twin-keys – Leisure and Money. They could not gain access to the Great Men of the Day, and those great great men could deliver their message to a limited number only. Today all this is changed . . . He who has something to tell his countrymen, something which it shall be to their profit to hear, can command an audience of millions ready to hand . . .'

(ibid.)

'It must not be presumed that the atmosphere of Savoy Hill is one of unbroken peace, nor that every listener who has a bone to pick with the programmes does so without showing his teeth. It is not always easy to placate the correspondent who calls everything that he does not like or understand "piffle" and all that really does appeal to him "not half good enough", and the feelings of some critics can never be allayed. There is a respectable gentleman living in a respectable suburb of a respectable town who does not permit his daughters to hear love songs or dance music. He, it is feared, will never again look leniently on the B.B.C. And the aunt (real) who was almost sure that she heard one of her clan say "Botheration" in the Children's Hour "one day last week" has doubtless carried out her intention of demanding the return of her licence money . . .'

(*BBC Hand Book*, 1928.)

'The wireless has been an immense boon to countless people, especially invalids and the dwellers in remote and isolated places. It might, too, be a great educative and civilising force if it did not adapt so many of its programmes to the lowest type of intelligence . . . I asked a friend of mine, the late Valentine Goldsmith, who had been with the B.B.C. since its earliest days, if he couldn't get them to improve the "popular" programmes. He answered cynically: "What does it matter anyway? The morons who listen to them keep their wireless going all day, so they get a little of everything." The wireless has done more than its share to gratify the passion for noise which is so characteristic of this singularly unaesthetic generation.'

(P. Colson, *Those Uneasy Years*, 1944.)

The Press

' "If only I could tell."

'These words are often on the lips of every husband and wife.

' "If only I could tell him about that irritating habit of

his that drives me mad!" "If only I could tell him that he is killing my love by being so secretive!" "If only I could tell her that I don't really love her!" "If only I could tell her that she is the most wonderful wife in the world!" "If only I could tell him of my past. It is haunting me!"

'Well, here's the chance to open your heart and tell the truth. Don't bottle it up any more. Tell the *Mirror*. Address immediately to "Secrets", *Daily Mirror*. Names and addresses will not be published.'

(*Daily Mirror* notice reprinted in H. Cudlipp, op. cit.)

'The *Daily Telegraph* wants a Ministry of Propaganda to be set up in peace-time . . . If there is to be a Propaganda Minister, the greatest propagandist in the town is Mr Geoffrey Dawson, Editor of *The Times* . . . The popular press is as nothing, in the way of propaganda, when compared with the unpopular newspapers. Put together the four popular papers, the *Daily Express*, the *Daily Mirror*, the *News Chronicle* and the *Daily Herald*, do not carry nearly as much propaganda as the other two.'

(*Evening Standard*, 24 May 1939.)

'To introduce the *best* daily newspaper: handsome gifts for husband, wife and children. Take the *News Chronicle* for eight weeks and make your own choice from the widest selection of good quality home articles ever offered . . .'

(Newspaper advertisement, 1936.)

Prizes

'First Prize: £500 and a Special 1936 Morris Ten-Four Coupe Value £215 and a 22 Gns. "Gloria" Radio with Electric Clock.
'Second Prize: £100 and a 1936 Morris Ten-Four (Sliding Head Saloon) Value £182. 10. 0 and a 22 Gns. Ferranti "Gloria" Radio with Electric Clock.

'Third Prize £80; Fourth Prize £60; Fifth Prize £40; Sixth Prize £30; Seventh Prize £20.
'Eight Ferranti Radios
'100 Expanding Suitcases
'100 Hampers.'

(*Sunday Chronicle*, 15 December 1935.)

'A friend of mine, endowed with the knack of solving puzzles, won in a single year a motor-car, five Christmas hampers, a collection of fountain pens, quantities of cigarettes and several cheques. I myself was invited to state that I always smoked a certain brand of cigarettes, the reward being offered being five thousand of them and twenty-five pounds.'

(P. Colson, op. cit.)

'Literary competitions are rapidly becoming part and parcel of our daily lives, thoughts and actions. Yes, Britain rules the competition wave.'

(*Everybody's Weekly*, 5 June 1937.)

'Taking the family away! No? Well, you may be doing it after all. There's a family holiday free for the winners of the second, third and fourth prizes in *Bullets*, No. 1080. Fares, week's accommodation and entertainments for two grown-ups and one or two children . . .'

(ibid., 17 July 1937.)

> 'Britain's Day.'
> 'To help Neville.'
> 'Can't go on.'
> 'Still unemployed.'
> 'As time passes by.'

(Some prizewinners.)

'You take two associated words of the same number of letters and endeavour to transform one into the other by changing one letter at a time – each change forming a genuine dictionary word.

```
'Hate into Love in four changes  Hate
                                 Date
                                 Dote
                                 Dove
                                 Love
'Love into Hate in four changes  Love
                                 Lone
                                 Lane
                                 Late
                                 Hate'
```

(An example of how to play a word game.)

'*Everybody's* football experts have given more correct Pool forecasts since the commencement of the season than any rival paper and have also been on top several times in the last nine weeks.'

(*Everybody's Weekly*, 21 December 1935.)

Sport

'These huge assemblages of people intent on one thing have a strange and at times sinister individuality. Listen dispassionately to the sounds they produce – the roar which rises to a crescendo as the ball approaches the goal, then dies away in mutterings of disgust, as the shot misses; the moans, the sighs, the inarticulate cries, the shrieks, the rattles. This is the many-headed monster indeed; and so it must have sounded in the amphitheatres of Rome when the issue was not victory for one or other of two teams, but life or death for one or other of two men . . .'

(M. Marples, *A History of Football*, 1954.)

'One of the commonest and probably one of the most well-founded charges against public schools is that of "athleticism", that the boys think far too much about games . . .

[Yet] it is not old public schoolboys who flock in thousands to league matches on every Saturday afternoon in the winter. It is not they who read columns and columns about these matches in next morning's Sunday paper, and not only about the matches, but about the heroes of them, their wives, their jokes, and their shops, and every conceivable and irrelevant detail of their private lives. It is certainly not only public schoolboys who fill Lords or the Oval, or a Scottish Golf Course at the time of an Open Championship like Epsom on Derby Day. It may be very cogently argued that the Englishman thinks too much about games, but the critic's lash should fall evenly on all British shoulders.'

(Bernard Darwin, *The English Public School*, 1929.)

'The Englishman likes to go and look at football and gets much excited in doing so. If this particular Englishman had been to a public school he would be less inclined to hoot at the poor referee and that is the main difference.'

(ibid.)

'ENGLAND IN DANGER OF COLLAPSE: FAST BOWLERS' WICKET'

(Newspaper headline.)

Politics

'I am talking of peace . . . Most of us, when we consider the subject, do not see great movements, deep moral or legal issues, groupings of "Powers" or any of those "huge, cloudy symbols". We catch our breath and think of something far more intimate, much more dear, the lives of our children and grandchildren, of the familiar sites and institutions of our own land, all the boundary stones of our spiritual estate. We live under the shadow of the last war and its memories still sicken us.'

(Speech by Stanley Baldwin, 31 October 1935, printed in G. M. Young, *Baldwin*, 1952.)

'Downing Street, when the Premier reached home last evening, was crammed with a crowd that became hysterical. A week before, boos and cries of "Save the Czechs" had been raised when the Prime Minister returned after his second visit to Hitler. Last evening it was one wild frenzy of cheering. A newspaper seller, crying his wares, expressed it in a phrase. "Public Hero Number One," he shouted, although it was not on his poster. Policemen wrestled in vain, seeking to hold the wildness in check . . . After yells of "We want Chamberlain", the crowd sang "Land of Hope and Glory" . . . Alone then a woman screamed raucously "Pack up your Troubles", a solo that the crowd applauded. Meanwhile, using newspapers as shelter, it actually kept off the rain with the peace terms Czechoslovakia had been forced to sign! This was the supreme irony of an evening in which you would think, when you heard the cheering, that Britain had really gained a great victory over the forces of Might.'

(Hannen Swaffer in the *Daily Herald*, 1 October 1938.)

'There will be no war this year nor the next either.'

(*Daily Express*, 19 September 1938 and many times until 7 August 1939.)

The Light and the Dark: A Sequence

'We were standing at a window of my room in the Foreign Office. It was getting dusk, and the lamps were being lit in the space below on which we were looking. My friend recalls that I remarked on this with the words: "The lamps are going out all over Europe; we shall not see them lit again in our generation." '

(Viscount Grey of Falloden, *Twenty-five Years*, Vol. II, 1925.)

'My first personal recollection of a visit to the cinema comes when I was five years old . . . We must have been seated in the first row, because I can remember trying to peer into the black pit below, being much more fascinated by the moving lights, as people came and went, than by anything on the screen, of which I have only a vague recollection.'

(Laboratory assistant, quoted in Mayer, op. cit.)

'At 9.50 torchlight procession arrives. Headed by local pipers. There are about 200 children, young men and girls – working-class – carrying torches, singing a marching song, and shouting. At least six torches are dropped. Shouts from the crowd. "Someone'll get burned." Boys and girls walk on, almost over burning torches on ground. They blaze for about a minute ... Cars and people close together. Crowd breaks on to golf course and streams towards bonfire. Up till now I have not heard a single remark about the Coronation ... Enthusiasm when the torchlight procession climbs the slope singing *Blaze Away* (two-step) and arrives beneath the bonfire at 10.20. With shouts and cheers the torches are thrown on the pile. Several torches are badly aimed and land in or near the crowd but no one is burned. Great flames shoot up from the bonfire. The embankment catches fire but nothing can be done owing to the heat ... Young boys of eight or nine run about near the flames.'

(*May the Twelfth: Mass-Observation Day Surveys 1937*. The reporter is from Prestwick.)

'The columns of smoke merged and became a monstrous curtain which blocked the sky; only the billows within it and the sudden shafts of flame which shot up hundreds of feet made one realise that it was a living thing and not just the backdrop of some nightmare opera. There were fire-hoses along the side of the road, climbing over one another like a helping of macaroni ... Every two or three minutes we would pull into the gutter as a fire bell broke out stridently behind us and an engine in unfamiliar livery tore past at full tilt: chocolate or green or blue, with gold letter-ing – City of Birmingham Fire Brigade, or Sheffield, or Bournemouth. The feeling was something you had never experienced before – the excitement and dash of fire engines arriving to help from so far away, and the oily, evil smell of fire and destruction, with its lazy insolent rhythm. It looked terrible and hopeless but there was a kind of *Götterdämmerung* grandeur about it.'

(Desmond Flower, *The War* (*1939–1945*), ed. Flower and J. Reeves, 1960.)

I I

The People's War and Peace

ASA BRIGGS

The second experience of international war in the twentieth century was very different from the first. After the speedy destruction of Poland it took months for the European War to burst into life. Yet by the end of 1941 the War had transcended the boundaries of Europe and become world-wide in scale, a war of many fronts. It was also a war of movement with little of the sense of stalemate or slaughter which had characterized the First World War. Many of the victims of the War were civilians destroyed in massive air attacks, yet these attacks did not break people's morale as had been feared when war was being anticipated with horror during the 1930s. There were neither the same heights of elation nor depths of despair as there had been between 1914 and 1918, though the horror of the concentration camp and the massacre of the Jews accentuated the sense of moral degradation which had been blunted before 1939.

The year 1940 was one of the most remarkable years in British history. It marked the end of the 'phoney war' and the beginning of what Churchill called 'the war of the unknown warriors'. In the summer, when France had been defeated, there was a threat of invasion: in the autumn there were the realities of sustained 'blitz' from the air. Yet by the end of the year the Battle of Britain had been won. Just as significant in retrospect as the great events was the new national mood – the determination to see the war through; the urge to break away from pre-war inhibitions; the willingness to carry out in weeks reforms which had been delayed for years before 1939; the hopes of a better world after the war both socially inside Britain and through peaceful international cooperation. The slogans – and the abstractions – were treated charily: it was at the level of the family, the neighbourhood and the village or town that the breakthrough was taking place.

As the war proceeded, more and more people were involved, including women and children. The mobilization of national resources had a profound effect on the experience of individuals and families. At the same time, it sharpened the awareness of social problems (for example, through the evacuation of children) and encouraged discussions of them (for example, through adult education in the Armed Services). At the highest level official reports were being published on health, social security, education and many other subjects, all of which drew a sharp contrast between the world before the war and the world as it might be. The very austerity of war-time, which was to continue after 1945, even in some respects – for example, bread rationing – to be intensified, meant an emphasis on 'fair shares for all'. This conception became relevant socially and administratively before it became a political slogan. So, too, did the conception of social solidarity. 'In a matter so fundamental,' wrote the authors of a Government White Paper of 1943 on Social Security, 'it is right for all citizens to stand in together, without exclusion based on differences of status, function or wealth.' The argument was not merely that administrative problems would be simplified if structures were to become 'comprehensive' or 'universal', but that through 'universal schemes' 'concrete expression' would be given to the 'solidarity and unity of the nation, which in war has been its bulwark against aggression and in peace will be its guarantee of success in the fight against individual want and mischance'.

Throughout the period covered in this chapter there was some kind of social consensus, created in 1940, which survived the change in 1945 from a 'National' government, headed by Churchill, to a Labour government – the first with a large majority – headed by Attlee. There were differences about nationalization and about fiscal policies, but when, for example, the National Insurance Bill was introduced in 1946, R. A. Butler, on behalf of the Conservative Opposition, said plainly:

'We regard this plan as part of the mosaic or the pattern of the new society ... This Bill forms part of a series of Bills ... which ... foresaw the pattern of the new society long before this Parliament was ever thought of ... The whole philosophy lying behind these measures, in which ... we have played our part and shall play our part, is that the good things of life shall be more widely shared.'

In the post-war world, however, or at least in post-war Britain, the fact that the 'good things' were still in short supply left the way open first for the growth of the black market (complete with 'spivs') and second for the demand for a restoration of the free play of market forces. There were contrasts in the attitudes of different generations as well as of different social and economic groups, and advertising came into its own as the distaste for official propaganda increased. Full employment, never achieved until the Second World War, stimulated the private expectations and aspirations of large numbers of people who had been 'deprived' before 1939, not always recognizing it. For those who preferred society to operate according to plan on the basis of one single aspiration, like winning the war or after the war achieving socialism, the new pluralism of motives and pressures and the growth of business agencies which could influence or canalize them were dangerous features of the post-war world which contained as yet unfulfilled potential. One thing was clear. No one wished to return to the 1930s, and no one talked of restoring 'normalcy' as they had done during the 1920s. That way back would have been deliberately closed even if it had proved possible to keep it open.

The violence of the Second World War – apparent not only in large-scale set battles, as in the Desert or on the Russian Front, but in the sporadic air attacks on towns and cities and in the emergence of civilian resistance movements – was not exorcized after 1945. Instead, the World War ended with the explosion of an atomic bomb on Japan which hinted noisily that whatever other freedoms might be won or guaranteed after 1945 freedom from fear would remain precarious. It was not until 1952 that Churchill, who had replaced Attlee as Prime Minister a year earlier, announced that Britain had carried out successful atomic bomb tests, but the preparations had long been continuous and highly organized. The first British atomic pile had come into operation in 1947, the year of the great fuel crisis, when in the coldest of winters the reactions of ordinary people were tested as they never had been since 1940 itself.

We can now see the whole of this period as one, transcending the greatest single event for those who were living at the time – the end of the wars against Germany and Japan and the shared excitement of Victory Day. Britain had emerged from the War changed but not destroyed, and George Orwell, who had vividly described the divided Britain of the 1930s, had great hopes that if British people 'can keep their feet, they can give the example that millions of human beings are waiting for'. This was still the mood when this chapter ends, even if it was shared for different reasons by different sections of the English people. Orwell's prophecies linked the future with the past. 'By the end of another decade it will finally be clear whether England is to survive . . . as a great nation or not. And if the answer is to be "Yes", it is the common people who must make it so.'

Prediction

'Poland was attacked from the air, and its bloody ruins occupied by tanks. Alsace and Lorraine were invaded after punishment from a German air fleet that left alive a mere handful of their people. The great forts, the network of trenches and gun emplacements on which France had spent labour and treasure so lavishly, were battled and pulverised into tumbled heaps of earth and steel and concrete.'

(Miles (S. Southwold), *The Gas War of 1940*, 1931.)

'And then, in a moment, the lights of London vanished, as if blotted out by a giant extinguisher. And in the dark streets the burned and wounded, bewildered and panic-stricken, fought and struggled like beasts, scrambling over the dead and dying alike, until they fell and were in turn trodden underfoot by the ever-increasing multitudes about them . . . In a dozen parts of London that night people died in their homes with the familiar walls crashing about them in flames; thousands rushed into the streets to be met by blasts of flame and explosion and were blown to rags; they came pouring out of suddenly darkened theatres, picture-houses, concerts and dance halls, into the dark congested streets to be crushed or burnt or trodden to death.'

(ibid.)

'The chief threat to defence in the near future comes from the effect, predominantly moral, of intensive air attack ... The best defence is the mobile form instead of relying on static positions ... Apart from air dominance, the chance of success in attack would depend upon raising the ratio of machine power – especially in quantity of tanks.'

(B. H. Liddell Hart, October 1938, *Memoirs*, Vol. II, 1965.)

'What is the city over the mountains
Cracks and re-forms and bursts in the violet air?'

(T. S. Eliot, *The Waste Land*.)

Sunday 3 September 1939

'We could eat no breakfast hardly, and just waited with sweating palms and despair for 11 o'clock.'

(Mass Observation: *War Begins at Home*.)

'Consequently this country is at war with Germany ... May God bless you all. May he defend the right, for it is evil things we shall be fighting against – brute force, bad faith, injustice, oppression and persecution; and against them I am certain that right will prevail.'

(Neville Chamberlain, broadcast of 3 September 1939, BBC Archive Disc.)

'I leant against my husband and went quite dead for a minute or two.'

(Mass Observation: ibid.)

'I walked round to the church to see if our wedding was on as arranged. After a satisfactory interview I started to walk back home. A woman poked her head out of a window and shouted: "It's war – war – we shall all be bombed to death within a few hours ..." I was caught without my gas-mask. I rushed into an air raid warden's house and grabbed one, put it on and arrived at our flat fully gasmasked. When Betty saw me, she eventually got hers too, and there we were, waiting for our wedding in about an hour's time, fully gasmasked!'

(Mr Kynvin, BBC Archive Disc.)

'The sirens started warbling and the whistles shrilling and the ARP Wardens patrolling the streets. We got past about a hundred doorways, and all the people indoors were coming out to see the war start.'

(Beatrice L. Warde, *Bombed but Unbeaten*, 1941.)

'I clasped my baby, sent aloft a prayer and waited for the worst.'

(Quoted in N. Longmate, *How We Lived Then*.)

'Pardon me, but have I time to get to Victoria before the devastation starts? I have to get a train for Haywards Heath.'

(*Daily Express*, 4 September 1939.)

'I was just leaving t'Sunday Schooil when t'Syreens went. I rushed back and took all't children dahn into t'Cellars. They'd nivver been dahn theer before.'

(Yorkshirewoman, oral record.)

'I got to Piccadilly about four and all was hustle and bustle there with the sandbags going on all round the Circus and round Eros, and we packed our flowers out on to our baskets . . . We didn't do much trade so we just sat there and waited for the blackout . . . the neon lighting and the advertising, that had all gone, it didn't seem like Piccadilly Circus at all.'

(Mrs Pegg, BBC Archive Disc.)

'When the sirens sounded for the first time I felt sick, and so did everybody else round me – sick, but at the same time curious and coldly defiant . . . As I dutifully trailed downstairs with my gas mask to the House of Commons shelters, my feeling was that this outrage was going to be punished and pretty soon. Journalists mingled with politicians on the last of the stairs, and I found myself descending with Mr Lloyd George ... He was cheerful and affable. [He said] "There's nothing new in all this to me. I've been through it all before." '

(J. E. Sewell, *Mirror of Britain*, 1943.)

1940: 'The Blitz'

'When the bombing first started people were rather nervous, but they didn't know what to do, but after a few days they soon got accustomed to this. When they came along to the shelters in the evenings, they fetched their belongings, insurance cards, the cash, the jewellery if they had any, a flask of tea, milk for the kiddies, boiled sweets, and the Council started dancing in the parks.'

(Mr Smith, BBC Archive Disc.)

'We shall defend every village, every town and every city. The vast mass of London itself, fought street by street, could easily devour an entire hostile army, and we would rather see London laid in ruins and ashes than that it should be tamely and abjectly enslaved.'

(Churchill broadcast, BBC Archive Disc.)

'They were confident if they were in the shelter they were safe. Of course they always had a little courage at the end of the week. They'd go very near the shelter to the little pub and if Hitler was a little bit kinder and he'd let them have an extra one, they came back merry and bright. In one of my shelters unbeknown to us they moved a piano in and the first I heard of it was that they'd all come out of the pub and it was like Barney's Fair over there.'

(Miss Rolph, BBC Archive Disc.)

'I was scared stiff of bombing, I don't mind admitting it. In those early days the tube shelters weren't anything to write home about. They had no sanitation as such. I remember once being driven out because much as I was afraid of the bombs the stench was so bad that I just had to get out. I remember eventually taking up residence more or less in the Regent's Park Tube, and I had a bunk there – these bunks were wire mesh – and I remember once after a particularly bad raid, patting the walls of the Tube and thinking Bless you, I don't care how long I'm in London I shall always be grateful to the good old London tube.'

(Mrs Blair-Hickman, BBC Archive Disc.)

'A lot of us, especially if we were from the North and thought we knew everything, imagined that the old cockney spirit was dead and gone. We thought the Londoner of today, catching his tubes and electric trains, was a different kind of fellow altogether, with too many of his corners rubbed off, too gullible, easily pleased, too soft; and we were wrong. This last grim week has shown us how we can take it. The Londoners, as the Americans are saying, can take it. ... There was a time when, like many North-countrymen who came South, I thought I disliked London; it had vast colourless suburbs that seemed to us even drearier than the ones we had left behind. We hated the extremes of wealth and poverty that we found cheek by jowl in the West End, where at night the great purring motor cars filled with glittering women passed the shadowy rows of the homeless, the destitute, the down-and-out ... But on those recent nights, when I have gone up to high roofs and have seen the fires like open wounds on the vast body of the city, I've realised, like many another settler here, how deeply I've come to love London, with its misty, twilit charm, its hidden cosiness and companionship, its smoky magic ... This then is a wonderful moment for us who are here in London, now in the roaring centre of the battlefield, the strangest army the world has ever seen, an army in drab civilian clothes, doing quite ordinary things, an army of all shapes and sizes and ages of folk, but nevertheless a real army, upon whose continuing and defiant spirit the world's future depends.'

(J. B. Priestley, broadcast of 15 September 1940.)

'Soon after ten o'clock at night a bomb fell on the School and I, along with a number of others, was ordered down. In one room I saw an AFS man lying on a bedstead, and his face looked as if it had been skinned. A little further along my brother officer bent down and pulled something out which he believed was a piece of bread, but it turned out to be part of a small child, the upper part, the limbs of a small child. This so upset us that we came out into the street. There were a number of bodies lying in the road. I stood and watched these for a few moments and eventually some of them stood up and they were not all dead.'

(Mr Peters, BBC Archive Disc.)

'. . . they lay quite still in their beautiful dresses, beautiful colours, covered in sawdust which must have fallen on them when the bomb had fallen down below . . . they looked like beautiful dolls that had been broken and the sawdust come out. Whenever I go down Coventry Street now I remember those bright, dead dolls with the dust on them.'

(Mr Jacobs, BBC Archive Disc.)

Austerity, Solidarity, Horror

'The fishermen are saving lives
By sweeping seas for mines,
So you'll not grumble, "What no fish?"
When you have read these lines.'

(War-time Jingle.)

'We just had to make things spin out as best we could. I remember one Monday I went out to look for something for supper. And I came back with a small jar of meat paste. It was all I could get anywhere.'

(BBC, *Woman's Hour* programme, 15 September 1969.)

'Cook a nice dinner, just get it dished up, sit down, on goes the siren, oh, yeah, of course, come back, it's stone cold, start again, off it'd go again, start running – yeah, we had some fun.'

(Housewife, BBC Archive Disc.)

'It's being so cheerful keeps me going.'

(Mona Lott in BBC, *ITMA* programmes.)

'Everyone in the land is a soldier for liberty. We must regard ourselves as one army. We're standing right up to it. Hitler's success will be brought to nought, and the name of Britain will go down in history, not as a great imperialist nation but as a marvellous people in a wonderful island that stood at the critical moment in the world's history between tyranny and liberty and won.'

(Ernest Bevin broadcast, BBC Archive Disc.)

'The whole of the warring nations are engaged, not only soldiers, but the entire population, men, women and children. The fronts are everywhere. The trenches are dug in the towns and streets. Every village is fortified. Every road is barred. The front lines run through the factories. The workmen are soldiers with different weapons but the same courage.'

(Churchill, *War Speeches*, Vol. I, 1951.)

'It was more than bricks and mortar that collapsed in West Ham on the 7th and 8th of September 1940, it was a local order of society which was found hopelessly wanting, as weak and badly constructed as the single brick walls which fell down at that blast.'

(Doreen Idle, *War Over West Ham*, 1943.)

'There had been – whether it was temporary or permanent who could tell – a moral as well as an economic revolution in our society.'

(Lord Woolton, *Memoirs*, 1959.)

'Those who have the will to win
Cook potatoes in their skin
For they know the sight of peelings
Deeply hurts Lord Woolton's feelings.'

(Ministry of Food Jingle.)

'The first words when you woke up in the morning and came out of the shelters. You just said, "Good morning, Thank God we're alive, girl, another night over."'

(Miss Rolph, BBC Archive Disc.)

'What is that sound high in the air
Murmur of maternal lamentation . . .'

(T. S. Eliot, *The Waste Land.*)

'It was really awful, one great crash and a big flash and then there was a big fire in the shelter and I lost my mother in there, and I lost my little girl in there. We went to the hospitals – nothing there – and they said, Well, why don't you go to the mortuary? Well, naturally I went round there, and he said, Well, we have one little girl here, not identified. When I looked down I'd never seen such a shock in all my life, all her little hair was burnt and her face where she'd put her fingers right across, all the fire was there, and I thought to myself – Oh dear, well, can it be true? And I thought to myself, well what about my mother. And we never did find anything of Mother at all.'

(Mrs Itzinger, BBC Archive Disc.)

'*Your* courage
Your cheerfulness
Your resolution
Will bring us victory'

(Ministry of Home Security Poster.)

'We were fishing for herring about one hundred miles from Aberdeen when two enemy planes came up flying so low that the wing tips almost touched the stem of the boat. They had five attacks on us before they finished us off.'

(Fisherman, BBC Archive Disc.)

'First, you mustn't waste any food. We want all the ships we can get to carry munitions. Are you eating wisely? Or are you just eating, and more than you really need at that? If you are, well cut it down, and let's have the shipping space instead.'

(Lord Woolton broadcast, BBC Archive Disc.)

> 'Pat-a-loaf, pat-a-loaf,
> Baker's man
> Bake me some oatmeal
> As fast as you can
> It builds up my health
> And its taste is so good
> I find that I *like*
> Eating just what I should.'

(Ministry of Food Jingle.)

'Sugar? Now really, I've heard a lot about sugar – can't you cut it down in wartime?'

(Lord Woolton broadcast, BBC Archive Disc.)

> 'We regret we are unable to supply:
> Vacuum flasks
> saccharines
> lipsticks
> rouges
> all types of vanishing cream
> all barley sugar sweets
> rolls razors
> rolls razor blades
> seven o'clock razor blades
> brushless shaving cream
> Nivea cream
> Until Notice removed.'

(Shopkeeper's notice.)

'When I arrived out of that shelter on the Saturday morning, the doors of which happened to be red hot, by the way, and twenty-one of us in that shelter – I found that station, name and everything had vanished along with the smoke of the bomb, and we had arrived at a stage that I as one person had always looked for – a stage of equality, a stage of no snobbery, a stage whereby here we met as human beings, sympathetic toward one another when we never were sympathetic before . . .'

(BBC broadcast, Archive Disc.)

'My street was as flat as this 'ere wharfside. My missus were just making me a cup of tea for when I come 'ome. She were in the passage between the kitchen and the wash'ouse, where it blowed her. The only thing I could recognize her by was one of her boots. I'd have lost fifteen 'omes if I could have kept my missus.'

(Hull Air Raid Warden, BBC Archive Disc.)

'Don't just relieve your symptoms with a pill or a powder. Don't put off the day of diagnosis. Let diagnosis come first and the proper treatment can follow. Sometimes, chronic indigestion is nervous indigestion, for the worries, the stresses, the frustrations of this harassing world have an uncanny way of expressing themselves through the stomach.'

(Radio Doctor broadcast, BBC Archive Disc.)

'If you are so unlucky as to have your clothes destroyed in an air-raid, special arrangements have been made to enable you, through the Assistance Board, or the Collector of Customs and Excise, to obtain sufficient coupons to set you up again with a stock of clothing. After you have got that stock, you will then be on the same footing as everyone else.'

(Captain Oliver Lyttleton broadcast, BBC Archive Disc.)

'Clothing was so scarce I pinched one of my mother's sheets, and I made myself a complete underset out of one of her sheets.'

(BBC, *Woman's Hour* programme, 15 September 1969.)

'I know all the women will look smart, but we men may look shabby. If we do we must not be ashamed. In war the term "battle stained" is an honourable one.

'We must learn as civilians to be seen in clothes that are not so smart, because we are bearing yet another share in the war. When you feel tired of your old clothes remember that by making them do you are contributing some part of an aeroplane, a gun or a tank.'

(Captain Oliver Lyttleton broadcast, BBC Archive Disc.)

'Their clothing was in a deplorable condition, some of the [evacuated] children being literally sewn into their ragged little garments. Except for a small number the children were filthy, and in this district we have never seen so many verminous children, lacking any knowledge of clean and hygienic habits.'

(*Town Children through Country Eyes*, 1940.)

'Dear Mum I hope you are well. I dont like the man's face. I dont like the lady's face much. Perhaps it will look better in daylight. I like the dog's face best.'

(Comment by a Liverpool girl evacuee.)

'A London worker visiting the reception area can only feel delight at the fit and happy children who surround her, alert with new interest and vigour. Commenting on this to a West Countryman he answered me, "Yes – I don't know what you Londoners do to them that they arrived looking the way they did." '

(M. Cozens, *Evacuation, A Social Revolution*, 1940.)

'In the new world that we have presently to build, is this evacuation experience to be one of the things that will force us to accept a levelling up of the insecure section of the community, even though we shall inevitably experience a levelling down of our comparative middle-class ease?'

(ibid.)

'Some children may try your patience by wetting their beds, but do not scold or punish; as this will only make matters worse.'

(Women's Voluntary Service pamphlet.)

Kinds of Fighting

'Hey, Gerry, tracer behind us . . .
All right Jimmy, hold on . . .
Where is he, Rear Gunner, can you see him?
Down . . . down, it's come down!
Did you shoot him down?
Yes, he's got it, boy, right in the middle.
Bloody good show!
All right, keep weaving, there's some flak coming up.
All right, don't all shout at once.'

(BBC Archive Disc.)

'The first generation of ruins, cleaned up, shored up, began to weather – in daylight they took their places as the norm of the scene . . . Reverses, losses, deadlocks now almost unnoticed, bred one another; every day the news hammered one more nail into a consciousness which no longer resounded . . . This was the lightless middle of the tunnel.'

(Elizabeth Bowen, *The Heat of the Day*, 1954.)

'You in Europe who listen to me now, you are the unknown soldiers. The Nazi official and the German soldier don't know you, but they fear you. The night is your friend, the "V" is your sign, and it's beginning to play on their nerves. There's a "V" sound – here's the letter V in morse.'

('Colonel Britton' broadcast, BBC Archive Disc.)

'I was at Tangmere and I was in the Ops room as a radio telephonist with direct communication with the pilots as they flew on their sorties against the Germans. And we used to see them out and then count them back, and then you'd wait, and there'd be some missing, then perhaps one or two would dribble back, and then you'd wait for some time and know that no more would be coming back. And then you got this awful sort of weeping in the various rooms at night, there was always, always, some weeping girl somewhere. It was just a sort of sound that always seemed to be behind the battle.'

(BBC, *Woman's Hour* programme, 15 September 1969.)

'They say that women, in a bombing raid
Retire to sleep in brand new underwear
Lest they be tumbled out of doors, displayed
In shabby garments to the public stare.

'You've often seen a house, sliced like a cheese,
Displaying its poor secrets – peeling walls
And warping cupboards. Of such tragedies
It is the petty scale that most appals.'

(Norman Cameron, *Punishment Enough*.)

'We have immense fun over "the lost men". Wherever you go in the desert, you come across little pockets of men camped by their vehicles: they are invariably unshaven, cheerful and brewing up tea in a petrol tin. Similarly they can *always* tell you which way to go ("Y Track, sir. Straight on till you get to the Rifleman's Grave; can't miss it, sir," or "Barrell Track, mate? W'y you just come from it.") Nine times out of ten they give you the directions wrong. They appear to belong to nobody, and they seem perfectly contented to camp out in the blue.'

(Commanding Officer, First Battalion, the Black Watch, in B. Fergusson, *Black Watch and the King's Enemies*, 1950.)

'The equipment carried by every officer and man was substantially the same. We were "self-contained", each man wearing web equipment with large pack containing all personal belongings, two grenades, ammunition for automatics and Brens, mess tins and five days' rations . . . An average pack weighed between seventy-five and eighty pounds. As our training progressed, "the jungle became our friend." '

(Lt. Col. R. C. Sutcliffe, in *Royal Artillery Commemoration Book, 1939–45* (1950).)

'When you go into action, it doesn't strike you you're in the army. You're more or less friends among yourselves. Everybody knows that his life depends on the next man. We all knew each other well.'

(Sergeant Maile, BBC Archive Disc.)

'Many times I have heard other men say, "I wish to hell my old woman wasn't above the age limit." '

(J. T. Murphy, *Victory Production*, 1942.)

War Work

'When Marion's boy friend was called up, *she* wanted to be in it too. So she asked the employment exchange about war work . . . In next to no time they had fixed her up at a Government Training Centre, learning to make munitions . . . And before long she was in an important war job. At last she felt she was really "doing her bit" . . . Jim was proud of her when he came home on leave. He knows how much equipment counts in modern warfare.'

(Ministry of Labour advertisement.)

'See some of the young chaps out of it that ought to go. Swinging the lead in here – whereas there's plenty of men my age could do a lot of their work – I've turned 60. I'm not prejudiced, but I think some of them should be turned out, those that I know are yellow.'

(Mass Observation: *People in Production*, 1942.)

'There's a lot of waste – shortage of skilled men all over the place and good men in the Army doing nothing.'

(Midland plumber, quoted in ibid.)

'I'm doing all right. I've got too much work. I'm the only carpenter left around these parts.'

(Carpenter, quoted in ibid.)

'I'm a Trade Unionist and I want an 8 hour Day, but owing to the War I realise we can't, so my 10 hours are about right.'

(Bricklayer, quoted in ibid.)

'I'm fed up with my job. I'm a fast worker, but a lot of girls take liberties. I've got a couple of days off, that's how I'm here. I get two days a month. It's shocking what the girls do coming late and going to the pictures in the afternoons.'

(Munitions girl, quoted in ibid.)

'I really think I work too long for my health sometimes.'

(Research chemist, quoted in ibid.)

'I shan't go into munitions unless I have to. I like to see a bit of life. I wouldn't mind the WAAFs but my husband doesn't want me to.'

(Tobacconist's manageress, quoted in ibid.)

'A: How do you like it?
'B: Well it's monotonous, but you think what it's for, you know.
'A: That's right; it makes all the difference, doesn't it, if you know what it's for.'

(Customer in a queue in a British Restaurant, Mass Observation Archive.)

'The most striking feature of the industrial situation here is the survival of strictly peace time procedure in the conflict between employers and men, which is still the predominant conflict here.'

(Northern manager, quoted in Mass Observation: *Who Likes and Dislikes Sir Stafford Cripps*, 1943.)

'This girl has so taken to machinery that she'd like to become an apprentice and go right through the works. This of course is not possible on account of Union agreements. There's a feeling among the men at the moment women must be in the factory solely because of the war but really women's place is the home . . .'

(Second Northern manager, quoted in ibid.)

'I was driving a crane and it was able to carry 20 ton. It was just like driving a tram. I was always frightened that I would drop these drums, because we had to go over these men that were working underneath, but I never did, but I was always frightened that I might do. And I was there from seven in the morning till seven at night, and I worked with lots of men and they first of all thought it was strange to have a woman driving this crane because it was so big.'

(BBC, *Woman's Hour* programme, 15 September 1969.)

Hope of the Future

'The men and women of this country, who have endured great hardships during the war, are asking what kind of life awaits them in peace. They seek for the opportunity of leading reasonably secure and happy lives, and they deserve to have it. How are we to provide our people with what they deserve? Here arises the disagreement between the parties.'

(Attlee broadcast, 1945.)

'The whole of the social and economic life of the nation has been uprooted by the war as by an earthquake. Normal life must be reestablished when peace comes, and every progressively minded thinker is determined that the social and economic evils and injustices for which the community suffered before the war must not be permitted in the new world which has to be created when the war is over.'

(B. S. Rowntree, letter of 1942, quoted in Briggs, *A Study of the Work of Seebohm Rowntree*, 1961.)

'The security plan in my report is a plan for securing that no-one in Britain willing to work while he can is without income sufficient to meet at all times the essential needs of himself and his family. The security plan is only a means of redistributing national income so as to put things first, so as to ensure abolition of want before the enjoyment of comfort.'

(Sir William Beveridge broadcast, BBC Archive Disc.)

'The world can never go back to the extent that it was prior to this Blitz. There'll be a better world, or ought to be.'

(Clydebank voice, BBC Archive Disc.)

Victory and Beyond

'This is the BBC Home Service. Here is a special bulletin, read by John Snagge. D Day has come. Early this morning the Allies began the assault on the North Western Face of Hitler's European fortress.'

(John Snagge, reading a news bulletin, BBC Archive Disc.)

'Hallo BBC. This is Chester Wilmot taking up the story of the Rhine crossing from an observation post in the tower of a building looking down on the Rhine itself . . . and that river at the moment is a sheet of burning water, because above it are streams of tracer shells and bullets from Bofors guns and machine guns . . .'

(Chester Wilmot reporting, BBC Archive Disc.)

'An official announcement will be broadcast by the Prime Minister at 3 o'clock tomorrow, Tuesday afternoon, the 8th May. In view of this fact, tomorrow, Tuesday, will be treated as Victory in Europe Day, and will be regarded as a holiday.'

(BBC announcement, BBC Archive Disc.)

'The German war is therefore at an end. Long live the cause of freedom! God save the King!'

(Churchill broadcast, BBC Archive Disc.)

'What a day. We gathered together on our bombed site and planned the finest party the children ever remembered. Neighbours pooled their sweet rations, and collected money, a few shillings from each family . . . and our grocer gave his entire stock of sweets, fruit, jellies, and so on. All the men in the neighbourhood spent the day clearing the site. The Church lent the tables, the milkman lent a cart for a platform, and we lent our radiogram and records for the music. We all took our garden chairs for the elderly to sit on. Someone collected all our spare jam jars. Black-out curtains came down to make fancy dresses for the children.'

(Cardiff housewife, quoted in N. Longmate, op. cit.)

'Until the end of May you may buy cotton bunting without coupons, as long as it is red, white or blue and does not cost more than one and three a square yard.'

(Board of Trade announcement.)

'Everyone rummaged in ragbags and offered bits to anyone who wanted them. That evening, ninety-four children paraded round the streets, carrying lighted candles in jam jars, wearing all manner of weird and fancy dress, singing lustily, "We'll be coming round the mountains when we come", and led by my small son wearing white cricket flannels, a scarlet cummerband and a Scout's hat, beating a drum. In the dusk it was a brave sight never to be forgotten.'

(Cardiff housewife, quoted in N. Longmate, op. cit.)

'We all walked to Buckingham Palace. As we got in front of it the floodlighting flicked on. It was wonderful, magnificent and inspiring and it seemed we had never seen so beautiful a building. The crowd was such as I have never seen. I was never so proud of England and our people. We then walked to Parliament Square and turned to face Big Ben. It was a few minutes to midnight. At one minute past, all fighting was to cease.'

(W.V.S. member, quoted in ibid.)

'It was this enormous sort of anti-climax in a way, it was almost like a bad film, in a way, one of those corny films that you see like Trader Horn ... and the dead people coming up in the sky afterwards. I saw them all, they all sort of came up in front of me, all their dear faces that ... died and this was the sort of feeling, of enormous happiness and enormous grief that they had lost their lives so young.'

(BBC, *Woman's Hour* programme, 15 September 1969.)

Back to Peace

'I was not sure, of course, just when my husband would arrive home, but he turned up at 11.30 one night and I had to get out of bed to let him in, trying desperately to get the curlers out of my hair. The children did not wake up, however, and I'll never forget Bill's face as he stood looking down at his small daughter, whom he was seeing for the first time, and at his son who had grown quite different from the baby he had left behind.'

(Woman, quoted in Longmate, op. cit.)

'For those who remembered the years between the wars the gradual climb back to prosperity was a long, dispiriting haul, echoing with pre-war memories of better days. For the wartime children it was different. Those years were not a return but a revelation. They were lit by surprises; between 1945 and 1951 we saw not only the first pineapples and bananas of our lives, but the first washing machine, the first fountain, the first television sets. The world opening before us was not a pale imitation of the one we had lost but a dip of extraordinary things we had never seen before. If later, we seemed to snarl with baffled rage at the disillusionment and apathy of our elders, perhaps this is why. They treated it all as a dreary mess; they forget that for us it could have been a brave new world.'

(Susan Cooper in M. Sissons and P. French (eds.), *Age of Austerity 1945–1951* (1963).)

'The process of turning over from war to peace is proceeding smoothly and quickly. It will mean a certain slackening of austerity at home but for the present it would be unwise to expect a large flow of goods for individual consumption in this country.'

(*Daily Mirror*, 4 June 1946.)

'Let me be absolutely blunt. If we and the rest of the world don't make the utmost sacrifice we can, men and women will die and children who have done us no harm will grow up weakly and crippled. The Government is treating this situation as a war crisis. Bread [rationed for the first time in 1946] means life. Don't waste a crumb.'

(Broadcast by Sir Ben Smith, Minister of Food, BBC Archive Disc.)

'Carrot Flan reminds you of Apricot Flan, but has a deliciousness all of its own.'

(Ministry of Food recipe book.)

'Whalemeat was a curious, powdery-textured substance resembling a meaty biscuit, with overtones of oil.'

(Susan Cooper, in Sissons and French, op. cit.)

'The public will take all we can give them, especially now the meat ration is cut.'

(Caterers' Association, 1947.)

'I've taken toilet paper from women's lavatories I've been to. There was a shortage of it a little while ago. When I was working in a pub part-time, I used occasionally to take packets of cigarettes – I gave them to my husband. Everyone else used to take them so I thought I might as well.'

(Housewife as reported by *Mass Observation*, 1949.)

'The spivs were tense, dubious, insecure. Yet the essence of spivvery was deeply English, a small, boyish lust for life, and eagerness to play practical jokes on the clumsy, long-winded motions of a bureaucracy.'

(David Hughes, in Sissons and French, op. cit.)

'Your doctor will give you a prescription for any medicines and drugs you may need. You can get these free from any chemist who takes part in the Scheme. In some country areas the doctor himself may dispense medicines. The same is true of all necessary appliances. Some of them will be obtainable through hospitals; some your doctor can prescribe for you. There will be no charge, unless careless breakage causes earlier replacement than usual.'

(Ministry of Health announcement, 1947.)

'So long as public health legislation was confined to environmental sanitation and the protection of the community from infectious diseases, there was no serious danger of confusion between preventive and curative medicine. Since the beginning of the present century, and more particularly in the second quarter, there has been an increasing tendency to introduce measures dealing with the care of the sick as part of the Local Authority services . . . The more important reason for adopting public medical care at that time, however, was that diseases of this kind were beyond the purse of the patient and his family, difficult as a rule for the doctor to attend and treat effectively in the home, and often so prolonged in their course that some form of institutional care had to be provided. It is right that the treatment of these diseases and others of the same category should now be returned to the fold of clinical medicine; and this has been accomplished under the National Health Services Act of 1946 . . . [Yet] we are in danger of falling into the same disorder as our predecessors of half a century ago, and for the same reason, that legislation for health and medical care lacks a single directive aim. The service is not growing like a tree, but only sprouting here and there in response to some specific pressure . . .'

(J. M. Mackintosh, *Trends of Opinion about the Public Health*, 1953.)

'I have heard so often the suggestion made . . . that if anything is done in this way by means of State provision, you will stop people saving. I can remember that suggestion being made at the time of the introduction of the old age pension of 5s a week at 70.'

(Clement Attlee in Parliament, 7 February 1946.)

'My son, aged nine, was rather peeved that his younger brother, aged nine months, should qualify for the new 5s family allowance, so we agreed that each should get half. There being some delay before we were able to collect our first payments I was able to place two certificates each to my two sons' credit in their War Savings accounts, and we shall continue to do this, so that they will have the benefit of the money when they are older.'

(*Picture Post*, 16 November 1946.)

'Won't it be nice when we have lovely lingerie, *and* Lux to look after our pretty things. Remember how pure, safe Lux preserved the beauty of delicate fabrics . . . And how easily it rinsed out. But while there is still not Lux, and you have to wash treasured things with the soap or flakes available, do take extra care . . .'

(Advertisement, 1946.)

'I was happier when I lay listening to bombs and daring myself to tremble; when I got romantic letters from abroad; when I cried over Dunkirk; when people showed their best side and we still believed we were fighting to gain something.'

(Woman, quoted in broadcast.)

'Just before the last stroke it had reached one minute past. A great cry went up and people clapped their hands. Something went off with a bang. The tugs in the river gave the V sign. *It was unforgettable.*'

(W.V.S. member describing V.E. Day, 1945, quoted in ibid.)

'We looked out towards the target and saw a vast ball of fire. After fifteen seconds the flame had died out and turned into a cloud. Exactly what that cloud looked like I do not suppose any words will ever describe. Unlike any other phenomenon the world had ever seen, it was possessed of some diabolical activity, as though it were a horrible form of life.'

(Group Captain Cheshire, broadcast on the Atomic Bomb, BBC Archive Disc.)

'What is the city over the mountains
Cracks and re-forms and bursts in the violet air
Falling towers
Jerusalem Athens Alexandria
Vienna London
Unreal.'

(T. S. Eliot, *The Waste Land.*)

12

Between Two Worlds

STUART HALL

The closer the social historian gets to his own times, the harder it is for him to be sure he has hold of what is essential about his period: the more difficult it is to separate the rich but incidental surface variety of social life from its underlying patterns. This chapter deals with 'The Long March of Everyman' through the 1950s and early 1960s. It is a period of rapid social change. It is also a period in which the pace and direction of social change itself becomes a topic of concern and public debate. The argument then was about whether the many indications of change really added up to a 'social revolution' for ordinary people. That argument is still not resolved: we are still living out its contradictory legacy. In the following commentary and extracts, I have tried to focus on what seem now to be major, powerful and significant strands in the period. But it remains, necessarily, selective, an interpretation – my interpretation. Its conclusions remain provisional, tentative. The witnesses I call on are still alive, and my '1950s' may not be theirs.

One of the most striking features of the period is the growth in scale and importance of the mass media of communication. Television on a mass scale first decisively intervenes in English social life in this period. It supplements, then overtakes, the already complex networks of communication – radio, newspapers, mass publishing – which are part and parcel of an advanced industrial civilization. These new means of communication massively document the social life of the period: they constitute a whole new documentary source for the social historian. Commentaries, witnessing descriptions, documentary material, which previously the social historian would have had to cull from printed sources, are now to be found, perhaps in their most 'primary' form, in our radio and television archives. I have drawn, wherever possible, on these sources, rather than on printed ones, for two reasons: first, because we find here the living voices and

273

speech rhythms of ordinary people talking about their experience of and response to the conditions of their lives; but second, because I want to give the reader a sense of how the new means of communication fundamentally reshaped, and reshapes, our sense of what our collective social experience is like. Extracts from archive material are not always as satisfactory as printed sources. They tend to be briefer, more heavily edited for a particular purpose: they have been inserted into a programme format, dictated by the special interest of a producer; speakers do not have the space and freedom to think their way around and into a subject in the way in which the diarist or the letter-writer of a previous period did. Moreover, the choice of archive material has been badly skewed. There is an over-abundance of 'official' material, linked with official public events; the voices and experiences of 'Everyman' are, characteristically, underrepresented. Yet it is in these voices that we can best grasp the movement of historical forces in the actual experience of the living witnesses: it is here that we hear the primary experience of ordinary men and women finding its own kind of articulacy. The contemporary social historian has no other alternative but to use these rich new sources as best he can.

Between Two Worlds

This chapter deals, exclusively, with the 1950s and early 1960s. The two worlds we are between are, on the one hand, the world of wartime Britain, and its immediate aftermath in the period of austerity: and, on the other hand, Britain now – Britain in Europe, Britain under inflation. The middle and late 1950s was the period of 'affluence': if we need a symbolic date for it, we might select the moment, after the defeat of the post-war Labour Government, when Churchill announced the 'bonfire of controls'. Slowly, at first, then with gathering speed, post-war Britain enters a period of rapid change. It is a period of growing prosperity, of a kind: a period when a great deal of money flows into the purchase of the newly available consumer goods; it is a 'prosperity' underpinned by the revolution in welfare, and by full employment. The rebuilding and reconstruction of the urban and suburban environment – made necessary, partly, by large-scale bombing and by the massive social neglect of the inter-war period – gets under way. New kinds of industry, based largely on the electronics revolution, come into being alongside the old – and without displacing them; the face of industrial Britain reveals two 'industrial revolutions', the second on top of, or within, the first. There is, therefore, a shift in the patterns of skills, and of work; there is also a shift in the composition of the labour force – more people either in clerical, highly skilled or service occupations, or pushed down into the semi-skilled or unskilled ranks of mass production, than in the older occupations. People begin to move about again, if they can; the changing patterns of prosperity as between the older and newer areas of industrial backwardness and growth pull people to where the jobs are. Many, of course – the majority – cannot or do not wish to move. The pattern of regional decline in the older industrial areas, and of hot-house, unorganized growth in the new areas (especially in the South-east) begins to emerge: the imagery of 'London' versus 'the North', which contributes so much to public debate, to literature and drama, to our whole sense of what the society is like in the period, is rooted in this aspect of change. In some areas and industries, the long, stable pattern of continuity from generation to generation persists: in some other areas, dominated by the newer industries, continuities are broken. The new housing schemes – the development of urban flats, of new housing estates and of the new towns – and the slow processes of rehousing certainly do not destroy the typical and traditional urban working-class environment; but they seem to make inroads into it, to warren and undermine it, even to rob it of something of its corporate stability. To the outsider, the social commentator, these begin to look like two contrasted, perhaps even opposed, 'styles' of working-class life. We begin to get, for the first time, the contrasting images of the 'extended kinship network' of the old working-class neighbourhood, and the 'family-centred' life on the new working-class estate. The densely-textured, corporate class culture of industrial working-class life, with its familiar urban landscape of 'back-to-backs', and its traditional spaces – the neighbourhood, the street, the pub, the corner shop, the 'occupied territory' of the first industrial revolution – is infiltrated, though not destroyed. An area like London's East End becomes a sort of living social laboratory for the social investigator: a place where, by patient *study, some little light might be thrown on the clear gap there is between what people think is happening to ordinary people, and what is actually going on: the gap between the image, or 'myths' of affluence, and contradictory reality. This kind of investigation – all that we have in the twentieth century to match the massive social investigations of the nineteenth – clarifies a little, but is in the end a thankless task. The real processes – new kinds of industry, rehousing, property speculation, the rise in consumption, urban planning and legislation, the inexorable forces of the market – continue to make on this landscape, and on the culture it sustains, an indelible imprint.*

'The first effect of the high density, high rise schemes was to destroy the function of the street, the local pub, the corner shop, as articulations of communal space. Instead there was only the privatised space of the family unit, stacked one on top of each other, in total isolation, juxtaposed with the totally public space which surrounded it, and which lacked any of the informal social controls generated by the neighbourhood. The streets which serviced the new estates became thoroughfares, their users 'pedestrians', and by analogy so many bits of human traffic, and this irrespective of whether or not they were separated from motorised traffic. It is indicative of how far the planners failed to understand the human ecology of the working class neighbourhood that they could actually talk about building 'vertical streets'. The people who had to live in them weren't fooled. As one put it – they might have hot running water and central heating, but to him they were still prisons in the sky. Inevitably, the physical isolation, the lack of human scale and sheer impersonality of the new environment was felt worst by people living in the new tower blocks which have gradually come to dominate the East End landscape.

'The second effect of redevelopment was to destroy 'matrilocal residence'. Not only was the new housing designed on the model of the nuclear family with little provision for large low income families (usually designated as 'problem families') and none at all for groups of young, single people, but the actual pattern of distribution of the new housing tended to disperse the kinship network; families of marriage were separated from their families of origin, especially during the first phase of redevelopment. The isolated family unit could no longer call on the resources of wider kinship networks, or of the neighbourhood, and the family itself became the sole focus of solidarity. This meant that any problems were bottled up within the immediate inter-personal context which produced them; and at the same time, family relationships were invested with a new intensity, to compensate for the diversity of relationships previously generated through neighbours and wider kin. The trouble was that although the traditional kinship system which corresponded to it had broken down, the traditional patterns of socialization (of communication and control) continued to reproduce themselves in the interior of the family. The working class family was thus not only isolated from the outside but undermined from within. There is no better example of what we are talking about than the plight of the so-called 'housebound mother'. The street or turning was no longer available as a safe playspace, under neighbourly supervision. Mum, or Auntie, was no longer just round the corner to look after the kids for the odd morning. Instead, the task of keeping an eye on the kids fell exclusively to the young wife, and the only safe playspace was the 'safety of the home'. Feeling herself cooped up with the kids, and cut off from the outside world, it wouldn't be surprising if she occasionally took out her frustration on those nearest and dearest! Only market research and advertising executives imagine that the housebound mother sublimates everything in her G-plan furniture, her washing machine or non-stick frying pan.'

(Phil Cohen, 'Sub-Cultural Conflict and Working Class Community', in *Working Papers In Cultural Studies*, No. 3, Centre for Cultural Studies, University of Birmingham, 1972.)

That passage certainly sums up one, representative *kind of* experience *in the period, though there were many which pointed the*

*other way: which suggested that, into and through the changes, and
behind the splurge of new consumer goods and gadgets which
advertising directed to the working-class home, the stubborn
continuities of working-class culture and life survived. But
'community' – a theme and topic which is unthinkable in English
social experience without the paradigm instance of the working-class
neighbourhood and the culture it supported – became, in the period,
a matter of widespread and fundamental concern. For behind these
clear manifestations of change, the meaning of which remains to
this day unclear, there emerged a connected, but different theme:
the question whether, as the conditions and patterns of social life
for working people changed, and as what money there was about
began to pour into the new consumer goods on offer, people might not
only be uprooted from a life they knew and had made to another partly
made for them by 'others', but might also be 'on the move', if not from
one class to another, then from one kind of class 'ideal' – solidarity,
neighbourliness, collectivity – to another: that of 'individualism', of
'competition' in the social struggle to 'get on', of 'privatization'.*

'It's true that the old pattern is changing. You get these
semi-detached houses with the privet hedges all right round
the house, and they have these great wide sun windows, and
the thing they do is cover the windows with muslin to sort of
shut themselves off. The result is that everyone is having
his own private little life, and his own little house, and
people don't share as much outside – with their neighbours.
People do tend to become much more – what you would
call 'middle class', and the same in their attitude to each
other – you know, the old attitude of middle class "keep
yourself to yourself . . ."'

'Nowadays, there's a tremendous change, an amazing
change, in fact, in just a few years. People have got television. They stay home to watch it – husbands and wives.
If they do come in at the weekend they're playing bingo.
They've now got a big queue for the one-armed bandit as
well. They do have a lot more money, but what they're
losing is togetherness.'

(Two extracts from *A Good and Comely Life*, BBC Archive Disc.)

'The majority of people do these little improvements in their houses – flush the doors, the idea being, you see, because it helps to modernise the place and helps to keep down dust and that sort of thing, I suppose. Quite a lot of people round here I know have installed geysers, you see, because we haven't any means of hot water other than the ordinary gas stove. It's a very old fashioned idea, you know. You have a pump on the wall out there to pump the water up into the bathroom out of an old-fashioned kettle copper, you see, which goes back to the prehistoric age.'

(From a programme about the Dagenham Housing Estate, *Forty Years Old*, BBC Archive Disc.)

'I'm not a snob by any means, but bringing the children up with – shall we say people with better income brackets rather than better educations – they tend to look for higher things in life.'

(ibid.)

But did these aspects of change mean what the speakers thought they did? Were muslin curtains in a small semi-detached a sign that you wanted to 'keep yourself to yourself'? Were working people losing their sense of 'togetherness'? Did a bit of 'do-it-yourself' around the house signify 'privatization'? What were the 'higher things in life' that children could learn from 'people with better income brackets'? If the changes these witnesses point to really did add up to one representative social experience, we must not forget how close the great majority of working people were to what the man from Dagenham called 'the prehistoric age'.

'I've got to carry my water; I got no coal house; we're living in one room – four of us – two bairns. I've got a bairn, two months, and one two-and-a-half. The walls are soaking. We can't use the other room for the rain that's coming in it. I've got to go down the stairs. I've got 20 stairs to go down: I've got to go down the street, along the back lane and into the yard for my water; and I've got no toilet, and until recently there's been three families sharing the one toilet.'

'Twenty-two was using the one toilet, a broken down wooden old shack which is not worth to put cats in let alone human beings.'

'It's damp, and the roof's falling in. The back bedroom's no good to sleep in, you can't sleep in that. The four of us have to sleep in one bedroom. A little girl, a little boy, me husband and meself. We've got a lavatory outside, no bathroom, cold water, got no hot water at all. I wouldn't know what a bathroom looked like. Nine people share the toilet with us. It's disgraceful. The wall's knocked down between the two toilets and you still can't go in if there's somebody in the next one. You've to wait until they're both empty, because you can see one another, you know. You sit side by side ... like that. Nobody wants that, do they? And the rats there – you have to dodge them. They get a bit rifely.'

(Three extracts from *Northern Slums*, BBC Archive Disc.)

'I come away with about £15 at the moment – four days – sometimes I'm on three. I was on three last week, which is only about £14. And I've got to give my wife £10 for grub and rent, £1 a week for electricity, £1 a week for gas, is £12. Thirty bob for the travelling, and of course I've got to pay the Union, and all the other different things – that takes a shilling here and a bob there. I'm left with about £1 a week to entertain me and the wife, and it costs me – if I go down to the Club on a Sunday night, it costs me about £2. 10. So I'm in debt, really. Don't smoke, have a drink, have a wee bid on the horses and that. No bank book, nothing in the bank. I have no car – I haven't enough money to buy a car. I've been married five years and we've never been on holiday yet.'

(From *More Equal Than Others*, BBC Archive Disc.)

Those, too, are representative 'affluent experiences'. It is – it was – difficult to distil any simple and straightforward pattern of change from such contradictory evidence, or to make sense of what meaning, in their own real experience, the variety of surface changes had for the majority of ordinary people in the society. Partly because the dramatic hiatus of the war had so interrupted English social life that almost anything would have been certain to have been experienced by the majority of people as new and different. The war imposed an over-simplified and over-dramatized imagery of 'before' and 'after' on the attempt to make sense of social change, and made the emergent patterns of change seem sharper, starker than in fact they were. Partly because such change as there was really does seem to have been moving across the face of the country at very different paces: composite social images, constructed out of a very partial experience of one corner of the South-east, utterly failed to net how far the 'pre-historic age' still survived in most other places – not excluding great areas of the South-east. But partly, also, because what people were trying to do was to forecast and anticipate the emerging patterns of social life; what they knew about was how change registered in their own experience in their own corner of the society. But there were strong temptations to extrapolate from these discontinuous social experiences, and build up from them a projected image of 'the future'. This is one way in which ordinary people try to come to terms and understand the forces which appear to be silently shaping their lives. Britain, entering a sort of 'affluence', was, at the same moment, trying to comprehend what 'affluence' was about. It was easy and tempting to take the highly visible and conspicuous indices of change for the 'real movement' underneath. It was a temptation which almost everyone fell into. Thus the terrifying 'myths of affluence' became inextricably interwoven with the contradictory 'experience' of affluence. No wonder one commentator, writing about Britain in the late fifties, called it 'Britain – Unknown Country'.

There was at least one other reason: television. The real spread of BBC television happened only in the early years of the fifties. Commercial television opened in 1955. This development fed the confusion in two ways. First, by monopolizing the channels of public discussion and debate in the society, television also centralized the power to make its images of social life stick. It communicated, at rapid speed, highly selective, if not distorted, images of one community or section of the society to another. It also helped to form

an overall image of where the whole *society was headed. Secondly,
it gave an almost tangible visibility to the quite limited rise in
consumption and in spending money. It signified the world in terms
of the 'goodies' produced in the new consumer industries and
seeking markets among the working class. It created the spectacular
world of commodities. Advertising, and the spurious social
images to which it was tied, represented only one way in which
television helped to obliterate the deep sources of change in a veritable
cornucopia of goods.*

*How far this imagery of consumption entered the lives and
imagination of ordinary men and women is now anyone's guess. It
seems, in retrospect, to have been wildly exaggerated. Where people
could test 'images' against 'experience', life may have felt glossier,
tinnier, fizzier than before – Hoggart, in* The Uses of Literacy,
*called it a 'candy-floss culture': it is to be doubted that they thought
they were on the threshold of a new Utopia of wealth. The 'telly',
like the piano before it, moved into the corner, and was at least
partly absorbed by the whole densely textured and structured life
around it: it made a difference – but it did not suddenly dismantle
the culture of working people, rooted as it was and remained in the
persistent structures of the English class system.*

'Yes, definitely classes. The whole set up of the nation is
built on class, regardless of what the newspapers tell us.
I mean, you just can't get away from it, can you? Even
the types of restaurants, hotels, things like that. They're all
built on it. Oh, it's a class society, yes.'

(From *More Equal Than Others*, BBC Archive Disc.)

'Night after night we sat in front of the telly with a ham
sandwich in one hand, a bar of chocolate in the other, and a
bottle of lemonade between our boots, while mam was with
some fancy-man upstairs on the new bed she'd ordered, and
I'd never known a family as happy as ours was in that couple
of months when we'd got all the money we needed. And
when the dough ran out I didn't think about anything
much, but just roamed the streets – looking for another job,
I told mam – hoping I suppose to get my hands on another

five hundred nicker so's the nice life we'd got used to could go on and on for ever. Because it's surprising how quick you can get used to a different life. To begin with, the adverts on the telly had shown us how much more there was in the world to buy than we'd ever dreamed of when we'd looked into shop windows but hadn't seen all there was to see because we didn't have the money to buy it with anyway. And the telly made all these things seem twenty times better than we'd ever thought they were. Even adverts at the cinema were cool and tame, because now we were seeing them in private at home. We used to cock our noses up at things in shops that didn't move, but suddenly we saw their real value because they jumped and glittered around the screen and had some pasty-faced tart going head over heels to get her nail-polished grabbers on to them or her lipstick lips over them, not like the crumby adverts you saw on posters or in newspapers as dead as doornails; these were flickering around loose, half-open packets and tins, making you think that all you had to do was finish opening them before they were yours, like seeing an unlocked safe through a shop window with the man gone away for a cup of tea without thinking to guard his lolly. The films they showed were good as well, in that way, because we couldn't get our eyes unglued from the cops chasing the robbers who had satchel-bags crammed with cash and looked like getting away to spend it – until the last moment. I always hoped they would end up free to blow the lot, and could never stop wanting to put my hand out, smash into the screen (it only looked a bit of rag-screen like at the pictures) and get the copper in a half-nelson so's he'd stop following the bloke with the money-bags. Even when he'd knocked off a couple of bank clerks I hoped he wouldn't get nabbed. In fact then I wished more than ever he wouldn't because it meant the hot-chair if he did, and I wouldn't wish that on anybody no matter what they'd done, because I'd read in a book where the hot-chair worn't a quick death at all, but that you just sat there scorching to death until you were dead. And it was when these cops were chasing the crooks that we played some good tricks with the telly, because when one of them opened his big gob to spout about them getting their man I'd turn the sound down and see his mouth move like a goldfish or mackerel or a minnow mimicking what they were supposed to be acting – it was so funny the whole family nearly went into fits on the brand new carpet that hadn't yet found its way to the bedroom. It was the best of all though when we did it to some Tory telling us about how good his government was going to be if we kept on voting for them – their slack chops rolling, opening and bumbling, hands lifting to twitch moustaches and touching their buttonholes to make sure the flower hadn't wilted, so that you could see they didn't mean a word they said, especially with not a murmur coming out because we'd cut off the sound. When the governor of the Borstal first talked to me I was reminded of those times so much that I nearly killed myself trying not to laugh. Yes, we played so many good stunts on the box of tricks that mam used to call us the Telly Boys, we got so clever at it.'

(Alan Sillitoe, *The Loneliness of the Long-Distance Runner*, 1959.)

In one section of the population, however, change did register in a peculiarly strong and visible way: among the young. The 1950s sees the rise to prominence, for the first time, of a distinct and identifiable 'culture of the young' – something different from the cold-shower culture of the private 'public' schools or the Guy Fawkes Night pranks of Oxbridge students – which touched, if not everyone, certainly all sections of the population. For ordinary young people, the war – which they had experienced, if at all, as young children – really did divide history into 'before' and 'after'; and they belonged, willy-nilly, to 'after'. This gave a strong genera-tional marking to the relationships between adults and 'youth'. If incomes had gone up a little for many working people, they had improved at a faster rate for young adults; and since their families had a little more economic security than between the wars, a higher proportion of what they earned was left over for spending on them-selves and their own recreations and pursuits. Affluent Britain was not a society which allowed spare cash to accumulate in anyone's pockets for long. The surplus in the pockets of young working-class boys and girls was quickly funnelled into the new industries servicing working-class leisure, and, out of this amalgam of forces, the distinctive youth styles which so marked the fifties emerged. This rapid translation of generational independence into style *was so striking that, for a time, 'youth' itself became* the *metaphor for social change.*

Two processes, not one, were in fact at work here. The new 'youth' styles, expressing themselves partly – as almost everything else in the period did – in terms of consumption patterns, also indicated subtle shifts in attitude and outlook: but no one changed their life-situation, life chances or social position by becoming a Teddy Boy or a Mod. The other process, the route up and out of the working class into the professional ranks via education – the Eleven Plus, the Grammar School, and the University – may have offered a more permanent route of social mobility: but far fewer could take it; and the social and personal costs for first generation 'Scholarship Boys' (there were, of course, fewer 'Scholarship Girls') were punishing – the loss of roots, of a sense of connection to the life of the community, even to one's own family.

'I went to a grammar school and I went to university because, apart from its being something I wanted, it was something they wanted as well.'

(The graduate son of a docker, BBC Archive Disc.)

'I made things very different for my boys. Different to how I had it. But to tell you the truth, I sometimes wonder if I was wise. I mean, if Frank hadn't got on, he might have got married and settled down near here and then there'd have been grandchildren. Frank's brilliant, you see, and I encouraged him to take a scholarship to Cambridge. He got a first-class honours degree and became a top-level specialist in aeronautical engineering. The Government sent him to Australia on secret work and he stayed out there with an Australian firm. We don't write: I don't even know his address. He's like Greta thingummy – he wants to be alone.

But there you are – I put him on his feet and he must go his own way.'

(A telephone engineer, quoted in P. Willmott and Michael Young, *Family and Class in a London Suburb*, 1960.)

The symbolic route seemed easier:

'We used to dress up like peacocks and parade on a Sunday morning down at Newcastle quayside at the market there. We used to meet fellers from Wallsend, everybody used to come and show their clothes off, you know, and this was the place where you got new ideas. If somebody came with a longer jacket than you, you know, you immediately went away and got a new jacket. You used to go to a tailor and used to get as wide a look as you can, measure a half-back and used to get about a ten inch half-back, 20 inches across your shoulders, although you never filled it. You used to get this, and the front of the jacket used to have one or two buttons and you used to have the break – Now the break of the jacket is where your first button meets, you know, fastens. You used to have this as low as possible, and quite often you got it below the natural waist of your trousers so that you could see this and you could have your long tie. In those days we used to wear hand-painted ties. At the knee the trousers were 24, 25 inches wide, and going down to 16 inches at the ankles, which gave an effect of having a man like a triangle . . .'

(From *Teddy Boys*, BBC Archive Disc.)

'Every night out, you know. There wasn't any home entertainments like television. I think they just – in that time, people had stopped playing the pianos in the house, you know, after the war, and you didn't have any real home entertainment. Sunday nights, you didn't – you had nothing else to do but walk around Newcastle, looking in shop windows, parading yourself again in your regular outfits. We used to get our 'kicks', as we call them nowadays, not from pills but just from laughter, really.'

(ibid.)

'If your bike is said to do 100 miles an hour, and it doesn't, you're a bit unhappy about it, and fiddle about with it and try and make it do the ton. But once you've done the ton, you're – well, I don't know: it boosts you up.'

(From *Burning It Up*, BBC Archive Disc.)

'I mean, they're not motor-cyclists: they're just, more or less coffee-bar cowboys.'

(ibid.)

'Short jackets, two little vents at the back, three buttons, single-breasted, maybe blazer stripes, wearing blazer, Italian rounded collar shirts, usually navy blue, white or red, trousers with no turn ups, usually 16 inch, 17 inch bottoms, pointed toe shoes, you know. That's about all. Oh, they wear big overcoats, with big pointed collars or macs, white macs, you know. It's all derived from the French and Italians.'

(From *Teenagers*, BBC Archive Disc.)

'I remember coming out of the Elephant & Castle, the big theatre at the corner – the Trocadero – and it was after seeing the Bill Haley film, *Rock Around the Clock*, and we all went down the Old Kent Road, and at the end of the Old Kent Road, all the fire engines were there, and they got their hoses all ready, and it was a big thing, terrible big thing. You felt you were it. Not only just because you were young, but you felt the rest of your lives would be, well, ordered by you and not ordered by other people. We thought we could do anything we bloody well wanted – we thought we could do anything at all – nothing could stop you. You were the guv'ner – you were the king. The world was free – the world was open.'

(Ray Gosling, extract from *Vox Pop 2: It's My Life* BBC programme.)

'The dreamland is always, like the win on the pools, just around the corner. The man with the big cigar from up

West who discovers The Boy, and buys him up, never arrives. Like the Education plan, and the premium bond, it can happen, but it rarely does, and always there is the fear that you have to sell what you have no right to sell. To reach the dreamy scene, the girl, or the boy in the teenage stories who is helped to a stage success by a Boy God in the end, finds true love, and happiness in the arms of the kid across the street who was jilted in her or his desire to be top. You have no right to sell your birthright. To be top you must lose your heritage, the love on the street that will never let you down. To be a God you have to make a deal with them, and they are never honest. They never play fair. They never treat you right. The haze that surrounds the life of the Boy is a fog of fear, and not the mist about to rise on a dazzling dawn of success. He lives in Birmingham, not Hollywood – a dead Empire in a sunset world, yet still hopes that somehow, an Eden will pull off the trick, Super Mac will open up those golden gates, and here along the M1 the orange trees of California will begin to blossom. There must be a lucky card somewhere, a permutation no one has found, a new body movement more appealing than the last. The man might come from Vernons. The man might come from the theatrical agency. The cheque, and the contract might be in his hand. Others may call apart from the rent man. If only he had the contacts. If only . . . And so this boy with everyone and everything against him, plays out his own private drama to the fuggy street, with his god on a chain round his neck, his girl clinging to his arm. Against all of them; in search of the heaven he sees on the glossy page, the screen, and the hoarding.'

(Ray Gosling, 'Dream Boy,' from *New Left Review* 3, May/June 1960.)

It can't be said that then – or now – adult members of the official culture displayed much sympathy for or insight into either of those 'dreams' – of freedom or recognition – which Ray Gosling gave voice to in those extracts. When the Any Questions *team – that repository of the conventional wisdom – was asked to comment*

on the events surrounding the showing of Bill Haley's Rock Around
the Clock, *Mary Stocks remarked that young people were merely
exhibiting 'a sort of unexpended animal spirits'; Lord Boothby
expressed the view that he'd 'rather they went off to Cairo and
started teddy-boying around there', and Jeremy Thorpe said that
'Jazz to me comes from the jungle and this is jungle music taken to
its logical conclusion. This is musical Mau-Mau.' It is hard,
thinking back, to recall the time when those references to 'Mau-
Mau' and 'Cairo' would have been good for a laugh. Still,* Any
Questions *reckons its audience in millions. Somebody out there
must have been listening.*

*For a good part of our period, the curve of popular feeling seems to
have been on the upswing. There's a good deal of optimism and
confidence about. Or at least, so the popular mood was defined by
those agents and powers in our society who are in a position to
define life for others. When, in the mid fifties, the* Daily Express
*began its advice column for inexperienced stock-market investors,
its voice rose to a crescendo:*

'The lucky slum kids of today can break through all social
barriers to become the millionaires of tomorrow. And if the
coffee-bar revolution has done so much for adolescents, the
Express is prepared to do just as much for adults ... As
stock markets climb Everest-high, more and more people
are venturing into holding stocks and shares. And they are
being openly encouraged to do so – with plans for workers
to buy shares in their own companies ... So, beginning
today, the *Daily Express* will guide you through the jargon
and the jungle.'

When the Economist *took stock of the situation, in 1959, what it
glimpsed – much to its pleasure – was nothing more or less than
'The Unproletarian Society' (16 May 1959):*

'The old-fashioned Conservative is one who looks out at the
comforts made achievable by rising incomes and the hire-
purchase revolution and who feels vaguely that the workers
are unfairly luckier than he was as a boy – that they are
getting above their station. The modern Conservative

should be one who looks up at the television aerials sprouting above the working-class homes of England, who looks down on the housewives' tight slacks on the back of the motor-cycle and family side-car on the summer road to Brighton, and who sees a great poetry in them. For this is what the de-proletarianisation of British society means; and the changes in social and industrial attitudes of mind it could bring with it are immense.'

And not only Conservatives. Mr Crosland, in his influential book, The Future of Socialism, *saw much the same trend – towards 'the threshold of the new era of abundance':*

'. . . even these poorer workers are themselves peering across the threshold; they have accepted the new standards as the social norm, and are already thinking of the day when they too will acquire these goods. All this must have a profound effect on the psychology of the working class . . .'

(C. A. R. Crosland, 'The Search For Equality', in *The Future of Socialism*, 1956.)

When the leader of the Labour Party, Hugh Gaitskell, faced the 1959 Conference at Blackpool after the third successive defeat of the traditional party of the working class at the polls, he certainly believed that these 'profound effects on the psychology of the working class' were part of a deep and permanent secular trend:

'In short, the changing character of labour, full employment, new housing, the new way of life based on the telly, the fridge, the car and the glossy magazines – all have had their effect on our political strength.'

One old Conservative who fully absorbed the new message recommended by the Economist *was the Prime Minister himself, Harold Macmillan:*

'Indeed, let us be frank about it: most of our people have never had it so good. Go round the country, go to the industrial towns, go to the farms, and you will see a state of prosperity such as we have never had in my life-time – nor indeed ever in the history of this country.'

(Harold Macmillan, in a speech at Bedford, 20 July 1957. Quoted in Anthony Sampson, *Macmillan*, 1967.)

When he went to the country in 1959, it was behind the slogan 'You've had it good. Have it better. Vote Conservative.' The affluent boom could not have been higher.

And then, suddenly, it turns down: the bubble bursts. When the mists and myths clear, it is still, recognizably, the same country we had known before. The poor are not only still with us – they are there in increasing numbers: poverty is 'rediscovered'. The 'economic miracle', which never happened, dissipates. The one per cent of the adult population who owned four fifths of all share capital and the ten per cent who owned four fifths of all private property had side-stepped the era of the 'redistribution of wealth'. Jimmy Porter, in John Osborne's play, Look Back in Anger *(1956), had observed that 'it's pretty dreary living in the American age – unless you're an American, of course. Perhaps all our children will be Americans.' But the American dawn failed to break. 'Affluence' crests – then breaks. The 'Macmillennium' is over. Britain 'Between Two Worlds' is also Britain between two moods: Britain which rises to a curve of feeling, then – stutters to a halt.*

There had been signs enough, for those who ran to read.

'I suppose people of our generation aren't able to die for good causes any longer. We had all that done for us, in the thirties and forties, when we were still kids. There aren't any good, brave causes left. If the big bang comes, and we all get killed off, it won't be in aid of the old-fashioned grand design. It'll just be for the Brave-New-nothing-very-much-thank-you. About as pointless and inglorious as stepping in front of a bus.'

(Jimmy Porter, in John Osborne's *Look Back In Anger*, 1956.)

'For, coming back to Britain is also, in many respects, like going back to the nursery. The outside world, the dangerous world, is shut away: its sounds are muffled. Cretonne curtains are drawn, with a pretty pattern on them of the Queen and her fairy-tale Prince, riding to Westminster in a golden coach. Nanny lights the fire, and sits herself down with a nice cup of tea and yesterday's *Daily Express*; but she keeps half an eye on us too, as we bring out our trophies from abroad, the books and pictures we have managed to get past the customs. (Nanny has a pair of scissors handy, to cut out anything it wouldn't be right for children to see.) The clock ticks on. The servants are all downstairs watching TV. Mummy and Daddy have gone to the new Noel Coward at the Globe. Sometimes there's a scream from the cellar – Nanny's lips tighten, but she doesn't say anything . . . Is it to be wondered at that, from time to time, a window is found open, and the family is diminished by one? We hear of him later sometimes, living in a penthouse in New York, or a *dacha* near Moscow. If he does really well, he is invited home, years later, and given tea in the drawing room, and we are told to call him Professor.'

(Lindsay Anderson, 'Get Out and Push', *Declaration*, ed. Tom Maschler.)

When the first ragged ranks of the Campaign for Nuclear Disarmament swung into view on the first day of their march to Aldermaston, one observer commented:

'This must be a bunch of bloody psychotics, trying to extrovert their own psychic difficulties, you know, to neither end nor purpose. It's like a bunch of tiny dogs yapping at the back door to the big house – it will accomplish sweet nothing.'

(BBC Archive Disc.)

René Cutforth, the radio commentator, however, risked the view that 'they might just be the only people left alive'. Certainly, the shadow of what Jimmy Porter called 'the big bang' lengthened across the whole face of 'affluent Britain' throughout this whole period, and nothing the 'bunch of bloody psychotics' did could raise it an inch. Yet the 'extra-parliamentary politics' which has so changed the face of political life in the western world in the succeeding decade, and which so powerfully crystallized the popular mood of protest and dissent against the enforced calm of 'prosperous Britain', had its beginnings here: it was fired in this highly respectable and law-abiding crucible. It was, after all, only two years between Harold Macmillan's remark, in an interview in the Daily Mail *(January 1961), that 'We've got it good. Let's keep it good. There is nothing to be ashamed of in that,' and his observation, to a hushed House of Commons, à propos* the Profumo Affair *(21 March 1963):*

'Here, I should tell the House that the Ministers did not know the contents. They were aware, and I was made aware, that the letter began with the word, "Darling". This was volunteered by Mr Profumo, who explained that, in circles in which he and his wife moved, it was a term of no great significance. I believe that might be accepted – I do not live among young people fairly widely . . .'

That little episode was, perhaps, a fitting epitaph to the latter end, the back-end, of the affluent era. It was, as Wayland Young remarked, 'scandal and crisis together'. It 'exercised some of the purgative and disruptive functions of a revolution' (Wayland Young, The Profumo Affair, *1963).*

In the 1950s, almost everything changed – a little. No segment of the society, no corner of the nation, no aspect of life remained untouched. So, one part of the story is this story of change, of emergent patterns, of new relationships and conditions for ordinary men and women, of a sense of discontinuity with the past. Change is not comfortable to live with, and not always easy to understand; in the 'society of affluence', which threw up such paradoxical signals, it was easy to project the problems which life presented into simple and stereotyped remedies:

'It is getting too bad now. They're too many in the country and they're over-running it. If they come into this country, they should be made to live to the same standards as we live, and not too many in their house as they always have done, unless someone puts their foot down. They bring in diseases and all sorts of things that spread to different people, and your children have to grow up with them and it's not right.'

(BBC Archive Disc.)

'They' in that passage were, of course, West Indian and Pakistani or Indian immigrants who, from the mid fifties on, came in substantial numbers into the booming cities and industries. The same motorcycle lad who said, of his parents, 'they just stay awake until I get in at night, and once I'm in they're happy. But every time I go out I know they're on edge', could casually remark about going 'down Notting Hill Gate . . . to punch a few niggers up'. Paradoxes.

Change, certainly. But 'a social revolution'? I doubt it. We need another term for a period of massive social upheaval which, nevertheless, leaves so much exactly where it was: which preserves even as it surpasses. I think ordinary men and women in the 1950s were caught somewhere inside that double process, trying to make sense of it. My aim in this chapter has been to catch, however provisionally, this contradictory movement.

Appendix

The BBC Radio 4 series, *The Long March of Everyman*, was an exploratory act of faith in the possibility of developing a history of the 'swarm life' of society's 'unknown soldiers', on the lines envisaged by Tolstoy in the excursus to *War and Peace*. It was conceived in terms of the mass media (a non-specialist audience); of the art of audio (communication through the 'total music' of all varieties of sound); and in relation to the newly developing field of 'oral history' – the tape-recording of first-hand historical evidence, particularly in the area of that day-to-day experience which has tended to be overlooked by the traditional history of 'great men and great events'.

The role of the historians who were the programme directors was to work out, in collaboration with their producers, the theme and scope which they thought proper to their programmes and possible in relation to the material which might be found. From the raw material which they provided (which could range from *actualité* sound recordings to the most indirect echoes of Everyman's voice in, say, a medieval court record), the programmes were composed on a pattern which aimed at a twofold 'symphony' – of voices, sounds, music, etc., on the one hand, and of concepts and images on the other.

The core of the whole enterprise was the recordings of these 'voices of Everyman', spoken as far as possible by contemporary equivalents of the original speakers. On the basis of what was known about the geographical origin, occupation and social group of the original speakers, a large-scale field-recording operation was organized, covering the whole of England, Scotland and Wales, and the five hundred tapes of 'vox pop' thus collected formed the main element of the twenty-six 45-minute 'sound symphonies'.

These were first broadcast, and repeated within the week, on BBC Radio 4 between 21 November 1971 and 24 May 1972. For the second repeat, from 30 September 1972 to 24 March 1973, additional introductions and epilogues were added, giving programmes of 55 minutes, and it is this final version which is now preserved in full in the BBC Sound Archives. The following list gives titles, subjects, programme directors, and the number of the programme in the BBC Sound Archives. The academic detail given for the programme directors is that which applied at the time of the making of the programme. The list gives details of all twenty-six programmes; this volume covers the second half of the series.

1. *Green Land, Red Bricks*
   (Prehistoric and Roman Britain)
   Barry Cunliffe, Professor of Archaeology at
   the University of Southampton   T 35060

2. *A Sigh on the Harp*
   (The Celts)
   Anne Ross, former Research Fellow, School
   of Scottish Studies, University of Edinburgh   T 35061

3. *Alfred's Jewel*
   (The Anglo-Saxons)
   H. R. Loyn, Professor of Medieval History,
   University College, Cardiff   T 35062

4. *Horsemen*
   (The medieval knight)
   Maurice Keen, Fellow and Tutor in Medie-
   val History, Balliol College, Oxford   T 35063

5. *The Village Church*
   (The medieval 'clerk')
   Paul Hyams, Fellow and Lecturer in Mo-
   dern History, Pembroke College, Oxford   T 35064

6. *Ploughmen*
   (The medieval peasant)
   Barrie Dobson, Senior Lecturer in History,
   University of York   T 35065

7. *The Sheep Hath Paid for All*
   (The transition from the medieval world)
   Rodney Hilton, Professor of Medieval
   History, University of Birmingham   T 35066

8. *Madrigal for Mixed Voices*
   (The Elizabethan Age)
   Joel Hurstfield, Astor Professor of English
   History, University College, London   T 35067

9. *London*
   (London in the seventeenth and eighteenth
   centuries)
   Valerie Pearl, Reader in the History of
   London, University College, London   T 35068

10. *The Holy War*
    (The Civil War)
    Christopher Hill, Professor of History and
    Master of Balliol College, Oxford   T 35069

11. *Nation of Shopkeepers*
    (The world of commerce and trade in the
    seventeenth and eighteenth centuries, with
    an excursus on the '45 Rebellion)
    Peter Mathias, Chichele Professor of
    Economic History and Fellow of All Souls
    College, Oxford   T 35070

12. *The British Gentleman*
    (The landed gentry from the seventeenth
    century to the mid-nineteenth)
    F. M. L. Thompson, Professor of Modern
    History, Bedford College, University of
    London   T 35071

20. *Poverty and Progress*
    (The later Victorian Age)
    Theo Barker, Professor of Economic and
    Social History, University of Kent   T 35079

21. *High Imperial Noon*
    (The British Empire from the 1830s to the
    eve of the Great War)
    V. G. Kiernan, Professor of History, Uni-
    versity of Edinburgh   T 35080

22. *The Inferno*
    (The Great War)
    John A. Terraine   T 35081

23. *Hunger March*
    (Working-class Britain in the Twenties and
    Thirties)
    Donald Nicholl, Reader in History, Uni-
    versity of Keele   T 35082

24. *Semi-Detached*
    (Middle-class Britain in the Twenties and
    Thirties)
    Asa Briggs, Professor of History and Vice-
    Chancellor, University of Sussex   T 35083

25. *The People's War and Peace*
    (The Second World War and the early
    Fifties)
    Asa Briggs, Professor of History and Vice-
    Chancellor, University of Sussex   T 35084

26. *Between Two Worlds*
    (The Fifties and Sixties)
    Stuart Hall, Acting Director, Centre for
    Contemporary Cultural Studies, Univer-
    sity of Birmingham   T 35085

The series was made in the BBC Radiophonic Workshop and the production team was as follows:

Associate Producer: Daniel Snowman
Technical Directors: David Cain and Dick Mills
Assistants: Norman McLeod, Richard Yeoman-Clark and Lloyd Silverthorne
Producer for the Voices of the People: Charles Parker
Field Recorders: John Merson and Jon Crook, assisted by Peter Warham, Bob Thompson, John Turtle, Alan Rodgers, Bill Cowley, Susan Fleming, Malcolm Freegard, Philip Donellan, Ann Catchpole, Keith Slade, Peter Yates, Bob Blair and Tony Wilson
Traditional Music Adviser: Madeau Stewart
Special music composed by David Cain
Production Assistant: Libby Maude
Production Secretaries: Brenda Piper, Valerie Dunn

The series was created and produced by Michael Mason.

The central consultants for the series were Professors Asa Briggs and Gwyn A. Williams. The literary consultants were Raymond Williams, University Reader in Drama in the University of Cambridge, and Michael Alexander, Lecturer in English at the University of Stirling. The ecological commentary throughout was given by Jaquetta Hawkes and the demographic commentary by Michael Drake, Dean and Director of Studies in the Faculty of Social Sciences, The Open University.

Acknowledgements

Grateful acknowledgement is due to the following for permission to reprint extracts in this book:

Mrs George Bambridge and Macmillan of London and Basingstoke for 'Tommy' and 'For All We Have and Are' by Rudyard Kipling; Faber & Faber for an extract from *The Collected Poems of Louis MacNeice*, extracts from *The Rock* and *The Waste Land* by T. S. Eliot, and extracts from *Old Soldiers Never Die* by Frank Richards; Lawrence & Wishart for 'A Young Miner Named Ford' from *Come All Ye Bold Miners* by A. L. Lloyd; Leo Cooper of London for extracts from *Recollections of Rifleman Harris*; Wm Collins Sons & Co. for an extract from *The British Seaman* by Christopher Lloyd; Macmillan of London and Basingstoke for extracts from *The Early Chartists* by Dorothy Thompson; Eyre & Spottiswoode, London, for extracts from *In London During the Great War* by Michael MacDonagh; The Society of Authors as the literary representative of the Estate of A. E. Housman, and Jonathan Cape Ltd, publishers of A. E. Housman's *Collected Poems*, for an extract from '1887'.

MORE ABOUT PENGUINS
AND PELICANS

Penguinews which appears every month, contains details of all the new books issued by Penguins as they are published. From time to time it is supplemented by *Penguins in Print*, which is our complete list of almost 5,000 titles.

A specimen copy of *Penguinews* will be sent to you free on request. Please write to Dept EP, Penguin Books Ltd, Harmondsworth, Middlesex, for your copy.

In the U.S.A.: For a complete list of books available from Penguins in the United States write to Dept CS, Penguin Books, 625 Madison Avenue, New York, New York 10022.

In Canada: For a complete list of books available from Penguins in Canada write to Penguin Books Canada Ltd, 2801 John Street, Markham, Ontario L3R 1B4